CALIFORNIA STUDIES IN FOOD AND CULTURE

Darra Goldstein, Editor

Beyond Hummus and Falafel

The publisher gratefully acknowledges the generous support of the General Endowment Fund of the University of California Press Foundation.

Beyond Hummus and Falafel

Social and Political Aspects
of Palestinian Food in Israel

Liora Gvion

Translated by David Wesley and Elana Wesley

UNIVERSITY OF CALIFORNIA PRESS
Berkeley · Los Angeles · London

*The author would like to thank the Kibbutzim College
of Education for its support for this project.*

University of California Press, one of the most
distinguished university presses in the United States,
enriches lives around the world by advancing
scholarship in the humanities, social sciences, and
natural sciences. Its activities are supported by the UC
Press Foundation and by philanthropic contributions
from individuals and institutions. For more
information, visit www.ucpress.edu.

University of California Press
Berkeley and Los Angeles, California

University of California Press, Ltd.
London, England

© 2012 Liora Gvion

Originally published in Hebrew as *Be-govah ha-beten:
ha-hebetim ha-hevratiyim veha-politiyim shel
ha-mitbah ha-'Arvi be-Yisra'el.*

Library of Congress Cataloging-in-Publication Data

Gvion, Liora.
    [Be-govah ha-beten. English]
    Beyond hummus and falafel : social and political
aspects of Palestinian food in Israel / Liora Gvion ;
translated by David Wesley and Elana Wesley.
        p. cm. — (California studies in food and culture ;
40)
    Originally published in Hebrew as: Be-govah
ha-beten : ha-hebetim ha-hevratiyim veha-politiyim
shel ha-mitbah ha-'Arvi be-Yisra'el.
    Includes bibliographical references and index.
    1. Cooking, Arab.   2. Food habits—Social
aspects—Israel.   3. Palestinian Arabs—Israel—
Attitudes.   I. Title.
    TX725.M628G8513   2006
    394.1'2095694—dc23
                                            2012026489

Manufactured in the United States of America

21 20 19 18 17 16 15 14 13 12
10 9 8 7 6 5 4 3 2 1

In keeping with a commitment to support
environmentally responsible and sustainable printing
practices, UC Press has printed this book on 50-pound
Enterprise, a 30% post-consumer-waste, recycled,
deinked fiber that is processed chlorine-free.
It is acid-free and meets all ANSI/NISO (Z 39.48)
requirements.

In memory of my parents:
Margalit Gvion (born as Paula Heitner) and
Raphael Gvion (born as Felix Grynbaum)

Contents

Preface to the American Edition

A couple of months after my book came out in Israel, I received a phone call from a Palestinian journalist who works for a major local television station. "We need to talk," he said in a tone I could not interpret with certainty. Having done many interviews as part of my research, I tried to get a sense of what the conversation was going to be about. He was, after all, the first and only Palestinian journalist who had expressed interest in my book.

More than being concerned about the nature of our talk, I was curious. A number of blog comments written by Palestinians in reference to reviews of my book were quite critical, to say the least, about the fact that a Jewish woman "dared writing about our food," as they put it. "We are tired of being folklorized and looked down on," said others. It made me feel uncomfortable. I had not intended to folklorize Palestinian food culture nor to look down on it while also capitalizing on it. If there was one thing I was proud of, it was my success in detaching Palestinian culinary knowledge from its folklorized version and constructing its narrative in a way that included all its complexities and hidden political dimensions.

"Why did you want to talk to me?" was my first question to the Palestinian journalist when we finally met. He looked a little uncomfortable as he told me that, upon receiving my book from a Jewish friend, he, too, had bristled at the idea of his culinary narrative being written by a Jewish scholar. He was tired of being an object of scientific investigation, of being observed by outsiders, especially those who claimed entitlement to the land he felt was his. The friend, I was told, promised he would buy the journalist dinner at a good restaurant in Tel Aviv should he still think, after reading the book, that the author had offended either the Palestinian people or their food culture. "I was looking forward to having this dinner," the journalist explained, "but about halfway through the book," he continued with a smile, "I had to admit that I, too, had fallen into ethnocentric pitfalls." When I asked what made him change his mind, he said, "Your interviewees told you things we never tell Jews, and you did not hide it from your readers. You just brought the reality straight to their faces." I do not think I have ever been moved by a reader's comment as much as I was moved by this observation. This particular compliment made me aware of the various attributes that, I believe, make this book important for both Israeli and American readers.

When I first started researching the Palestinian kitchen in Israel, I encountered a lot of resentment—mostly from political activists, but also from some colleagues, both Jews and Palestinians, who questioned the legitimacy of my study. Many of them felt it was not proper for a Jewish Israeli woman to penetrate the Palestinian kitchen. "Their cuisine is for them to study" was a sentence I heard throughout my fieldwork. No answers were given to my questions: Why is it okay for Jews in general, and Jewish men in particular, to study Palestinians' political views, voting patterns, incomes, or educational achievements—but not their culinary culture? Why would my study encourage the appropriation of Palestinian dishes, while studies on marriage or family patterns were not seen as an obstacle to women's mobility or a questioning of their virtues?

To this day, I am not sure what caused these reactions. Was it my determination to touch on the topic of food—a topic many scholars see as frivolous and unworthy of sociological investigation? It was only recently that I realized the reaction was something more than the general disrespect food scholars often encountered. In fact, for many Palestinians food was far from frivolous. Palestinian food and eating habits were one of the few topics Jewish scholars had not touched on, and thus food represented one dimension of life over which Palestinians had total control. As I proceeded with my study, I came to understand that social, political, financial, and gender issues lay behind daily food practices, and that food revealed social relations, tradition, pride, and resistance, all put in a pot and cooked—not necessarily to everyone's liking—into a multilayered repast. I was not a natural guest at these meals. I was an intruder who worked her way through pots, pans, pantries, and spices, a guest who asked questions, helped children with their homework, accompanied women in their shopping and to their social gatherings, and always accepted an invitation to join a meal.

I believe that my reading of Palestinian cuisine and the social practices involved in food production, as acknowledged by the Palestinian journalist, reveals how limited the contacts and interactions between Jews and Palestinians in Israel are. The astonishment expressed by the Palestinian journalist at my understanding of Palestinian attitudes toward food also emphasizes the political dimension that underlies all interactions between the two peoples. The two groups accept each other as individuals; sometimes friendships are even formed and sustained. At the same time, Jews have difficulty accepting Palestinians as a group that is entitled to social recognition even as they preserve their distinctive features. I met Palestinians who accused my people of showing disrespect to and a lack of interest in their food culture, and who feared that the lack of mutual respect between us would hinder the chances of Palestinian citizens realizing their full civil and political rights.

My intention was not only to bring forward the Palestinian narrative on food. I also wanted to interweave the story of food with stories of the daily lives of the Palestinian citizens of Israel, relating food practices with the politics of identity and the economic reality in which Palestinians live. I wanted to explore such questions as: How do political conditions shape the Palestinian culinary repertoire? How has the cessation of domestic agriculture affected the Palestinian rural family? And to what extent do daily or occasional encounters with Jews—as fellow workers, neighbors, professionals, or soldiers—influence and change the Palestinian diet?

My contribution, I hope, is not only in pointing out the distinctive features of Palestinian cuisine and its modes of food consumption. I intend to show how food positions the Palestinian citizens of Israel as a distinct social group with particular concerns and interests. Their social, economic, and political interests are different both from those of Jewish Israelis and from those of Palestinians in the West Bank and the Gaza Strip. The ongoing support of Palestinians in Israel for an independent Palestinian state has led to a general neglect by the Jewish public, the Israeli government, and the Western world, all of whom fail to realize the unique needs and interests of Palestinians in Israel. It has also contributed to a widespread assumption that the eventual establishment of a Palestinian state will solve problems for the Palestinian citizens of Israel as well. I hope that my book conveys the particular position of the Palestinian citizens of Israel, who struggle to have their own interests recognized within Israeli society, on the one hand, and to support the Palestinian struggle, on the other hand.

Let me take you on a journey to a foreign culture of the people who live in geographic proximity to me. Some of them are my next-door neighbors; others are my students, colleagues, physicians, or plumbers. And yet before I embarked on this study, I knew little about their food, and they know not much about mine. This book is a journey to kitchens that are often better equipped than my own, and for one major reason: new kitchen technologies enable the preparation of traditional dishes in less time and with less effort and thus make possible the preservation of those dishes.

Together we will look at the domestic knowledge involved in food production and learn about the ways in which Palestinian women use food as a means of negotiating positions both in the home and in the broader community. I argue that despite the large amount of culinary knowledge at their disposal by virtue of their being responsible for feeding their families, Palestinian women only moderately and informally negotiate the extent of their dissent from the existing social order. Although they experience a dual subjugation—both at the hands of the patriarchal system of Palestinian society and as female citizens in Israeli society—they go no further than asserting the informal power that their role in the family and the community grants them.

My study of Palestinian kitchens and their modernization exposed me to the ways in which food becomes a major component of identity. By studying food I could detect the process through which a Palestinian Arab identity has emerged in Israel in the shadow of a dominant Jewish culture and show how, in light of the above, Palestinian cuisine combines tradition and modernity. Interestingly, the home and its women are the agents of modernity, while restaurants preserve traditional foods and portray traditional social relationships.

I am often asked what I am left with, now that the work is finished. I have learned that I need not fear the study of the unknown. I have realized over and over again how welcoming my informants were when I asked questions about what for them was "common sense." The contradictions I encountered, the critics of Israeli society, the dissatisfaction of my informants from their position in Israel are all brought forward for you to read, so that you may evaluate and draw your own conclusions. I was lucky to have interviewed women and men who were grateful and proud to deliver their truth, and I feel fortunate that I had the chance to listen.

Preface to the Original Edition

As If We Were Eskimos—A Most Personal Opening

I was sitting in the living room of Samira's spacious home in Galilee when I felt, for the first time during my fieldwork, like an oppressor.[1] The feeling inched up from my stomach past my chest, causing discomfort, if not embarrassment. "Eat, why aren't you eating my cake?" she pressed. She was about to serve me a second piece, although I had hardly finished the first one. "Beirut Nights," she called it, a delicious cake I could not bring myself to enjoy. Had I not known that Samira defines herself as a Palestinian citizen of the state of Israel, I would have thought of her as a typical Jewish mother. We were talking about food. The conversation was technical and strained—I hadn't managed to break through the wall separating researcher from informant; I could not get through to her. We sounded like distant acquaintances exchanging recipes. Yet here and there, interwoven in the conversation, were threads not typical of women's conversations. The longer Samira tried to accommodate me, the more strongly I felt I was not reaching her. She weighed every word as though she were speaking from her head and not her stomach. And it was her stomach I wanted to hear. She kept asking whether the information she was conveying to me was relevant, whether I was learning new things from her, and especially whether the information she was providing would enable me to write an authentic and accurate cookbook. "Because I don't cook according to an exact number of cups and tablespoons, as you do," she said.

Suddenly I understood, and with the understanding came the colonialist feeling: Samira thought I was writing a cookbook. She thought that I was going to write in my own name a book about her culinary culture—a book that perhaps would have been written by one of her own people, had they been a group with equal rights whose culture was accepted and sought out. I could understand her reservations, which were evident despite her courtesy and amiable readiness to assist me. I was just one more person who came and took notes, tasting a bit of her culture in order to present it as my own. "I'm not writing a cookbook," I said, trying to keep the uneasiness out of my voice. "The amounts aren't important. I'm trying to understand what has happened to you, to your culture, and especially to your food since you and I have been living here together." Incredulous, she responded: "You're not writing a cookbook? Then what are you writing?" At that moment she remembered: "Yes, you did tell me that you're a sociologist and want to know us through food and to understand how our kitchens have changed since we have been living side by side. I forgot. For a moment I thought you were just another female journalist coming to ask, take notes, and write about our food in the paper as if we were Eskimos." She let out a brief giggle, adding: "Sometimes they write as if it were the food of their own mothers, without even mentioning us."

One phrase of Samira's kept echoing in my head, more than any other I had heard in the course of the hundred interviews I had conducted: "Since we have been living side by side." Ostensibly just a slight nuance apart from "living here together," as I had presented the matter, but the expression revealed a different perspective. Whereas I had presented a Zionist view, Samira had presented a delicate version of her reality; she did not say "since we have been living alongside *you*," which would have emphasized the inequality in our relations. Rather, she gave expression to the distance between us without saying openly that the situation, in which "Israeliness" carries more weight than does "Arabness," discriminates against her.

Because of this inequality, for a female Jewish author of Ashkenazi origin to write a book about Arab food was a challenging mission. As objective as I might be, as neutral and attentive to the information flowing in my direction, would I succeed in shedding the cultural burdens, stereotypes, and perceptions of the Arab minority that had been implanted inside me during my many years in Israel? Would it be Jewish eyes that did the observing, and an Ashkenazi palate that did the tasting? On the other hand, I was fascinated by the possibility of penetrating a world that was not mine, a world nearby geographically—sometimes no farther than ten minutes from my home—but, at the same time, very far from me, closed to me, the gap between us difficult to bridge. This world's geography was not a part of mine; it was a world of towns and cities that were nothing more than blurred names on signs at turns in the road that I had never explored. And its culture—with its odors wafting out of the houses, its habits of dress and etiquette, its rules for receiving guests, and its norms of everyday behavior—was completely foreign to me.

Finally, curiosity won out over apprehension. Filled with the desire to meet those with whom I share a disputed land, and aware that I would need to learn alien codes and assign other meanings to familiar words in order to understand things properly, I set out on a compelling journey to other kitchens and eating customs. I entered a world in which traditional odors and new fragrances blended in one pot, in which wild plants, homemade cheeses, and sun-dried wheat watched over by a scarecrow came together with the technology of the microwave oven and home freezer, and in which a group that is a minority in its own land struggles between the need to define a distinct national identity and the constraints and desires involved in being part of the whole and its culture.

The journey was fascinating. People opened up their pantries, kitchen cupboards, and refrigerators for me and invited me to join them for meals. They let me in—not always consciously—to the secrets of their culture, their economic situation, the family hierarchy, and their feelings toward Jews and toward building their own national identities. I accompanied women on their shopping trips to markets or to local shops. I scooped out vegetables to be stuffed and helped pinch pastry dough before it was placed in the oven. Only after I understood that "the odor of Jewish cooking" is an expression meaning food that doesn't whet the appetite did I realize that the opportunity accorded me to help with the cooking was a great compliment—as if the odors of Jewish food had not stuck to me and wouldn't adhere to their food.

During our encounters, my interviewees—who were mostly women—attempted to map me cognitively according to the categories with which they were familiar. I quickly understood that my way to their culinary knowledge led through this mapping. I was asked questions that became stepping stones toward defining myself for them and mitigating the sense of strangeness between us, such as: How many children do I have? Who takes care of my children while I'm here with them? Did I study before or after I was married? Am I also a teacher? What do I cook? But there was one question that caused me discomfort and was hard for me to answer because it signified gaps that were difficult to bridge: "Does your husband let you move about this way and meet people?" Educated women asked this question out of curiosity; less-educated women did not always grasp my ability to act as an independent woman who is not subject to the permission of her husband. This question caused me to wonder about the differences between a Jewish woman, educated and working in Israel in the twenty-first century, and an Arab woman in a comparable situation. How do Palestinian women perceive women's liberation?

There were also moments in my fieldwork that caused me to reexamine my attitude toward my own culture and to ask myself questions about my Jewish identity. For example, one time I asked to interview an intellectual couple living in Haifa on the Jewish New Year. There was a pregnant silence on the other end of the line, after which the man said: "All right, you can come if you wish. I didn't think you would want to come to interview us on Rosh Hashanah." I quickly explained that I don't observe Jewish traditions. When I arrived for the interview, my hosts received me with the greeting "Happy New Year," and they served me honey cake "so it would be a sweet year." I am certain that they had no intention of embarrassing me; on the contrary, this was a desire on their part to honor my holiday. After this interview, I decided that I would not conduct any further interviews on Jewish holidays: if I gave the impression that I didn't even honor my own traditions, then what might be surmised about my honoring anyone else's?

When I embarked on this journey, I had no idea what Palestinian food in Israel was, and even now that my journey is over, I'm not sure how to define it. I set out equipped with the common Israeli knowledge that Palestinian food meant hummus, tahini, *mjadara* (made of rice), *seniyeh, labaneh, ful, kubeh,* baklava, and small cups of sweet, strong black coffee. Those proved to be the tip of the iceberg of a rich cuisine that makes use, in season, of all that grows nearby—a cuisine of those who do not have cash on hand at all times but who are familiar with the fruit of their land and know how to make good use of it. I wondered why we Jews learned to love hummus and *ful* to the point of making them our own, while we remain completely unfamiliar with such dishes as *melukhiye, hubeizeh, frike, shishbarak, m'khamar, mansaf, maklubeh,* or *matfune.*[2] Are we like the Americans who rejected Mexican cuisine both because of the hostility between the two countries during the nineteenth century and because Mexicans were among the poorest ethnic groups in American society? Do we reject foods harvested from the garden or the field near the house because they are eaten by those identified in the public consciousness as our enemies, and whom we associate with poverty, privation, and perhaps even a lack of culture?

At the same time many more questions arose, and I was confronted with numerous surprises. For example, alongside the seasonal wild plants in Israel, the local Palestinian kitchen had also embraced dishes and ingredients from elsewhere. Macaroni, lasagna, Chinese specialties, dairy treats, cornflakes, cakes, schnitzel, pizza, and quiche were all found on the shelves of refrigerators and pantries after having been adapted to the Palestinian palate. Should foreign foods be regarded as part of the Palestinian kitchen? Does their appearance on the Palestinian menu mean that this cuisine has lost its traditional national character? Does their presence indicate that Palestinian society in Israel is in the process of searching for its own identity, in an attempt to define its place between "Israeliness" and a distinct Palestinian existence? Or does it perhaps reflect exposure to global trends in a world whose culture is growing increasingly homogeneous? Finally, what can be learned from the Palestinian kitchen about Jews and their culture, about the identity being shaped inside Israel's borders?

These questions, which began to engage me on a personal level and not only as a sociologist, made it more difficult for me to write, sometimes to the point of literary paralysis. On the one hand, Arab culture felt alien to me, and more than once it seemed presumptuous on my part to write a book about the Palestinian kitchen in Israel. On the other hand, I felt too much involvement, too close and too fond of the people I had met. Along with these mixed feelings I also felt confusion and embarrassment: more than once, upon returning home from an interview in the villages, I felt shame because people were living so close to me in conditions resembling those of the third world—without good roads, proper infrastructure, or a decent educational system. My distress was described well by a friend who commented, whenever I sounded overwhelmed, "So you've been 'abroad' again, have you?" Unlike the journalists Samira would host in her home, I didn't want to write about Eskimos and about the rest of the world, and I didn't want to appropriate food that was not mine and treat it as if it were. Wrestling with these questions eventually led to some insight about my own activity and its context: through learning about the Palestinian kitchen, I was seeking a way to understand and present an existing culture that was constantly renewing and redefining itself in relation to the Jewish and Palestinian reality in the region.

I have shared with you the distress, uncertainty, and hesitation that accompanied me as I wrote this book, if only so that you will read it with the understanding that food is more than an array of proteins, carbohydrates, vitamins, and calories. Rather, food is a rich package of cultural and social relations, and a means of creating personal, gender, or national identity. If I succeed in conveying this sense of what food is, I will have achieved my objective.

I wish to thank the hundred men and women who agreed to be interviewed and who hosted me in their homes or offices and enabled me to discuss my concerns and interests with them. My thanks to the Institute for Israeli Arab Studies, which first sparked my curiosity about the Palestinian kitchen in Israel. Special thanks to Professor Shaul Mishal, for the wonderful name he gave to the Hebrew version of the book and for his generous help in finding a warm home for the manuscript, and to Professor Emanuel Marx, for his unstinting support. Without them, this book could not have come into being.

Introduction

Food, Ethnicity, and Identity

Food is one of the means through which distinct national and ethnic identities are formed and practiced. This chapter illuminates the social processes through which food contributes to the national and ethnic identities of groups that share a single territory but perceive themselves as distant and different from one another politically, culturally, and economically. I also look at the circumstances under which food serves as a bridge between two such groups: Palestinians and Jews who are citizens of the state of Israel. An examination of the processes that shape national and ethnic cuisines and enable continuity, along with incorporation of changes into the daily diet, reveals the connection between the politics of identity and the daily culinary practices held in both the private and public spheres. Although food is an integral part of Palestinian daily life, its symbolic, social, and political aspects have only recently been acknowledged as a means by which Palestinians distinguish themselves from Jewish Israelis.[1] Decisions relating to food are not merely gastronomic choices; they also reflect individual tastes, along with social identity; class, national or ethnic membership; and the way we choose to present ourselves to others.[2] This book, then, contributes to the theoretical dimensions of the discourse on food by analyzing the political and social processes that shape Palestinian cuisine in Israel and by examining the kitchen as a political and cultural text that emerges and changes in the context of the formation of a national identity.

Food is a prism through which it is possible to present, write, and reconstruct history, and it thereby reveals relationships of control, exploitation, and denial of or derogation of rights accorded to the culture of the other. As we shall see, scholars have largely discussed the theoretical elements having to do with the formation of nations, ethnic group consciousness, and colonialism. They have also addressed the relevance of these sorts of political processes to the formation of national cuisines and the institutionalization of culinary knowledge. Written history becomes a reservoir of common and assumed knowledge that links individuals and serves as the basis for agreement about a shared heritage.[3] Such a history constructs tradition, transforms it into a medium that embodies the unique culture of a national group, and defines the means of sharing this culture with other groups. But history, Frances Fitzgerald argues, is written by the dominant group: the agent that constructs its own history as well as that of minority and ethnic groups that reside in the same territory.[4]

In his book *Orientalism,* Edward Said sees the colonialist discourse as an example of the production of knowledge about non-Western regions.[5] This constitution of knowledge reproduces ideologies, power relations, and existing institutions and practices, as well as the image of the other as "primitive." Deconstruction of the colonialist discourse reveals the centrality of the themes of race and eroticization of the primitive, and poses questions about the existence of an alternative to the European historical knowledge of the other.[6]

Robert Stam and Ella Shohat identify colonialism with Eurocentrism—the ideology upon which Europeans base their economic, political, and cultural hegemony in third-world countries.[7] This hegemony is built more upon a cognitive process than upon a concrete institutional one. Eurocentrism attributes to the West constant progress from autocratic regimes to democratic ones. It emphasizes the undemocratic traditions prevalent in non-European countries and blurs the limitations of European democracy. This justifies the appropriation of non-Western cultures and leads to paternalism, glorification of the West, and deprecation of everything not European. The alternative to appropriation, according to Stam and Shohat, is for third-world writers, poets, and filmmakers to create texts of their own history. Such texts counter the Eurocentric perception and allow third-world artists to institutionalize control over their image, identity, and history. Writing their own past is a way to rewrite the present and change the pattern of existing power relations.

The awakening of national culture often plays a role in the process of political liberation. Frantz Fanon emphasizes the importance of delving into the original culture in order to mobilize sources for action and for new political content.[8] Colonialism, for Fanon, is not only territorial control of a country but also a process that empties the minds of the native population of content and revises their past and their history. Conquerors present themselves as having come to light up the dark world of the natives, to rescue the natives from themselves. The local culture, mobilized by national liberation fighters, represents daily life, celebrates the actions of individuals for their own nation, presents the face of resistance, and produces new content. In other words, culture becomes a tool in the national struggle and provides a basis for creation of a national identity with the establishment of a nation-state.

The establishment of nation-states involves the development of a national consciousness, culture, and identity.[9] As part of that process, reservoirs of culinary knowledge become an integral part of the national culture. Still, they do not turn into a means of developing a national or political consciousness of resistance. National kitchens developed in nation-states, leading to unique dishes that sharpened the distinction between one nation-state and its neighbor.[10] Until the rise of nationalism, culinary borders were defined on the basis of class and lifestyle—in other words, as "beyond" ethnic or regional differences. For example, aristocrats throughout Europe ate similar foods with no connection to where they lived, so that the kitchens of wealthy Italians more closely resembled those of wealthy French people than those of poor Italians. Printing technology contributed to the culinary expression of nationalism by enabling recipes to be published, giving them a material permanence and transforming them into a stock of cultural knowledge unique to a particular nation-state and accessible to all readers.[11]

Crystallization of the national cuisine created a link between the nation-state and the food products, eating habits, and main dishes that became its symbols. In the eighteenth century, for example, the Prussian political elite consumed potatoes as a status symbol. With the passing of the years and changing economic and political circumstances, in northern Germany, the potato became a basic food consumed by all.[12] In addition, the kitchens of immigrants were forced to adapt to their new surroundings. For example, the new settlers who came to America wanted to recreate the English kitchen, but they discovered that the climatic conditions differed, and the absence of essential basic ingredients compelled them to establish a new kitchen dependent upon local meat and agricultural products. In this way, corn and turkey became staples in the American diet.[13] Similarly, the combination of steak, chips, and salad became identified with the French kitchen, and pasta was associated with the Italian kitchen.[14]

DIASPORIC COMMUNITIES

The rise of the nation-state also gave birth to local ethnic groups: historically and symbolically small communities whose national identities differ from those of the nation-state in which they are located. In some cases, amid problems of economic, social, and political mobility, these ethnic communities experienced geographical and cultural exile. Such ethnic diasporas, in which many individuals develop a sense of belonging to a symbolic community that is not necessarily geographically coterminous with the country in which they live, are a familiar characteristic of the modern world.[15] William Safran defines a *diaspora* as a community geographically separated from the center, located in the periphery.[16] Such a community preserves a memory or myth of its country of origin along with a desire to be accepted as an equal in its new country. It sees in the land of its forefathers a place to which it aspires to return if and when a suitable time arises; thus, it sustains a commitment to national liberation and independence. André Levi and Alex Weingrod add that among contemporary diasporas there are minorities whose cultures and rights have been repressed.[17]

Geographically, émigrés and diasporic ethnic communities dwell inside the absorbing society, but economically, socially, culturally, and symbolically, they live outside it.[18] They assume the role of foreigners, enabling them to experience a certain degree of freedom and to develop a politics based upon the imputed past as the source of their self-definition. In this way, the past becomes the basis for the unique content of their ethnicity, the ground out of which its strategies for action arise, and the repository of the symbols that nourish its empowerment.[19] Sometimes, a diasporic culture acquires a private, even secret, dimension, but that does not prevent it from contributing to a multicultural and democratic climate.[20]

Diasporic communities may also grow out of national or cultural feelings, without the trauma of territorial exile that is usually accompanied by the dream of a return to the homeland. Such diasporic communities are likely to develop and form their collective identities through religious practices, written traditions, and culture without a longing for territory.[21] These include groups of voluntary émigrés, refugees, foreign workers, and ethnic communities whose stores of knowledge include historical perceptions, cultural meanings, and alternative geographical maps. Some wish to belong to the absorbing society and to preserve the myth of returning home at the same time, distinguishing themselves both from the community in their land of origin and from that of the land in which they presently live.[22]

By living a diasporic existence accompanied by the development and preservation of a myth of returning home—even if only symbolically—migrants are in certain political circumstances transformed from a minority group into an ethnic group. While a minority group experiences only the relationship of inequality fostered by the dominant group, an ethnic group builds a collective that shares common beliefs, culture, identity, and behavior. Its members identify themselves and are identified by others as being distinct from the surrounding society.[23] To what extent is ethnic identity a matter of personal or group choice and to what extent is it defined by the dominant group? The answer depends on the access of the ethnic group to the system of rewards and benefits controlled by the dominant group.[24] Many ethnic groups, like the Palestinian citizens of Israel, do not succeed in breaking through the barriers set by the labor market, which is divided on an ethnic basis, and they find themselves on the lower rungs of the occupational ladder.[25] The stigmatization of the minority group also makes it more difficult to become mobile through acquisition of education or to realize the potential of that education—if it has been acquired—in the occupational hierarchy. Thus, minority groups remain closed among themselves as they reproduce their culture and experience conflicts between it and the culture of the absorbing society.[26]

The overlap between state and nation in Israeli society has given birth to an encounter between the official Zionist narrative of the dominant Jewish nation-state and the narrative of the national Palestinian minority group. Israeli political rhetoric, which is cast in terms of violent ongoing conflict, defines the Arab citizens of the state as a "dangerous" national minority. In terms of citizenship, Palestinians are included within the general polity, but at the same time, they are socially excluded on the grounds of their supposedly unbridgeable foreignness.[27] According to Sammy Smooha and Oren Yiftachel, this is why Israel is a deeply divided ethnonational state that must prove that the rights it bestows upon its Arab citizens entitle it to inclusion in the family of democratic nations.[28]

THE DEVELOPMENT OF A PALESTINIAN IDENTITY

In 1948, only 160,000 of the 900,000 total Palestinians remained in the part of Palestine upon which Israel was established. They currently constitute 19 percent of Israel's population.[29] Although granted formal citizenship, these Palestinians live in an "ethnic state" in which national identity is not inclusive of all citizens, but rather is limited to the members of one ethnic group. The Israeli state developed an extensive system for marginalizing and controlling Palestinian people based on segmentation, collaboration, and dependence.[30]

The interface of the Jewish and Palestinian populations in the new state of Israel was accompanied by the enactment of emergency regulations that defined restricted military-administered zones until 1966. Thus, two distinct political regimes were created. Adriana Kemp refers to these as two different ecological systems—the first, a polity administered according to democratic principles and striving for normalization of the lives of its citizens, and the other, a polity administered according to emergency regulations based upon a definition of ongoing war. This definition enabled the state to control its Palestinian citizens and to shape the web of its social relations with them. Regulations gave broad authority to military governors, allowing them to limit the movement of Israeli Arabs, confiscate land, translocate residents from place to place, grant work permits or marriage licenses, and determine the conditions of medical care. By defining the Arabs inside Israel as loyal supporters of the enemy, the military government became necessary to control their actions. Members of the Palestinian minority group were entitled to equal rights as citizens of the state. But the definition of ongoing war led to the perpetuation of institutional discrimination against them by the Jewish citizens.[31]

This rhetoric shaped and defined the relations between the two groups as an ongoing conflict.[32] In this context, Majid al-Haj suggests that Palestinian identity in the state of Israel may be examined in relation to four spheres, or dimensions: local, national, regional, and religious.[33] In the local dimension, the Palestinian population has undergone a process of accelerated modernization leading to a rise in the level of education and standard of living, a change in patterns of consumption, and the partial adoption of the lifestyle of the Jewish public.[34] But Azmi Bishara observes that, while modernization has affected the Palestinian citizenry in Israel, it has bypassed the localities in which they live.[35] The Arab villages and towns have remained undeveloped and unable to adapt to residents' demands or needs. Moreover, while the Palestinian population aims to present itself as modern, state agencies encourage the theme of authenticity, commodifying Palestinian traditional culture and portraying Palestinians as a group that modernization has skipped. Palestinian population centers and rural locales are reevaluated as potential markets: the former are commodified as sites of ethnic tourism, and the latter are reimagined as places of country hospitality.[36]

Simultaneously, a politicization of the Palestinian population has manifested in the appearance of young leadership—educated and with well-formed political awareness—to replace the traditional leadership. This new leadership has set up organizations that act through extraparliamentary bodies such as Sons of the Village (Ibna Al-Balad) and the National Committee of Chairmen of Arab Local Authorities. Although exposure to democratic political apparatuses did not, at first, lead to increased political awareness or a will to organize in order to achieve civil rights, the younger generation has been struggling for civic partnership and equality between Jews and Palestinians in the state of Israel.[37]

In the national dimension, Palestinian citizens of Israel face the consequences of the Law of Return, which defines the state of Israel as a Jewish state and hence excludes Palestinian citizens from participating in projects with national objectives, such as "Judaizing" Galilee. National identity, as distinguished from religious and demographic differences, impinges on the economic processes that have shaped Palestinian society in the state of Israel. The expropriation of land, which left many families with plots too small to develop their commercial agricultural potential; the widening entry of technology into the realm of agriculture; and the founding of agricultural marketing cooperatives closed to Palestinians all combined to leave the Arab population unable to compete with Jewish agriculture. Thus, agriculture ceased to be a main source of income for the Arabs.[38]

Neutralization of the economic capability of the Palestinian population prevented it from developing its own streams of income and led to dependence upon Jewish employers.[39] Manufacturing investments in the military domain have been carried out at the expense of development of other infrastructure in both Arab and Jewish population centers. Such investments have prevented the establishment of independent income sources in the Arab sector and have contributed to the perpetuation of employment discrimination against Arabs and to a limitation of the variety of occupations available to them.[40]

Several trends have been evident in the labor market over the years. First, the overall number of employed Palestinians in Israel has increased, and they have begun to work primarily for Jewish employers. Second, the rate of participation of Arab males—especially older men—in the labor market has declined, for several reasons. Many Arab men had only a low level of education and were manual laborers. Therefore they were able to work in their occupations for only relatively short periods of time, and they did not have the benefit of professional training that would facilitate their absorption into new branches of the labor market. Third, although the education gap between Jews and Arabs has lessened, even today educated Arabs struggle to translate their credentials into suitable employment and higher income.[41] For example, graduates of the life sciences faculties have difficulty finding work in their field of specialization due to the barriers imposed on the grounds of national security. Many have no alternative but to turn to teaching, although a few have found high administrative positions in government offices, such as the Ministry of Education.[42]

The limited opportunities for suitable employment, along with limited access to state infrastructure, have impacted Palestinian identity. During the period from 1948 to 1967, Palestinians sought security and accommodation and thus attempted to integrate into life in Israel. Until 1967, the pan-Arab element was dominant in the identity of Palestinian citizens of Israel. The Six-Day War of 1967 created direct contact between the Palestinian population and leadership in the West Bank. The latter accused the Arab citizens of Israel of having collaborated with the Israeli regime. Consequently, the Palestinian component of these Arab citizens' identity was awakened, connecting them with the consciousness of Palestinian suffering. From 1973 through the 1990s, the Palestinian component of their identity has been further strengthened. This tendency was reinforced with the eruption of the First Intifada (1987–1993), a Palestinian uprising against the Israeli occupation in the Palestinian Territories. The uprising began in the Jabalia refugee camp and quickly spread throughout Gaza, the West Bank, and East Jerusalem.[43] At this time the Palestine Liberation Organization (PLO) was recognized by Palestinians as their sole legitimate representative.[44] The mobilization of Palestinian citizens of Israel in support of their brothers and sisters gathered momentum from the outbreak of the Second Intifada.[45] Also known as the Al-Aqsa Intifada or the Oslo War, this second Palestinian uprising was a period of intensified Palestinian-Israeli violence that began in late September 2000.[46] One indication of increased momentum was the growing number of Arab academicians who were then being absorbed in institutions of higher education in the Occupied Territories.[47]

In the religious dimension, contact with Palestinians in the Occupied Territories brought Muslim Palestinians in Israel closer to religion. Young Israeli Arabs began to immerse themselves in advanced religious study in institutions in the West Bank and became leaders of the Islamic movement inside Israel. Economic hardship also played a part in accelerating the turn to religion. The Islamic movement grew in strength with the passage of time, and the socio-religious movement became a politico-religious one, represented in local government and in national Arab organizations.[48]

The economic, social, and political processes to which Palestinian citizens of Israel have been exposed since the establishment of the state have also brought about changes in the structure of the Arab family in Israel. Through massive confiscation of Palestinian Arab lands, Palestinians became economically dependent on the state's infrastructure.[49] Small family farms no longer provided a steady source of income, and young Palestinian men started working as unskilled day laborers for Jewish employers. Consequently, the traditional extended family unit living off the land broke into nuclear family units.[50]

Previously, all members of the family were dependent on agriculture for their income, working on farmland owned by the father of the family. Children, even those who had already established their own families, were subject to their father's authority. It was only after the father's death that the land was divided among the children, who retained mutual responsibility for the family land. When young people began to work outside the village and a monetary economy took root, relations between fathers and sons changed, as did patterns of residence. Young brides also played a part in accelerating the dissolution of the *hamula* (clan): their subordinate role via-à-vis their mothers-in-law and the difficulties of comanaging with the other women in the household increased pressure on the husband to break up the extended family and build an independent residence for his nuclear family. In this way the economic dependence of young men upon their fathers was replaced by an economic dependence upon the Jewish sector, and within the nuclear family a new generation of parents arose that placed the interests of its children first and foremost. This new family structure is reflected in changing patterns of consumption, a decline in the birthrate, a new arrangement of and furnishings for the home, and an investment in education.

The political rhetoric that shaped and defined the relations between Israeli Jews and Arabs as a violent ongoing conflict gave birth to civil limitations, institutionalized discrimination, and an ethnically divided labor market. It also shaped a Palestinian political and cultural identity distinct from the Jewish Israeli one. Palestinians in Israel have at least three identities: Arab, Palestinian, and Palestinian Israeli. No single identity dominates over the others and each relates to a different content of meanings and plays a different role in their identity repertoire. The Palestinian identity emphasizes a sense of national pride and solidarity on behalf of cultural heritage. The Israeli identity is relevant as a democratic system that assigns high priority to individual rights but also as a system that stresses Palestinians' marginalization.[51] To challenge this marginalization, Palestinians in Israel choose selective venues for paving their participation in Israeli society while expressing their right to uphold a distinctive culture and identity.

This book analyzes just one element of cultural identity and course of action: changes that have occurred in Palestinian food in Israel following its encounter with the Jewish Zionist state. I show how culinary knowledge, primarily female, has become a cultural reservoir preserving a distinct national identity. Kept within the boundaries of the community, food has turned into a means of institutionalizing opposition to attempts to appropriate resources belonging to the Palestinian population and transform them into the general body of Israeli culinary knowledge. An economic and political analysis of the Arab kitchen in Israel helps us understand why certain changes are accepted and others rejected.

Furthermore, the book deals with the innovations and culinary ideologies and principles that underlie the Arab kitchen in Israel. I argue, in the first part of the book, that despite the geographic proximity between Palestinian and Jewish citizens of Israel, the infiltration of "Jewish" dishes into the Palestinian kitchen has been limited to those that suited the structure of the Arab meal and existing eating habits and those that enabled the preparation of the traditional dishes by advanced cooking technology. Simultaneously, the very limited adoption of Palestinian dishes into the Jewish Israeli kitchen is interpreted by Palestinians as a symbolic expression of the lack of respect and interest exhibited by the Jewish public towards Arabic-Palestinian culture. This lack of respect leads to an unwillingness to regard Palestinian citizens of Israel as an ethnic group entitled to realize its civil and political rights in full.

THE CULINARY MANIFESTATIONS OF NATIONAL AND ETHNIC IDENTITIES

Studies have looked at the role that food plays in the process of identity formation among immigrants, minorities, and ethnic communities. Scholars have also given attention to the connection between the status of minority and ethnic groups and their cuisines.[52] By focusing on Palestinian citizens of Israel, I look at how the cuisines of minorities reveal negotiations over both social inclusion and self-identification. I consider how food may reflect relations between ethnic communities and the dominant group, how it finds expression in the colonial discourse, and what role it plays as a part of the cultural assets of the nation-state.

Food, according to Arjun Appadurai and Warren Belasco, represents the collective and states who we are, where we came from, and who we want to be.[53] It is a cultural product through which ethnicity is constructed.[54] Our food preferences reveal the extent to which we wish to include others in our collective and the extent to which we acknowledge their culturally distinctive features.[55] Cooking and eating, therefore, are means of constructing social boundaries between those incorporated into the national food culture and those we do not trust enough to include in the collective. Pierre Van den Berghe claims that ethnic food developed out of mutual contact, because it was only after immigration that the immigrant realized the difference between his culture and that of the dominant group.[56] The immigrant's daily practices become anything ranging from exotic to bizarre, strange, and unacceptable. Simultaneously, food becomes a medium through which minorities express themes of inclusion in and exclusion from the society in which they live and recapture the totality of their old way of life.[57]

Several factors redefine and change immigrants' food practices. First, immigrants must seek out local substitutes for basic ingredients or import them from the mother country.[58] For example, early Italian immigrants to the United States were dissatisfied with American cheeses and pastas and instead preferred to import these products from Italy, even if doing so was seen as a health threat.[59] Similarly, starting in the 1980s, Iranian immigrants in Los Angeles and Indian immigrants in the San Francisco Bay Area opened stores selling imported spices and basic ingredients—and even prepared foods—intended for their own use. These stores also helped to reproduce the traditional role of the Indian or Iranian woman. With instruction offered by the staff of such stores, immigrant women were able to preserve their culture within their households. Only after they had gained a certain economic well-being and security about their place in American society did the immigrants begin to sell their food products and spices to other Americans, presenting their diet as an exotic cuisine that would diversify American eating habits.[60]

Second, encounters in the new land oblige the immigrant group to adapt its food to the existing culinary categories of the dominant national group. For instance, lunch, the central meal of the day in Europe, became a small meal for Italian and Russian immigrant communities in the United States, while the evening meal gained prominence. Serving a traditional meal faithful to the patterns of eating in their homeland was usually limited to weekends, holidays, and celebrations such as weddings.[61] Also, certain ingredients require social revaluation. An example is the change that occurred in the attitude of the Russian community in the midwestern United States: homemade noodles, which had been consumed on a daily basis in Russia, became exotic and were consumed only on special occasions. In other cases, immigrants adapt their dishes to the basic categories of the absorbing society. Erica Wheeler and Tan Swee Poh describe how Chinese women in England adapted the Chinese distinction between hot and cold food to their children's demands to eat the school lunch in order to fit in with the English children.[62] Because most of the foods served in the school were fried, the women treated them as hot foods, and when the children came home, their mothers fed them foods considered cold by Chinese culture.

Changes also occur in the patterns of serving, snacking, and the refreshments customary in the land of origin. Maris Gillette, for example, studied the way in which Western dishes, which contradicted Islamic food and hygienic laws, entered the diet of the Muslim community in China.[63] Chinese Muslims purchased these foods for the younger generation, with the intention of exposing their children to Western culture. Leslie Prosterman, who researched the menu offered at Jewish weddings in the United States, found a controlled break with the culinary boundaries of traditional Jewish culture.[64] Even if Jewish dietary laws were preserved, most of the menus were put together from fashionable dishes that appealed to the tastes of the younger generation, whereas the traditional dishes were served as side dishes, mostly to satisfy the generation of grandparents. Similarly, countries that have only recently begun opening up to Western culture have applied their own interpretations to the fast-food industry. The dizzying success of fast-food restaurants in China, Israel, and Russia testifies to the fact that globalization does not erase ethnic or national cultures but rather is interwoven with them.[65]

Third, immigrants are often confronted by the stigmatization of their food. Immigrants experience difficulties selling their food outside their communities, due to the general public's distaste for ethnic food. Sales, therefore, often remain within the boundaries of their communities. Thus, ethnic entrepreneurs open ethnic restaurants intended solely for immigrants. In addition to food, these restaurants sell nostalgia and a connection with the home country: music typical of the land of origin is played there, the native language is spoken, and only members of the community gather there.[66]

Joseph Conlin describes the history of mines in the United States through the story of their food.[67] He emphasizes the role played by Chinese immigrants, who lived near the mines during the Gold Rush in the middle of the nineteenth century, in introducing Chinese food to the American kitchen. Americans had an aversion to Chinese food because of its short cooking time and unfamiliar ingredients. However, the Chinese were almost the only ones who opened restaurants near the mines. Their restaurants were cheap, and some of the few dishes they served were adapted to the American palate. The rest is history: once the Chinese kitchen succeeded in penetrating the boundaries of suspicious American society, it became one of the most popular cuisines in the United States.[68]

Mexican immigrants in the United States and their food underwent a more degrading experience during the same period.[69] American miners saw Mexican food as the food of the enemy and the poor, and they refused to eat it. It was only during the 1980s that the Mexican kitchen in the United States blossomed, mostly due to the establishment of ethnic fast-food chains serving processed and industrialized products suitable for the American lunch, and as a result of the tortilla's transformation into a convenience food, able to be prepared in minutes for a family supper.[70] In American cities today, Mexican restaurants of varying degrees of authenticity cater to a heterogeneous clientele.[71]

Scholars point to the connection between the status of the ethnic group and the attitude toward its food. Lynn Harbottle, for instance, shows that Iranian restaurants in England since the 1980s have mostly been owned by students who suddenly became illegal immigrants following Khomeini's rise to power in their country.[72] Lacking other possibilities for earning a living to finance their studies, they opened "Persian" restaurants and served what they themselves had eaten all their lives:

homemade Iranian food. Restaurateurs refrained from presenting themselves as Iranian, saying that customers would not patronize an Iranian restaurant because of the low status of Iranians in England.

Immigrants and minority groups differ in the opportunities they have to marshal their food as a means of either economic mobility or bridging the cultural gap between themselves and their host society. Moreover, political discourse contributes its own criteria to distinguish between dishes that win acceptance in the local culinary realm and dishes that elicit disdain. The kitchens of groups in positions of power and prestige enjoy culinary appreciation; people are curious about these groups' culinary heritage and are willing to taste their food, even when it is costly or made of unfamiliar ingredients. Conversely, the food of minority groups is considered unhealthy, undistinguished, devoid of taste, and unclean. A political discourse along these lines in Israel contributes to the relatively low prices in Arab restaurants and positions them as popular restaurants with wide appeal, yet not for the taste setters. As an indirect result, the mobility—especially the social mobility—of the Palestinian population in Israel has suffered.

Cookbooks are another terrain in which culinary knowledge is gathered and disseminated to the public. As cultural texts, cookbooks reveal relations of power by means of the ways in which the dominant group and ethnic groups write, rewrite, and construct their past, their culture, and their public image.[73] Roland Barthes defines *text* in this context as an aggregation of quotations through which the reader simultaneously transmits, screens, and creates knowledge.[74] As such, the text places knowledge in a particular historical context, and the reader creates the text by instilling his or her own meanings into the time and place in which it is read. The meanings of texts, therefore, are constantly changing based on who interprets and integrates the knowledge contained within them, and into which particular cultural world. Textual analysis reveals under what conditions minority and ethnic groups write their own histories and cultures; how texts represent minority groups, and under what conditions minority groups' self-images and histories undergo change.

Cookbooks are also social spaces with their own rules. They gather, evaluate, and contrast knowledge, mark its boundaries, establish formal stocks of culinary wisdom, and allow for a simultaneous presentation of various cuisines in simple and practical language. Consequently, they contribute to the weakening of culinary boundaries as the secrets of one group become available to others.[75] Food writers negotiate and present ethnicity and take it upon themselves to transmit ethnic knowledge to those outside the ethnic community. By including recipes either as authentic or in a modified form, food writers integrate ethnic culinary knowledge, reveal relations of power, and turn food into a commodity to be consumed by everyone and on diverse occasions. Janet Theophano notes the difficulty Chinese women have finding recipes in American cookbooks that are suitable for their families, and she describes the attempts of some of them to compose cookbooks that will translate the Chinese kitchen in a way that will be accessible to Americans as well.[76]

Additionally, cookbooks enhance collective memories. They mean different things to different social groups, and often their very concept is foreign to immigrants and minorities, who tend to transmit culinary knowledge orally. Cookbooks written by either immigrants or minorities turn ethnicity into a reservoir of practical knowledge that can be integrated within the boundaries of the local culinary knowledge. In other words, when immigrants and minorities think there is a potential clientele for their food, they are willing to disseminate their culinary heritage in a form and content that is potentially appealing.

The dissemination of culinary knowledge out of the community of its holders does not merely express the demand of ethnic groups to realize their rights in a multicultural era. Rather, it is part of the process of cultural globalization that blurs the distinctive features of national and ethnic cuisines functioning within the same borders. For example, it is possible to find dishes such as pizza, pasta, hamburgers, and falafel, whose historical roots have been forgotten, in many countries. Globalization has not skipped over the Palestinian cuisine in Israel. Openness to new markets and products, advanced cooking technologies, and the accessibility of modern channels of communication have exposed the Palestinian population to new dishes, some of which they adopt and adapt to their own traditional tastes and some of which they reject.

The emerging and changing culinary culture of Palestinian citizens of Israel is also influenced by other factors, such as geography. Climatic conditions determine the accessibility of certain ingredients and thereby also determine the character of the menu. Fish dishes, for example, are more abundant in Arab localities close to the sea than in those located in the hills or plains. History is another factor. The various conquerors that followed one another in the region left their imprint in the Arab plates as well as in other domains. For example, stuffed vegetables reached the Palestinian kitchen in Israel by way of the Turkish kitchen. Culture, too, contributes its part by assigning symbolic meanings to certain dishes, and by determining who will eat them and under what circumstances. For example, Palestinian Christians eat a shelled-wheat pudding known as *burbara* on December 4 in memory of St. Barbara, an early Christian martyr; many Muslims also started eating *burbara* as an expression of solidarity with Christians. Social relationships, such as the division of labor between men and women, also shape the Arab kitchen in Israel. Palestinians of both sexes expect women to manage the domestic kitchen but men to cook in the public domain. Religious precepts are yet another influence on culinary practices: in Islam, eating pork is proscribed, as is drinking alcohol. Finally, economic considerations shape the daily menu in accordance with the family's financial means. While the rise in the price of bulgur (cracked wheat) caused many to give it up in favor of subsidized rice, the low price of industrial noodles made the preparation of homemade noodles not worthwhile.

Certain developments in the Palestinian cuisine in Israel are unique. With the founding of the state of Israel, Palestinians became a minority group living on their own land, yet excluded from the social and cultural boundaries of the collective. Some of the changes the cuisine underwent resemble changes in cuisines of immigrants, even though the Palestinian citizens of Israel did not experience physical migration. While the food of immigrants usually changes, as we have seen, by being exposed to the dominant culture, receiving approval from it, and acquiring an exotic aroma, Palestinian cuisine underwent a more complex transformation. On the one hand, neither the establishment of the state of Israel, nor exposure to Jewish society, interrupted the continuity of the Palestinian kitchen. It retained its unique features, while innovations were adopted selectively, consistent with the needs and tastes of the population. Arab society in Israel was also not cut off from the basic products to which it was accustomed, and many families continued to grow fruits and vegetables, culture their own sour milk and cheeses, preserve meat, prepare bulgur, bake bread, and harvest and use wild plants. On the other hand, dishes that demanded intensive labor either disappeared or were replaced by technologically innovative substitutes that shortened preparation time and by prepared foods such as breakfast cereals, fast foods, dairy desserts, and canned goods.

Similar to immigrant societies, Palestinian citizens of Israel also kept most of the elements of their cuisine in the private sphere, not so much due to the reluctance of the Palestinian population to expose its food as to the suspicions of the Jewish public toward Arab food. Some, but only relatively few, of its components were appropriated by Jewish knowledge agents and became identified as "Israeli" dishes, in that their source was ultimately forgotten or not acknowledged. This was the fate of falafel, hummus, tahini, baklava, and *labaneh*. But contrary to the kitchens of other migrant groups throughout the world, Palestinian cuisine in Israel has not yet been tapped for nostalgic flavor during holidays or family gatherings, because it lives on actively in daily life and continues to be passed down from generation to generation as part of women's socialization. The Arab kitchen thus remains a reservoir of knowledge possessed by the Arab community.

The first generation of immigrants and diasporic communities tends to preserve and reproduce its food and eating habits in the home, both out of habit and in an attempt to overcome a sense of alienation.[77] The familiar food, with its fragrances from the land of origin, is a source of comfort in the daily confrontation with a different culture; a labor market often necessitating occupational retraining, low wages, or lack of prestige for one's work; and a host society unaware of the unique needs of the immigrants and exiles. Members of the second generation, more receptive to the dominant culture, tend to include that culture's dishes in their daily and holiday culinary repertoire, even at the price of alienation from their parents' culture.[78] The third and fourth generations of immigrant families, according to Herbert Gans, feel secure enough to return to their roots and home country traditions.[79] They are familiar with the codes of the dominant culture, do not have traumatic memories of migration, and are able to see in the culture of their parents and grandparents an exotic decoration of their daily lives—a spice enabling institutionalization of symbolic longing for the land of origin, along with trips in search of their roots, ethnic festivals, and learning the language of their parents.

The boundaries between an immigrant group and its host society are frequently flexible and diffuse, enabling the selective passage of knowledge, including culinary knowledge, between the groups. But in this regard, the situation of the Palestinians in Israel is different, as they are defined as hostile toward the state. Consequently, the territorial and social boundaries between Palestinians and Jewish Israeli society find expression in the kitchen as well. The fact that Palestinian cuisine in Israel has remained within the domestic sphere since 1948 is both a matter of personal choice as well as a manifestation of the sense of social and political marginality experienced by Palestinians in Israel. Publicly and politically, the longing for Palestine—a state not yet in existence—has changed form and content over the years; that longing has grown more concrete, until it is now part of the Palestinian strategy for realizing civil rights in the state of Israel. At the same time, it has prevented dissemination of their culinary knowledge outside the boundaries of the community.

In order to understand how Palestinians use food to develop a distinctive ethnic identity and the circumstances in which food serves as a bridge between Jews and Palestinians in Israel, we must identify the agents of culinary knowledge among Israeli Arabs. These agents are charged with preserving and disseminating culinary knowledge within both the private and public spheres. This book examines the strategies used by these knowledge agents to transform food into a tool for institutionalizing both a distinct identity and an intercultural bridge.

Palestinian women in Israel are the leading culinary agents at the level of the home. They use their position as domestic cooks both to modernize their cooking repertoire and to sustain traditional Palestinian culinary knowledge within the boundaries of their community. On the one hand, they use Palestinian food as a milestone for the construction of a diasporic identity distinct from Jewish society. Simultaneously, they exchange recipes and food with their Jewish neighbors and friends, introducing their families to foods they are likely to eat out of the community. Men, conversely, sustain the image of Palestinian food at the level of the restaurant, by maintaining the division between home food and restaurant food.

As knowledge agents operating in the domestic sphere, Palestinian women participate in the construction of a Palestinian identity. Through their cooking they make a connection between a distinct female identity and national liberation, between liberation at the level of the home and liberation from the system of colonial relations. These issues lead to a consideration of the extent to which the models of Western feminism are applicable to ethnic and minority groups. Some studies have examined the role of migrant women and their subjection to a double suppression—once as women and once as members of a minority group.[80] Both women and men from ethnic groups integrate mostly into the lower ranks of the labor ladder, but in most cases, women are more willing than men to accept their low status.

The popular as well as the professional discourse on food revolves around two pivots: One sees national and ethnic cuisines as bounded reservoirs of culinary knowledge based upon dishes, ingredients, and methods of cooking subscribed to by members of the community. The second sees national and ethnic cuisines as an aggregation of dishes cooked and consumed at the homes of members of a particular national ethnic group. Both perspectives assume the existence of various knowledge agents and various techniques of information dissemination.

According to the first approach, professional knowledge agents disseminate culinary knowledge and preserve it as a fixed doctrine. Moreover, the identification of culinary boundaries, ingredients, and rules of mixing and cooking can—at best—describe a national kitchen in its present state. This approach would have trouble explaining previous and contemporary transformations and innovations, especially those that challenge the culinary habits or the traditional cooking techniques that cross national barriers. Furthermore, this approach does not take into consideration changes of fashion, taste, eating habits, and political processes that are typical of modern societies. Advanced technologies, sophisticated marketing, or the ever-present desire to resemble another group influence the palate of the modern person; taste becomes more uniform across intersociety boundaries, and authenticity fades away.

The second approach attributes a central role to women as knowledge agents. Unlike the first approach, which does not see culinary knowledge as bounded by location, content, or time, the second approach emphasizes the accessibility of culinary information to all. Its advantage lies in its ability to explain changes that occur in the public and domestic kitchen and changes in culinary practices. This approach would view everything cooked and eaten by Palestinian citizens of Israel as Arab food, including *bamba* (a local and popular snack food among children), chocolate, cornflakes, margarine, soup made from frozen vegetables, and schnitzel.

This second, more flexible, approach is, among other things, a product of the transition from a modern to a postmodern view of the world. Modernity, as understood by Jürgen Habermas, focuses on the emergence of defined spheres of knowledge controlled by experts.[81] According to Michel Foucault, in modern times knowledge became a central means of accumulating power and controlling the subjects of a regime.[82] The culinary sphere has not been immune to these developments; from the nineteenth century onward, great chefs have developed methods of cooking that broke with existing culinary traditions and argued for the autonomy of the culinary domain.[83] On the other hand, postmodernists cast doubt upon the ability to create and define metaspheres that bestow legitimacy upon a particular sphere of knowledge.

While modernism consolidated disciplines, postmodernism deconstructs the knowledge domains created by modernism into small narratives and creates the pluralism that enables the combination of elements that had been separate in the past.[84]

This process takes place in the culinary sphere as well. For example, beliefs that French cuisine is based on a wealth of cream-based sauces or that Italian cuisine is synonymous with pasta are gradually replaced by the understanding that current cuisines emerge out of social, economic, and political processes that occur outside the culinary domain, such as technological developments, disappearance of seasonal agriculture, accessibility of new ingredients, massive immigration, changes in traditional gender-based division of labor, and a national awakening among ethnic groups. All these are fertile grounds for the blending of culinary traditions that had been historically and geographically separate. In other words, postmodernism in general, and its culinary manifestation in particular, emphasize the fact that national cuisines (including those already in existence for hundreds of years) are not homogeneous and closed entities as is commonly supposed. Rather, they are collections of individual items, cultural assumptions, political climates, and accessible technologies that together constitute contingent entities. For these reasons, it is difficult today to speak of "French," "Italian," or "Chinese" cuisines. Rather, we have national cuisines as texts that gather and produce the constituents, ideologies, and technologies that exist at a given moment for a particular audience.

The Palestinian cuisine in Israel has not escaped this process. Daily links with the Jewish population and exposure to new cooking products and technologies have introduced changes in Palestinian culinary practice and have redefined its traditional culinary boundaries. The entry of new ingredients of every kind has given birth to combinations that depart from the traditional kitchen, such as lasagna using lamb meat, *sfikhah* from frozen pastry dough sold in the supermarket, and other items for daily use, such as ketchup, dry cereals, and dairy products. Thus, culinary practice among the Palestinian citizens of Israel differs from that found in Jordan, Lebanon, or any other Arab country, as each community adds to its culinary repertoire those elements to which it has been exposed in its country of residence.

The perception of national cuisines is challenged from another direction as well. Starting in the mid-1970s, an increasing number of Western cookbooks have asserted that chefs and authors have overstated the importance of national cuisines and that regional kitchens are no less dominant—and possibly more dominant—than national ones.[85] In Italy, for example, there is a real difference between the southern kitchen, where pasta is widely used, and the northern kitchen, where rich dishes are more prevalent. In many Middle Eastern countries as well, regional kitchens are found: In Egypt, a distinction is made between the rural kitchen and the urban one and also between the kitchen of the poor and that of the wealthy. The main distinction in Turkey is between the Istanbul kitchen (characterized by fish and seafood, rice, and delicate seasonings), the Izmir kitchen (characterized by Syrian dishes such as *kubeh*), and the Anatolian kitchen (where the Balkan influence is prominent). In Iran, the most noticeable differences are between the Persian-speaking and the non-Persian-speaking regions.[86]

One could assume that at a time when culinary boundaries are blurred and ethnic culinary knowledge more than ever before is recruited from and integrated into the culinary knowledge of its surroundings, authenticity is giving way to pseudoethnic cuisines. These focus on food as a means of making a living and emphasize the potential similarity of the various cuisines rather than their differences. Culinary agents of the ethnic groups negotiate with the dominant group about the limits of reciprocal influence and appropriation of dishes by the dominant culture.[87] Although limited in their power, ethnic groups manage to draw on their own reservoirs of knowledge to contribute to and enrich the dominant culinary culture, while maintaining a certain degree of culinary autonomy. Moreover, they gain control over the public image of their ethnicity and food.[88] The social interactions and negotiations that I describe in the next chapters comprise countless personal choices and decisions made by individual actors. It is when these are aggregated into emerging macrolevel social and political definitions and forms of action that the process of social negotiation comes into view.

Palestinian citizens of Israel negotiate the extent to which their culinary culture wins acceptance among Jews and the form and content of its dissemination out of their community. Questions are asked as to whether and how Palestinian cookery should be preserved during an era of increasing exposure to new foodstuffs. What is the nature of culinary exchanges between Palestinians and Jews in Israel and how should they be organized? Do these exchanges stem from an attitude of mutual respect, equality, and reciprocity, or do they simply institutionalize the appropriation of Palestinian food?

These negotiations take place at both the domestic and the public level. At the household level, Palestinian women take the lead. Being responsible for feeding the family, they make daily decisions regarding the dishes that will reach the family table. They are also agents for change in the domestic culinary repertoire as they introduce their families to new foods. At the public level, Palestinian men engage in negotiations from their positions as breadwinners. In their position as restaurateurs, they define and shape the nature, boundaries, and substance of Palestinian cuisine in Israel and the reciprocal relations that exist between it and what Palestinians perceive as Jewish cuisine. Cooking on the public level is based on a more limited repertoire of dishes from the household kitchen. At the same time, it serves as a bridge between Palestinian and Jewish Israeli societies, a display window of Palestinian cuisine, and an indication of the dishes that the Palestinian public seeks in restaurants. Via the Palestinian public kitchen, the Jewish population is invited to taste, recognize, and experience new but not overly unfamiliar foods, whereas for the Palestinian community, and particularly for Palestinian women, the public kitchen provides an opportunity to rest from everyday foods and kitchen chores and to enjoy dishes that are not an integral part of the daily repertoire.

This book provides a peek into the pots and plates of Palestinian women and men in Israel. Part 1 focuses on the nature of Arab food and cooking in the domestic sphere. By analyzing food as a system of knowledge, I reveal the connection between food and the status of women and show how food becomes an informal means for women to negotiate their position both in the home and in the Palestinian community. The focus on Palestinian women as active agents of culinary knowledge sheds light on the nature of Palestinian women's minority status in Israel. I also examine the ways in which Palestinian women's social position prevents them from developing a feminine identity that challenges traditional social conventions. I argue that despite the vast culinary knowledge at their disposal, Palestinian women are careful when mobilizing that knowledge as a means of ameliorating their position in the family. Their ability to make decisions in their lives and control their fates—that is, to negotiate the extent of their dissent from the existing order—is limited. Although they experience a dual subjugation—both at the hands of the patriarchal system of Palestinian society and as female citizens in Israeli society, they go no further than asserting the informal power that their role in the family and the community grants them. As different as their lives may be from those of their mothers, they still feel they cannot write a social culinary text of their own that would redefine their position in the domestic household and public-political systems.

Part 2 discusses the Palestinian kitchen in Israel on the public level. In connection with modernization I claim that there is a link between the culinary knowledge exposed in the public sphere and the processes of forming ethnic identity characteristic of symbolic exile. The discussion revolves around the diverse content that Palestinian citizens of Israel assign to their perception of modernization, and examines its expression in light of the changes in dishes and cooking technologies over the period of ongoing contact with Jewish society. Moreover, I focus on the connection between the emergence of a Palestinian Arab identity in the shadow of the dominant Jewish culture in the state of Israel and the development of a cuisine that combines tradition and modernity. I point to the social factors that support or prevent public recognition, both Jewish and Arab, for the Palestinian Arab kitchen. For that purpose I analyze the ways in which Palestinian restaurants in Israel compete for clientele outside the Arab community.

The research on which the book is based is the result of one hundred in-depth interviews conducted with Palestinian women and men living in Israel. The respondents come from urban and rural backgrounds and include Muslims and Christians. All but two, who lived in the Negev, resided either in Galilee, in the Triangle area, or in small towns in the vicinity of Tel Aviv. Only a few of my informants perceived themselves as Israelis; some defined themselves as Palestinians, and the rest saw themselves as Arab citizens of the state of Israel. This book adopts the definitions invoked in the particular cases. Purely to simplify and unify the book, the expression "Palestinian citizens of Israel" is used throughout to signify Arabs who are citizens of the state of Israel, and the term "Palestinians" is used to denote Palestinians living in the Occupied Territories. In making that decision I do not mean to challenge in any way the independent definitions of self used by the two groups.

Since the book's central focus is the social meaning and role of food, along with its political connections as perceived by the population under study, I have devoted less attention to the culinary differences between the various regions in Israel, between urban and rural populations, and between those living in so-called mixed cities and those living in all-Arab towns or villages.[89] These differences are noted explicitly in only a small number of instances, when such information was relevant.

This interpretive focus enables me to concentrate in greater depth on information relating specifically to food and to devote less attention to institutional aspects that accompany culinary activity and organize the dissemination of culinary knowledge.

Now that I have defined the focus of the book, let us allow the cooks—men and women—and the food, smells, spices, and utensils to have their say.

PART ONE

What Palestinian Women Must Know

Food in the Home

Souad seasons a mixture of rice and ground meat with salt, black pepper, cinnamon, and *baharat* (a spice blend). Using this mixture, she fills summer squash halfway up and packs them into a deep pot, layers two or three peeled tomatoes on top, splashes some olive oil over it all, and covers the mix with a stainless steel tray. She places the pot over a medium flame, and we sit down in the living room for coffee and conversation. An hour later, Souad stands up. "It's ready," she announces. "How do you know?" I ask. "I know," she responds and goes to the kitchen to remove the pot from the fire and set the table.

This brief encounter conveys in a nutshell the essence of women's culinary knowledge. Starting at a young age, Palestinian women, as part of their socialization, acquire cooking skills through trial and error and daily practice. Armed with a life of culinary knowledge, Souad is able to prepare dishes without tasting them during the course of their preparation. At the domestic level, women are active practitioners and purveyors of culinary knowledge; conversely, men disseminate Palestinian culinary knowledge in the public sphere. As professional cooks men prepare only dishes that are nor regularly eaten in the Palestinian home.

The first part of this book concerns women, analyzing the traditional Arab kitchen as a reservoir of women's culinary knowledge. The discussion focuses upon home technology, economic constraints, and the ways in which the webs of family relations shape the kitchen and the

Palestinian household repertoire in Israel as they preserve power relations within both the family and the community.

I first examine the components of female knowledge, its culinary and cultural boundaries, and the ways in which that knowledge is expressed and renewed in practice. Within the territory of the home, women create, develop, and archive accumulated culinary knowledge, passing it on from one generation to the next. In doing so, women are also agents of change, adapting new recipes to accommodate the tastes and needs of the surrounding community. The domestic kitchen, as we shall see, has three distinctive features. First, domestic culinary knowledge is based on familiarity with the reservoir of products and dishes available to Palestinian citizens of Israel and with the existing technologies of home cooking. The latter are what determine methods for cooking, food preservation, and storage.

Second, domestic knowledge requires familiarity with the natural environment and the ability to mobilize free or inexpensive food sources throughout the year. This knowledge enables women to identify potential food sources, make use of all their components, and diversify the culinary repertoire.[1] Generally speaking, kitchens are based on modes of thought that determine the use of products, the rules of cooking and serving, and the adaptation of foods for specific populations. For example, cultures in Asia distinguish between "hot" and "cold" foods, believing that hot foods warm the body and create energy, while cold ones have a calming effect and promote coolness and comfort. It is expected that women in these cultures will know not only what a "cold" food is and what a "hot" one is but also to whom and under what circumstances they should serve these foods.[2]

Third, domestic culinary knowledge is organized around a distinction between culinary events, such as family meals versus festive ones. Women master knowledge of the various meals that constitute the institutional basis of Palestinian hospitality and the culinary exchanges that take place between members of the community.[3] Furthermore, culinary practices reinforce the status quo and a gendered social hierarchy in the Palestinian home. The dishes a woman serves to her guests, the quantities she chooses to prepare, and her ability to suit the meal to the event all testify to her level of culinary knowledge and feminine skill.

The discussion considers three central aspects of culinary practice and their wider context. I examine the connection between the positions different family members hold in the household and the way in which those positions influence what is eaten at home. The culinary sphere opens up a place where women make decisions in the home, but this does not challenge the system of family power relations. This system perseveres even when women join the workforce outside the home, as they turn to their mothers for help with cooking.

Moving beyond the isolated home and individual family, culinary activity contributes to community formation, as women share daily life, exchange cooking tips and practices, and work together to prepare meals for special occasions.

Finally, I show the extent to which women's culinary knowledge is integral to their daily social experience in Palestinian society in Israel. The ability to cook has become an essential commodity in the social capital of those about to marry and start their own families. As mothers, women prepare the coming generation, retaining and processing culinary knowledge, thus paradoxically serving as agents of change who introduce innovations into the household while adapting them to the tastes of the family.

CHAPTER I

Women's Ways of Knowing

Culinary knowledge is at the core of social identity for Palestinian women in Israel. Women acquire culinary knowledge and master certain food preparation skills as part of a normal process of gender socialization. First and foremost, women must learn to prepare, preserve, and store foods on a family budget. They must also master the accepted culinary norms and social practices of Palestinian family and society, particularly as they govern hospitality and the practice of hosting guests from the larger community. Women's cooking is based upon obligation and reciprocity, and it ensures the continuing life of a family and the community at large.

Knowledge at a technical level includes proficiency in the techniques of cooking, storage, and baking: Should one cook using gas or coals? Bake in the *taboun* or in an electric oven? What means of storage and refrigeration should be used? And should dough be kneaded by hand or mechanically? Technical knowledge also requires a response to changing household technologies.[1] For example, when it became possible to prepare dough in commercial quantities, the technology of baking at home gradually disappeared from the knowledge reserves of Arab women in Israel. As a result of new household technologies, there has been a decline in home preparation of dishes such as baklava and *kishik,* a dish made from dehydrated sheep's milk mixed with bulgur.[2]

On the level of day-to-day culinary organization, women's knowledge involves familiarity with the criteria for selecting products and putting them to maximal and varied use. Women in general, and especially those in developing societies, are adept at finding food in ways that depend as little as possible on a monetary economy. In many societies, women raise crops for domestic use and exchange goods and services with other women.[3] Among Palestinian women in Israel, this proficiency expresses itself in the ability to select vegetables for cooking that are inexpensive and nourishing, and to locate natural sources of food that do not cost money, such as edible wild plants that grow in yards and fields. Palestinian women are skilled at preparing meat dishes from fresh meat and making use of all parts of the animal; they are also able to serve meat dishes that contain very little or even no meat. The function of women as food suppliers increases their value in the family and in the community but does not challenge power relations in the home.

In Palestinian culture, women are generally responsible for preparing meals in the home. The meal is an expression of the level of female culinary knowledge, since it demonstrates a woman's ability to translate into practical knowledge not only the theoretical knowledge of cooking but also the semiotic system and the popular cultural beliefs invoked by food. Women thus become responsible for organizing the structure of the meal, the tastes and aesthetics of its serving, and the rules of food classification. The culinary knowledge held by Palestinian women in Israel may be understood as part of the development of their female identity and the institutionalization of the gender definition of roles in the family and in the community. Culinary knowledge also serves as a means of constructing the distinct cultural identity of Palestinian citizens of Israel.

THE TECHNOLOGICAL LEVEL

Food preparation in the traditional Palestinian domestic kitchen is based upon simple technology. Until the 1960s, baking, cooking, and food preservation and storage were carried out by female manual labor in a traditional spirit. Starting in the 1960s, electric appliances became accessible and popular. Concurrently, some of the simple means of food preparation have gradually disappeared, while others have survived and continue to be used—especially among the older generation—alongside modern means. In this discussion, I focus on the two main technologies most common in the kitchens of Palestinian citizens of Israel: the technology of preserving and storing and the technology of baking. We shall discover how these technologies both strengthened the gender division of labor in the Palestinian community and helped to institutionalize community ties.

"We No Longer Make Kishik": Food Preservation and Storage Technologies

Before the 1960s, most Arab villages and towns in Israel lacked the infrastructure necessary to support the use of electrical appliances in the home. Under military rule, Arab localities were of less concern to Israeli politicians, who often considered the provision of proper infrastructure as a return for Arabs' expression of loyalty to the Jewish state. In the absence of electric means of refrigeration that would enable the long-term storage and preservation of meat and milk products, Palestinian women in Israel developed alternative methods based on keeping food in cool places, preserving it in oil, or drying it. Practically speaking, these three solutions enabled women to store food instead of discarding it or allowing it to spoil. Socially, these preservation and storage methods reinforced community boundaries, since they were based upon a gendered division of labor and institutionalized trust among women. They also accorded well with the transition to a monetary economy, built upon relations of trust between women as consumers and salespeople in local shops.

First and foremost, these preservation technologies responded to the needs created by the times: the absence of an electrical grid and economic means that kept electric appliances out of the villages for quite a long time after the establishment of the state of Israel. Most Arab families did not eat meat every day, for economic reasons; their aim was to keep a herd of sheep as a permanent source of milk products. On holidays or for special occasions, they would slaughter a sheep, and after all had eaten, they would store the leftover meat under conditions that ensured its preservation for several days at least. Keeping the meat in a cool place was the short-term solution—effective for two or three days—and demanded very simple expertise: meat was stored in a covered ceramic pot. Some hung the container high up—on a lamp shade, for example—and others lowered it down a well, hanging it above the water, to exploit the coolness there. Nabiya from Majd-al-Kurum explains:

> After we slaughtered a sheep and ate, my mother would take the leftover meat and put it into a jar. On the jar she would place cloth or dough.

Sometimes she would tie it with rope from a light fixture; sometimes she would lower it into the well so it would stay cool. It would keep that way for a day or two.

To keep meat for a longer period of time, other techniques were employed. The most popular was to store the meat in its own fat. After cutting it into cubes and cooking it until it was three-quarters done, says seventy-year-old Um George, from the town of Rama:

> When the fat was like oil, we covered the meat in its fat to enclose it and put it in a ceramic container. Whenever we needed meat, we opened up the fat, took out as much as we needed, and covered the meat again.

Another simple preservation technique is drying meat. In Arab society, drying and salting meat was less common than storing it in oil. Turkiya, a sixty-year-old cosmetics shop and grocery store manager from Jaffa, relates that before there was a refrigerator in their home, her mother preferred drying leftover meat to storing it in oil:

> She used to cut the meat into cubes and cover it with a lot of salt so all the liquid was removed. Then, she put it in a basket, covered it with a cloth, and hung the basket on the chandelier so the cat couldn't reach it. We could keep the meat two weeks that way.

All three techniques were based on cutting meat into small cubes—a method that suits many dishes commonly consumed by Arabs. Additionally, all three techniques reflected a gendered division of labor, according to which women cook, preserve, and store meat after men have slaughtered the sheep. The slaughter, preservation, and storage of food enabled regular family and community life by ensuring a constant supply of food for the family as well as for broader circles.

The creation of an accessible supply of milk for the periods when goats and sheep are not lactating satisfied similar needs. Certain milk products were stored in oil or dried, similarly to the meat. The most common and best-known example of a milk product of this type is *labaneh,* which in the Arab sector is stored and sold covered with olive oil. Today, in the era of the refrigerator and commercial *labaneh,* olive oil serves as a garnish and also imparts flavor and a sense of authenticity. *Labaneh* is prepared in the summer, when goats produce richer milk. Using the traditional method, women took ten to twenty liters of goat's milk and put it in small sacks, hanging them to drain the fluid. Once the milk had drained sufficiently, women added salt, formed balls, and put the balls into jars, covering them with olive oil. Isam, a literature teacher from the village of Kabul who now lives in Haifa, says that his mother still prepares *labaneh* every summer for her extended family:

> She brought us about twenty jars a year and a half ago. Today I straightened out the storeroom and found one jar. It still tastes superb!

Another traditional technique for preserving and storing milk is still used today: milk is dried or transformed into a solid, so that with the addition of liquid, the milk can be reconstituted. In the Palestinian kitchen in Israel milk is stored as hard cheese that can be changed into *laban* that is suitable for cooking. The two most popular products serving this purpose are *kishik* and *jibne,* the Arab cheese. These products serve as milk reservoirs that free women from needing to seek out fresh milk.

Ethnologists, linguists, and historians have had difficulty ascertaining the origins of *kishik.* According to Françoise Aubaile-Sallenave, who analyzes the linguistic and use aspects of *kishik,* the source of the word is the Persian *kishik.*[4] *Kishik* is known outside of Israel in Iran, Azerbaijan, Armenia, Kurdistan, Lebanon, the Arabian Peninsula, and Egypt. Despite its variations, *kishik* can be identified by its main ingredients: sheep's milk mixed with a grain (especially bulgur). Methods of its preparation are varied: in Iran it is prepared from yogurt and preserved in small balls; in Turkey it is defined as sour dried milk; in Syria, Lebanon, and Israel it is known to be boiled milk mixed with bulgur and then dried in the sun.

Along with the development of domestic technology and amid a growing economy in Israel, refrigerators were introduced into the home and sales of commercial milk products jumped. For these reasons the preparation of *kishik* in the home became superfluous and not worth the effort, until it eventually disappeared from the culinary scene.

In the past, the custom was to prepare *kishik* from boiled sheep's milk. After the milk had cooled and bulgur had been added, it was all moved to a cloth bag and the liquid was drained out. When the milk had drained, a large heavy stone was placed on the cheese thus produced for several days in order to squeeze out the small amount of moisture still remaining. Then the cheese was coated in salt, a string was run through it, and it was hung to dry further in the sun. To transform the *kishik* to *laban,* a piece of it was pounded very fine, and it was mixed with water until it became a thick liquid.

Nabiya, a sixty-year-old single woman from Acre, still prepares *kishik* every summer in order to preserve the waning tradition. For years she tried to convince her niece to learn to prepare *kishik* in order to assure continuation of the tradition, but her niece believes there is no room for *kishik* in the modern daily menu. Nabiya explains:

> It takes a lot of work, and you need to feel it in your fingers before you set it out to dry. It takes me fifteen days to prepare it. In winter I use *kishik* to prepare *laban* for cooking. Unfortunately, the younger generation of women would not hear of it.

In Jerusalem and the Occupied Territories, *kishik* is called *jibjib*, and some think it tastes sourer and is "as dry as stones." Today, even though the small amounts of *kishik* and *jibjib* made in the home are still prepared by women, most of it is sold to stores. As my interviewees put it, these food products are purchased only in stores perceived as being "as clean as my home." The merchant middleman who earns the confidence of his clientele is thought of as the supplier of a traditional product that liberates women from the labor of preparing it. Reina, who works in a Jerusalem barbershop, explains that for her to purchase *kishik* at the store she needs to be convinced the place is clean:

> I go into a store several times, check out the salesperson, his hands, the floor, and his utensils. If it is all clean, I buy. I still place the *kishik* in boiling water so no germs remain.

Reina uses *kishik* mostly for the unique taste that it imparts to food, rather than as a way to provide milk: its sour flavor lends dishes such as *shishbarak* their particular taste. But unlike her mother, who used to crumble the *kishik* by hand, Reina uses a mixer.

The purchase and preparation of *kishik* was an important part of a Palestinian woman's realm of knowledge, which responded to the practical and social needs of the community. Women were expected to be adept at the techniques of preparing *kishik,* storing it, and turning it into *laban* for cooking. At the same time, the use of *kishik* enabled them to develop trust and exchange relations with those producing *kishik* in their stead, thus bringing them within the boundaries of the community.

Like *kishik,* Arab cheese provides a means to prevent milk products from spoiling, and thus creates a way of storing milk, a vital protein in the Arab diet. Cheese, too, is able to change form and taste according to the needs of the dish, since it is possible to soften it and neutralize its basic salty taste. When one wants to prepare *knafeh,* for example, one soaks the cheese in water, changing the water every few minutes until the saltiness is gone, and then kneads the cheese to the desired texture.

In the past, cheese was prepared at home from sheep's milk. With the spread of pediatric clinics in the cities and villages and an increasing concern for hygiene and awareness of risks associated with raw milk, women who still prepare cheese at home have begun to pasteurize the milk. Fatma, from the village of Barta'a in Wadi Ara, says:

> I make cheese at home like my mother did, but I buy something in the pharmacy to put in the milk to make sure the cheese is clean.

As with *kishik,* the technology used in preparing cheese is no longer an integral part of women's knowledge. More and more women buy cheese from village women who still prepare it at home or from a storekeeper who has won their trust. Alia, from the village of Reine in Galilee, says:

> I wouldn't buy cheese from someone I don't know. You Jews taught us that there are diseases in cheese and we need to be sure that it is clean. Because of that there are fewer sicknesses among us now.

Despite knowing who has made the cheese, most women pasteurize it again when they bring it home. Nadia, from Makr, who stopped making cheese fifteen years ago when she started working outside her home, buys cheese from a woman she has known for many years. Yet she still makes sure the cheese is pasteurized and safe for eating:

> I don't trust her completely. I put the cheese in boiling water and then remove it from the water and put in on a plate. If the cheese returns to its form, that's a sign it's all right. I keep the cheese in lots of water and salt in the refrigerator so I know it's one hundred percent clean.

Storage and preservation technologies both responded to practical needs within a developing context. Changing technologies and access to pasteurized and processed cheeses represent a certain level of liberation for Palestinian women. Technological change also altered women's relationships to the larger community, as they came to trust store owners who purvey hygienic food products.

From Taboun *to Oven: The Technology of Baking*

Like technologies for the preservation and storage of meat and milk, the technology of baking employed in the Palestinian community reflects the level of baking technology in Israel as a whole.

Bread has always served as a metaphor in speaking about poverty, wealth, and simple technologies as compared with advanced techniques.

As such, it has been a key focus of imitation by the lower classes. In eighteenth-century Europe, commercial bread, made from white flour, was a status symbol of the upper class; it therefore became an object of imitation by members of the lower class, who until then had only eaten dark bread or bread that was not made entirely from wheat. Flour was milled at home, and bread was baked in the domestic oven. Accelerating industrialization in Europe beginning in the mid-eighteenth century enabled white flour to be manufactured in large quantities. At the same time, it became customary to purchase bread made from white flour at bakeries located near residential areas, and baking bread at home was restricted to those who could not afford commercial bread. Women who worked outside the home and had difficulty balancing that work with their domestic obligations, or women whose financial situation permitted it, took advantage of the relatively low price of bread as well as the variety offered in the bakeries, so that home baking was no longer worthwhile.[5]

Over the past hundred years, the Palestinian sector in Israel has undergone a similar transformation. In the past, women gathered wheat in the fields and milled it into flour at home. Technological innovations and improvements in Palestinians' economic situations made it possible for them to mill wheat in the village flour mill rather than grinding it by hand at home. Women prepared dough early in the morning and baked bread in a *taboun*—an oven made of clay and dug into the earth, with just its dome visible above the surface. The low structure of the *taboun* required women to bend down beside it as they rolled out dough and baked it on both sides. Animal dung and the remains from the olive harvest—which were accessible to all—were burned at night to eliminate bad odors, and then used as fuel. In the morning the coals were covered with stones from the riverbed, and bread was baked on the raised surface. The glowing coals were not extinguished during the day, so that the *taboun* remained available for additional use. Ziad, a biologist born during the 1950s in the Triangle, a region on Israel's border east of Netanya, recounts:

> I remember that at night during the '50s the entire village was permeated with the smell of burnt dung. Sometimes I long for that smell. During the '60s the era of the *taboun* came to an end and we entered the era of kerosene. Later women switched to electric ovens, electric pots, or wood-burning ovens in the yard.

In Arab villages some families still prefer to bake their bread in the *taboun*. Aida, a religious housewife and a teacher by training whose husband works as a chef at a hotel in the center of the country, explains that even though they can afford to buy bread, she prefers the taste of home-baked bread:

> I get up in the morning and make bread so my husband can have freshly home-baked bread when he returns from work. The children also like warm bread from the *taboun*. I have an oven in the kitchen, but the *taboun* is something else.

When men began to work outside the village, their families were exposed to the cash economy. Later on, when women joined the labor market, their families' economic situations improved further. One of the first manifestations of the improvement was the ability to purchase milled white flour. From there it was but a short step to the purchase of ready-made bread from local bakeries and stores. Nawaf, a doctor from the north, learned about white bread from his parents' neighbor:

> She began to buy white flour and later white bread from the store and my mother learned from her. It was considered a sign of style, showing everyone that we were well off. During these past ten years, bread is no longer baked at home; everyone purchases it.

Adnan, a government-employed social worker from the Triangle, relates that during his childhood, he and his friends identified the consumption of white bread with Israeli soldiers. And for all that, the imitation of Jewish eating habits began with bread:

> One day my uncle came to the house with a loaf of the bread the Israeli soldiers used to eat. We each tasted a bit so there would be enough for all of us. Now that our financial situation has improved and women work outside the home, you'll find a loaf of bread everywhere you go: sliced bread, low-calorie bread, and also what you call *pita*.

And indeed, from the sixties onward, along with the growing consumption of industrial baked bread, kerosene and electric ovens were used more in the home. Fewer women continued to bake bread in the *taboun* at home. Electric pots, widely used during the seventies by Palestinians in Israel, made baking easier. Samira, a teacher who lives in Acre, relates that she couldn't get used to the taste of store-bought bread, and that she felt a sense of relief when her husband bought her an electric "wonder pot."[6] She takes the pot out of the kitchen cupboard, puts it down on the stove, and plugs it in. When it heats up, she returns to check the dough. When I ask why she sets the "wonder pot" on the gas burner, she laughs:

> You know, I never noticed. Maybe because it is called a pot and it has the shape of a pot that I put it on the gas. It's even tastier than the bread

my mother baked in the *taboun* and in much less work than my mama had to do.

The entry of electric appliances into the Palestinian home in Israel did not completely replace the traditional baking methods. Rather, it imposed new knowledge that women had to learn and most chose to adopt. Prior baking knowledge is retained and drawn upon during times of economic hardship that necessitate conserving electricity and expenses. Families with limited budgets can cut down on their electricity bills by exchanging their electric oven for one that burns logs. While in Jewish society the fireplace is a status symbol, an indication of economic well-being and personal style, in the Arab sector, it is a sign of economic hardship. "My mother lives in the village," says the owner of a grocery in Baka al-Gharbiya. "Recently she started preparing bread at home." At first he thought it was out of nostalgia; afterward, he saw that she had a wood oven. She had less money, and that's how she economized. In other words, tradition is a reservoir of knowledge that can be tapped in times of need to keep down the family's expenses.

Changes in everyday life habits also influence the extent to which women bake. Baking bread was a core part of Palestinian women's daily experience and activity in Israel. Even today, baking bread at home is a sign of a woman's competence as a mother and wife. Modern technologies, such as the electric oven, freezer, and microwave, make it possible to bake bread once every few days and store it without impairing its freshness. Thus, the woman is perceived as both one who fulfills her traditional gender roles and one who knows how to perform them alongside new responsibilities, such as sharing the burden of earning a livelihood.

Older women have only partially adapted to modern baking technologies. A Galilee surgeon claims that his mother can immediately identify homemade bread, but with the changing times she has learned to combine traditional principles with modern technologies:

> At the very most she'll buy from the man who goes around the village with his car selling to everyone, but she's not happy with that. When I was a boy, I would wake up to the odor of fresh bread. Now she's older and it's hard for her, so she bakes every few days and puts the bread in the freezer.

This statement, like many similar ones I heard, reveals that the appearance of modern technology has changed home labor, often causing people to exchange products that had been a central part of their food consumption for modern substitutes. At the same time, modern technology enables continued consumption of products that would otherwise have disappeared from the daily menu because of the intensive work entailed in their preparation. The new technologies of preserving, storing, and baking, and the possibility of replacing food products that in the past had been prepared at home with ready-made products, ease the physical burden borne by women, but the responsibility to prepare food for the entire family is still theirs; the traditional division of labor remains unchanged.

Despite the convenience of using a refrigerator, oven, and electric pot, the traditional aromas have not completely disappeared, but have only become subtler. New technology allows Palestinian women to choose whether to adhere to the traditional patterns of food preparation or to adopt those that lighten the work burden at home. In other words, cultural content alongside instrumental needs determine the ways in which technology is used.[7] While most women rely on store-bought bread and cheese, other women continue to bake or prepare cheese at home. These two trends exist simultaneously and are not considered contradictory. As we shall see, this duality is characteristic of the Palestinian kitchen in Israel.

DAILY CULINARY ORGANIZATION

As agents of culinary knowledge who shape and sustain the Palestinian culinary heritage at home, Palestinian women in Israel preserve power relations in the Palestinian family and community. Culinary organization in everyday life includes selecting products and preparing them while watching the family budget. A woman will be appreciated if she chooses and prepares the proper vegetables for filling, selects suitable fresh meat in the market, uses all parts of the animal, and serves meat dishes that contain little or even no meat. This ability establishes her as a wise woman, responsible and thrifty. The internalization of culinary knowledge strengthens women's position in the household and family without challenging the position of the men of the house.

The Preparation of Vegetables and Wild Plants

The ability to obtain and prepare food is an important part of women's knowledge in Palestinian society. It is also an indication of a woman's readiness for married life and her ability to manage a household efficiently and economically. Women are expected to know how to choose the best ingredients in the market, how to prepare them, and how to make the best use of them.

An example of a basic skill that Palestinian women must acquire in the course of their socialization is the purchase and preparation of vegetables to be stuffed. First, one must know which eggplant, squash, potatoes, carrots, and root vegetables are suitable for filling and which should be left for other dishes. Mary, a forty-seven-year-old Christian woman from Ramla, explains the principles of selecting vegetables as I accompany her on her shopping trip to the market:

> It's important to choose small, wide vegetables. Otherwise, it's hard to make an opening for filling. If the vegetables are long and thin, it's hard to scoop them out. They break apart and their taste isn't right for filling.

Second, one must learn how to prepare the vegetables for filling. With the help of a special curved knife, women scoop out the vegetables with a turning movement and remove elongated pieces. It's important to know how far to dig in to the vegetable in a way that ensures that the sides and bottom don't collapse. Experienced women, who devote half a minute at most to each vegetable, manage to leave about half a centimeter on the walls of the vegetable to prevent crumbling. Sixteen-year-old Abir, from Galilee, who has been engaged for the past year, relates that learning to stuff vegetables was the first task her mother assigned her after her engagement. Her fiancé did not want her to go to school, so she stays home and learns how to cook under her mother's supervision:

> She would call me and say, "Come, see how I prepare the stuffed vegetables." I would watch and afterward I would try. On my first try, I broke the squash, but slowly I improved. Today I sit and prepare squash by myself.

Third, one must learn how and with what to stuff the vegetables. Experienced women know to stuff the vegetables only halfway, so that the stuffing does not spill over and the dish is not spoiled, which would arouse doubts about her skill. The stuffing usually consists of rice with spices. If the budget permits, small pieces of lamb meat and pine nuts are added. Aisha, a nurse who has been married for the past five years, learned to cook only a short time before she was married, because she was a full-time student at a nursing school. She was not an experienced cook when she got married, and the first time she decided to make *makhshi* it took her two hours to scoop out the insides of the vegetables:

> I stuffed the entire cavity with rice and put it in the pot with tomatoes on top and cooked it the way my mom explained to me over the phone. As I opened the pot, all the rice spilled out, and the vegetables broke apart. Luckily my husband laughed. Slowly, I learned.

Fourth, Palestinian women must be thrifty with the vegetables even though they are relatively cheap. Putting them to maximum use indicates a high degree of cooking skill and a developed sense of responsibility. When vegetables are emptied out before being filled, some make use of the inside of the vegetables to prepare another dish. The inside part of the squash, for example, can be fried with spices and eggs. The result is a thick omelet that is a meal in itself. Another possibility is to prepare *tridi,* a vegetable dish made of small slices of vegetables, or chickpeas mixed with leftover squash and served with small slices of pita.

The ultimate marker of female knowledge is the ability to vary the menu within the bounds of the budget and the supply in the market, and to create a sense of the richest possible home menu. A woman who knows how to vary her dishes and create the sense of an abundant kitchen is considered to be an outstanding housewife, and her social prestige increases. Younis, a carpentry shop owner, tells me that he evaluated his future wife's expertise according to the variety of her culinary repertoire:

> I asked her, "What do you make with eggplant?" All in all she mentioned fourteen things. I thought to myself: "She will be a good wife. With her there will always be food at home."

Moustafa, a restaurateur from Jaffa, says that he was envious of a guest in his restaurant who bragged about how right he had been to marry a Syrian woman instead of a local Palestinian woman "who might be modern":

> He said that his wife could prepare twenty-four different dishes from eggplant and about thirty dishes from squash. She makes about fifteen kinds of *kubeh.* They've been married for two years and she has never made him the same food twice.

Questions about a woman's ability to vary dishes and make use of the products at her disposal are considered legitimate. They provide vital information to the man who is about to tie his life to hers. Arab men consider culinary knowledge to be one of the resources that determine a woman's value in the marriage market.

Grains and vegetables, more than other foods, are products through which a woman can show her ability to diversify the menu. Eggplant, for example, is the basis for a large variety of dishes. A woman with experience knows that eggplant can be pickled, stuffed, fried with vegetables and spices, cooked with rice (*maklubeh*), or baked with other vegetables and covered with tahini. A well-known and widely served dish made from eggplant is *menazali,* which can be prepared several ways: some are satisfied with a dish from pieces of eggplant fried with tomatoes, onion, and sometimes also chickpeas; others, like Um Yussuf from Jaffa, will prepare *menazali halabiah:*

> I alternate layers of fried eggplant stuffed with a mixture of fried onions and lamb meat seasoned with *baharat* and black pepper with layers of sliced potatoes. Finally I add tomatoes and all that remains of the meat. Then I cover it with just a bit of water and cook it.

Another popular dish is *musaka,* or eggplant stuffed with meat and cooked in *laban.* Unlike the Greek version of *musaka,* the Palestinian version of the dish is made from two slices of eggplant connected to each other on the bottom in a kind of sandwich. The "sandwich" is filled with spiced ground meat and then fried or cooked in goat's-milk *laban.*

Potatoes, too, benefit from a variety of recipes. In the past, they were usually cut into cubes, cooked quickly, and seasoned with lemon, olive oil, parsley, onions, and garlic. Today, potatoes receive more attention. Like eggplant and squash, potatoes are stuffed with lamb meat that has been fried with onions and spiced with nutmeg, black pepper, salt, *baharat,* and cinnamon. Potato dishes that have entered the menu as a result of Jewish influence include potato salad with mayonnaise and potato pie.

Soup is another way to economize and ensure full utilization of ingredients. If a soup is thick and rich, as red lentil soup is, it constitutes a full meal. The lentils are cooked in water containing fried onions, *baharat,* salt, and bouillon powder or cumin until they practically melt and form a very thick dish. Another version of lentil soup is *rishta,* in which green lentils are cooked with onions and seasoned with salt, pepper, and chicken bouillon powder. While the lentils are cooking, dough is prepared from flour and water. It is folded several times and cut into thin strips. When the soup boils, the strips of dough are added to create a lentil soup with noodles.

A similar range of dishes can be prepared from garbanzo beans as well. The slow cooking of rice and garbanzo beans—either in water in which meat has been cooked or in tomato sauce seasoned with salt, pepper, and *baharat*—is a meal in itself. Instead of rice it is possible to use bulgur and to prepare *blili* and garbanzo beans—garbanzo beans cooked with either lamb or beef and bulgur. The dish is eaten hot or cold with *laban* and fresh onions. One who cannot afford meat can prepare fava bean *blili*—a dish made from green fava beans and bulgur.

A soup made from a base of water in which meat has been cooked serves as gravy. Alia, a social science student from the Triangle region, explains that in the traditional meal, each of the diners gets an individual bowl of soup. The meat and rice plate is shared by two diners or more, each eating from his own corner:

> We dip the rice in the soup. The soup is gravy for the rice. It's eaten together. Everything is put on the table at the same time.

Ramona from Kafar Barta'a adds:

> After I cook the chicken or the meat, I save the water. Then I put in the rice or frozen vegetables or potatoes or carrots, season it, and there is more food. We eat it with the meat.

Wild plants, grains, and legumes are commonly found in the traditional Palestinian kitchen and are essential and central to its cuisine. Foraged foods are cheap and readily available, as they can be gathered and don't need to be bought. Wild plants take only a short time to cook, and therefore can be prepared during a break from work in the field or after a workday outside the home. They can be cooked with legumes, thus providing an excellent source of protein that also keeps well. Although wild plant leaves shrink during cooking or are absorbed into the liquid of legumes, such dishes have a large volume; with the addition of bread, vegetables, and *laban*, they make an inexpensive and nutritious meal. Sometimes pieces of meat are added to the dish to make it even more substantial.[8]

The use of wild plants requires that practical knowledge be passed from one generation to the next. Children learn to identify wild plants and men recognize them, but women process the knowledge with the intention of transforming the plants into food. Wild plant expertise entails identifying edible plants and knowing when to harvest them, how to clean and cook them, when to serve them and to whom, and how to recognize the unique traits of each of them. One needs to know which plant is suitable for a meat dish and also how to freeze wild plants so that they remain accessible and nutritious when not in season.

Hubeizeh is a well-liked wild plant. It grows in winter near the house, has dark-green leaves and a sharp taste, and is rich in iron and beneficial to intestinal functioning. To prepare it, one fries onions in oil, adds washed and finely chopped *hubeizeh* leaves, and seasons them with dill, salt, and pepper, or lemon juice with a little salt. The dish is eaten with cold *laban*. The Bedouins cooked *hubeizeh* leaves in boiling water, stirring with a wooden spoon. When the leaves began to give off liquid, they added whole-grain flour and salt to the mixture. The result was a very thick soup that was eaten with sheep's-milk *laban* and eggs fried in *samneh* (clarified butter).

Other wild plants are used for either cooked dishes or salads. Women prepare salad from chicory, which is sold today in markets. The stem of the *selika* plant is boiled in water and seasoned with garlic and lemon. The boiled leaves of the *saiyena* (literally, "wild tongue") are served with rice, *frike*, or meat, or made into a filling for dough. *Arum*, the spiciest of all the wild plants, serves as a condiment for meat. *Zaatar* (a blend of Middle Eastern herbs with sesame seeds) is made into salad or ground into a powder to be used as a spice. *Hurfesh* is fried in olive oil and seasoned. *Sunara* is a thorny plant that grows near the home and is found mostly in Galilee. Its stem can be eaten as is, in a salad seasoned with olive oil and lemon, or fried with onions, salt, pepper, and mushrooms. This last dish is served as a main course and eaten with rice and *laban*.

Unlike most wild plants, which grow near the home and thus can be cooked without advance planning, *akub,* a thorny plant with an edible stem and flower, grows in the mountains, and harvesting it becomes a family outing. After the family returns home with full baskets, cleaning begins, requiring time and expertise. First, the thorns are removed. Second, the stems are separated from the flowers, which are referred to as the *akub's* "eggs" (slang for testicles), and they are cleaned. Then the "eggs" are fried with onions, garlic, and lemon and eaten with bread and *laban*. *Akub* can be used as a filling for dough or in salad, or it can be fried with lamb or veal and served with rice. Over the years, the number of people going out to pick *akub* has declined. Many of the younger generation don't recognize it, and it is losing its place on the daily menu. In Haifa, Acre, and Jaffa I met women who had heard of *akub* but had not eaten it often. Nadia, an elementary school teacher, grew up in a mixed city in a family that wasn't used to eating *akub*. At a young age, she married a fellow from one of the Galilee villages. Her mother-in-law cooked *akub,* so she became familiar with the dish, but she never went out to pick it and never cooked it. For her, *akub* seemed to be folklore—a remnant of the premodern period during which people were compelled to eat what was available and not what they thought was tasty. Her friend added:

> My mother told me about *akub*, but at home they never made it. You need to remove the leaves with a pair of tweezers and soak the root in water. My sister's mother-in-law, Nur, is a good cook. At her place I ate *akub*.

Hindbah, found mostly in the center of the country, is a wild plant whose leaves resemble lettuce leaves. It grows in winter near water sources. Like *akub, hindbah* is picked in season—a custom that is fast disappearing. On rare occasions it is found in the markets in Lod, Ramla, or Jerusalem. Jaffa women buy *hindbah* either from Ramla women who sell their merchandise in the market in Ajami (the Arab section of Jaffa) or from relatives who live in Ramla or Lod. Lod women on a limited budget recount that on sunny winter days, they still go in groups on foot from Lod to Ben Shemen to pick *hindbah*. Fatma, a cleaning lady who works in a major hospital, went picking a week prior to our encounter, "before the herbs dried." On her way back she and her friends carried baskets on their heads with a yearly supply of *hindbah*:

> I came home, cleaned the leaves, and half-cooked them. Then I put them into bags and into the freezer. I mix them with oil, tahini, and lemon and eat them. Sometimes I put them in a sandwich that I take to work in the hospital.

A popular cultivated plant that holds special status in the Palestinian kitchen is *melukhiye*. Unlike the wild plants that grow in one's backyard, *melukhiye* is sold in the city markets of Lod, Ramla, Jaffa, Jerusalem, Haifa, and Acre and in local markets in Arab villages. Its price sometimes rises to as much as twenty Israeli new shekels per kilogram. Its handling requires dexterity and a delicate touch, as its leaves can be easily spoiled. For the leaves to remain unblemished, they are cleaned as soon as possible after purchase. Skilled women are able to clean the leaves without their absorbing water. To accomplish this, the women wipe the leaves one by one with a damp cloth and dry them in the sun. After drying, the leaves are chopped and fried or made into soup. When cooked, the leaves exude a liquid that imparts to the dish a viscosity resembling that of okra. *Melukhiye* can be served as soup alongside a meat dish, mixed with meat or chicken, or eaten with rice and *laban*. It is a festive dish, usually served on holidays or at family gatherings.

Another popular, though less festive, dish featuring *melukhiye* is *bsara,* which is made from dry fava beans that are soaked in water with baking soda and cooked until soft. Dried *melukhiye* is added to the fava beans along with a mixture of tahini, crushed garlic, lemon, and hot pepper. The result is a dish with the texture of soup that is eaten along with bread and vegetables. Since *melukhiye* grows in the summer, many women dry and freeze it for use in the winter as well. Abed, a Hebrew teacher from the northern part of Israel, tells me how happy he was to discover that *melukhiye* keeps well in the freezer, making it readily available during the winter. Several years ago Abed decided to freeze one kilogram of *melukhiye* to see how it kept. The experience proved successful and he has frozen twenty kilos of *melukhiye* at the end of the summer ever since:

> I purchase it on a Friday, and all evening and on Saturday morning I sit and clean the leaves. We half-cook it and pack it in small bags. My wife laughs as she explains that my love for *melukhiye* turned me into a more considerate man who helps her at home.

Grains, like wild plants, also form the basis for inexpensive dishes that make it possible to feed many mouths while using little meat. Women know when wheat should be harvested, how to prepare a store of wheat and *frike* for the winter, and how to prepare bulgur. The wheat for use in the home is harvested in two stages. In the first stage, one month before the wheat is ripe, green wheat is harvested to be used in preparing *frike*. It is smoked and ground into flour that can be kept for a long time. Once the *frike is* cooked, the result is a dish that is a substitute for rice. Sometimes *frike* is added to lamb or chicken soup, making a complete meal.

In the second stage, after enough green wheat has been cut to prepare *frike* for the coming year, the ripe wheat is harvested. Some of the wheat is ground into flour for baking, and the rest is used to prepare bulgur. Women usually prepare three kinds of bulgur: bulgur for tabbouleh, bulgur for *mjadara,* and very fine bulgur that remains behind and is used in preparing certain kinds of *kubeh.*

In the past, women used to prepare enough bulgur to last throughout the year. When the state of Israel was established, the price of bulgur rose, and many women began to replace it with rice. The principal of a high school in Galilee tells me that where previously, the average Arab family consumed 250 kilos of bulgur and only about 60 kilos of rice in one year, since the establishment of Israel, the relative amounts have switched: wheat has become more expensive than rice, which is subsidized.[9]

Traditionally, bulgur was prepared in a ceremony directed by women with the participation of children. Village women removed the stones, peels, straw, and foreign particles from the wheat, cooked it, moved the pot onto the roof, and spread its contents out to dry. The children acted as living scarecrows, keeping watch to prevent the birds from pecking at the drying wheat. Today, even though many women prefer to buy bulgur from stores or from other villagers, some still prepare it themselves at home for the sake of cleanliness or nostalgia or to save money. Khishmi, a teacher from Kafar Yasif, recalls that her mother used to boil the wheat over a fire outside the house and ask her daughters to clean the house roof. Khishmi and her sister would watch their mother climb to the roof of the house with a pot of wheat on her head and then, with a large spatula, pour a thin layer of wheat on the roof to cool. After three or four days, they would gather the wheat with a brush, bring it into the house, and clean it of stones and peels:

> After the grinding, three strainers would be brought: one with large holes for bulgur to make *mjadara* and *shulbato*, another strainer for bulgur to make *kubeh*, and a third for very, very tiny bulgur to be used in tabbouleh. It is all put into sacks, and you have bulgur for the entire year. I still do it this way myself.

The ability to make the best use of legumes and make from them a variety of dishes is an additional indication of female knowledge. *Mjadara,* for example, is a popular dish favored among the Jewish public—so much so that its Arab origins are forgotten by and large. It consists of a combination of lentils and grains (rice or bulgur) served either dry or as a thick stew. In Jaffa and in the Triangle, under Egyptian influence, *mjadara* is prepared from rice and small green lentils. The first stage in preparation is cleaning the lentils and rice. The lentils, covered with rice, are then cooked in water with salt and cumin. At the same time, onions are cut and fried in oil, sometimes until they are burnt—depending on the preference of members of the family. It is recommended that olive oil not be used, because it burns and blackens the food. The onions are added to the dish and it is seasoned with salt and black pepper. The result is dry *mjadara,* which is eaten as a main dish along with *laban* and salad. The dry version of *mjadara* made from rice is also known in the north as *metakta'ah.* It is eaten less frequently than liquid *mjadara,* which resembles a thick stew. Sausan, who lives in

Jaffa but comes originally from the village of Reina in Galilee, makes *mjadara* from rice, unlike her mother, who made *mjadara* from bulgur:

> My children don't like bulgur. I burn the onions as my mother did. Then I pour water on the onions, boil, and grind the onions. It makes the *mjadara* red.

Mjadara made from bulgur, lentils, and onions—either dry or liquid—is typical of the north. When the price of bulgur rose, bulgur *mjadara* changed from a poor person's food to a nostalgic one that only those financially well off could afford to eat regularly. Like rice-based *mjadara,* this dish can be prepared soupy or dry. Maria, a resident of Acre, says:

> *Mjadara* with bulgur is tastier and healthier. I select the amount that feels right to me, heat it with small lentils, fry onions, and put it all together. I add only salt and make the dry kind.

The most popular version of *mjadara* from bulgur and without lentils is *shulbato,* or *lubatiyeh.* To prepare it, you fry onions in corn oil (though it used to be prepared with olive oil), add bulgur and tomato juice, and cook until the bulgur is soft enough to eat. The same dish without tomato juice is called *jarisha.* Another version, called *yalanji* (bulgur with thin slices of tomato, onion, parsley, and mint), is also used as a filling for grape leaves.

Mugrabiya, a Palestinian version of couscous made from garbanzo beans and bulgur thickened with semolina and served with chicken, is another way to add variety. To prepare *mugrabiya,* one prepares *couscouson* made of bulgur and semolina by wetting one's fingers and rolling the grains in flour. The particles grow larger and separate from one another and are steamed over chicken soup. Meanwhile, chicken or lamb soup cooks in one pot, while onions and garbanzo beans cook in another. The soup created from the chicken is seasoned with *baharat,* cumin, saffron, and cinnamon. To serve, one fills a plate with *couscouson,* pours on soup, and adds fried onions, garbanzo beans, and a piece of meat.

The female territory of the kitchen becomes the zone for practicing and applying culinary knowledge. Here, women teach each other and show their husbands that they know how to avoid a monotonous menu. In the kitchen, women also make use of existing and new culinary knowledge while exploiting and transforming modern technology, thereby broadening their stores of knowledge. Finally, women's culinary knowledge and efforts strengthen their traditional role as women, while also serving as a means of expressing their position in relation to the family. A woman who cooks is said to be fulfilling her destiny, and the quality of her cooking determines her reputation with regard to her goodness, faithfulness, and efficiency. We shall examine how these qualities are expressed in Arab women's attitude toward meat.

The Preparation of Meat

The purchase and preparation of meat are related to the prevailing cultural perceptions that shape Palestinian cuisine in Israel. As with vegetables and cheese, there are clear criteria for determining what fresh meat is suitable for purchasing, what it is best to leave in the store, and how to economize on the use of meat. The methods for preparing meat mostly rest on the principle of using the minimum amount of meat needed to impart a meaty flavor to a dish. The introduction of new meat products to the Palestinian kitchen depends upon their compatibility with accepted principles for handling meat.

More than anything else, the special status accorded meat by the Palestinian kitchen in Israel reflects the interweaving of cultural principles, technical skills, and economic constraints. The disappearance of home butchering has created a new problem: a decreased supply of fresh meat. Consumers look for a butcher able to provide fresh, high-quality meat in what they judge to be a clean environment. The perceived reliability of a butcher is increased by the constant presence of customers in his store, which gives him an advantage over other butchers even if their shops are cleaner. Miriam, a university graduate who recently married an academic from the Triangle, joined her husband's family in buying lamb for her sister-in-law's wedding. They went to the main street of Baka al-Gharbiya, an area in which she was not familiar with the meat shops, and looked at two stores. In one, the meat was hanging in good order; all was shining clean. In the second store, everything was full of bloodstains. There were large pieces of meat everywhere, and all was in disarray. She said to the rest of the group:

> How is it that you buy meat in such a place? Let's go to the other store where it's clean and pleasant. They told me, "Why do you think it's so clean and neat? Because nobody buys there, so he has time to clean and put things in order. This store has customers all the time, which means the meat is fresh."

Many scholars have described meat as a symbol of life and masculinity, strength and power. Its freshness, flowing blood, and red color signify life.[10] In Arab culture as well, meat symbolizes life and vitality—qualities that the Palestinian public feels disappear in the process of freezing meat. Frozen meat, though cheaper, is deemed repugnant, unclean, and unsanitary. Women who buy frozen meat are perceived as not appreciating the importance of their task and their family. They are seen as taking the easy way out instead of investing effort, attention, and thought. The suspicions against frozen meat are typical of both women and men of all classes, levels of education, and religions. To them, frozen meat symbolizes the inanimate and the dead—the opposite of what meat is supposed to represent. Sylvia, a resident of Acre and the widow of a policeman in the Mandatory government, shares with me:

> Frozen meat disgusts me. You can't see what the meat looks like. I don't know where it comes from, how long it has been sitting in the freezer, when the animal was butchered.

Varda, a teaching instructor with a master's degree in education from Haifa University, argues that it is not normal to buy a hunk of ice that twitches after lying several hours on the drain board. She is repulsed by the idea of an animal, after it has died, oozing blood and softening. Her Jewish friend from university kept telling her it did not make sense to buy fresh chicken and stand and clean it for hours. When Varda finally decided to buy a frozen chicken at the supermarket a few years ago, she realized that she did not know how to select a frozen chicken, all wrapped in a package, and how to distinguish between a good chicken and a bad one.

> I chose one whose skin I thought I could see through the nylon. I came home and defrosted it, and what do I see? Feathers! Not many but two or three. What can I tell you? It disgusted me so much that I threw out the chicken.

When I tried to understand why a few feathers on a frozen chicken skin would arouse such repugnance, while feathers on a fresh chicken indicated cleanliness, I was introduced to a cultural understanding of the laws of purity and impurity. A fresh chicken is in its natural state; therefore it is considered clean. The feathers and skin are an integral part of the chicken, and they are an indication of its freshness—its recent transformation from living to dead. It is the woman who will carry the chicken through the next stage, from dead to cooked. A frozen chicken, on the other hand, is considered impure because of the intervention and preservation that it has undergone at the hands of a stranger, whose training is unknown. The freezing process unnaturally separates the chicken from the living and leaves it "dead" for quite a long time without enabling the immediate process of cooking or rotting. Defrosting transforms the meat to "as though it were alive"—a category that is unnatural. Therefore, its skin and feathers do not indicate freshness but rather the process of preservation. If the fresh chicken is defined as clean because of its proximity to the living chicken, the cleanliness of the frozen chicken is artificial and the doing of human beings; thus the feathers on its skin testify that the cleaning work was not carried out properly.

Women's insistence on using fresh meat does more than reinforce cultural perceptions about the significance of the living and the impure. It is also a manifestation of female skill, along with an expression of the respect women have for their husbands. According to Anne Murcott, a good, devoted housewife pleases her husband by having a hot home-cooked meal, prepared from only fresh meat, ready for him upon his return from work.[11] The use of purchased frozen meat is interpreted both as disrespectful on the wife's part and as an indication of her inability to fulfill her duties fittingly. The use of fresh meat entails more work: the meat needs to be bought close to the time it is cooked, it needs to be washed several times, the bones need to be separated, and the meat needs to be cooked and seasoned. In general, more and more fast foods are entering Arab kitchens. Yogurt with fruit cereal, soup mandels, and frozen vegetables are all found in kitchen pantries, but frozen meat is still absent from most home freezers. Jamal, the owner of an advertising firm specializing in publicity in the Arab sector, says:

> Frozen meat is too large a jump. It would be the equivalent of a meat substitute or even meat without roots. People will suspect there is something wrong with it, especially in a kitchen where meat is respected.

I press Jamal and ask how it would be possible, despite that, to sell frozen meat to the Palestinian public, and what images are worth using for that purpose. He responds that one must draw on images of the Palestinian woman and not make use of the modern connotations that sell other frozen foods so well. He believes that perhaps the only way would be to show a man eating chicken and complimenting his wife on the wonderful dish, not realizing she has used a frozen chicken:

> I wouldn't use sentences such as "Using frozen chicken has provided me with more time for myself" or "It has helped me balance my budget." That

wouldn't be well received. I would emphasize that the taste could be the same and, most important, that the husband is satisfied.

Recoiling from purchasing frozen meat does not contradict the prevailing trend to freeze fresh meat in the home freezer, however. That freezing takes place after the meat has been examined and declared fresh and clean and is performed not by a stranger but by a woman whose skill is recognized in her household. Domestic freezing assists women who work outside the home and need to prepare a cooked meal, and it frees them from the burden of daily trips to the butcher. The possibility of freezing also strengthens the traditional trend of purchasing large amounts of meat. Purchasing only a small amount of meat is considered a declaration of the buyer's insecure economic situation. Ziyad, the principal of a northern high school, says that he always buys at least one kilo of meat, even when his wife needs only three hundred grams. The habit, according to Ziyad, remains from the time when Palestinians butchered sheep and were left with a lot of meat:

> I can't bring myself to purchase a small amount of meat. It seems to me to be not honorable, as if I'm being stingy. So we buy a large amount each time and freeze it. That way, if my wife needs meat, we always have some in the house.

Hiyam, a social worker from Haifa, claims that the conflict between the traditional way of life and the modern one influences the purchase of meat. Although it is irrational to buy a kilo of meat when one needs only a quarter of a kilo, or to buy only fresh meat when frozen meat costs approximately half the price and is also more hygienic, wholesale buying and home freezing preserve both traditional eating habits and female expertise:

> Sometimes I think that people would have a lot more money if they bought rationally, but that's contrary to our tradition. It's difficult for me to tell people that if they bought only the amount of meat they needed and if they used frozen meat, they would have more money left for education. It's a very delicate subject.

While industrialized freezing is thought to be impure, domestic freezing is perceived as a means of purifying meat and ensuring its freshness. Lubna, the wife of a Mandatory policeman, believes that certain meats need to be frozen before they are eaten in order to prevent illness:

> Calf meat needs to be in the freezer for fourteen days. Inside it is a fungus that needs to die. The cold of the freezer kills it. After

fourteen days the meat can be eaten without worry about the fungus.

When I asked if there weren't fungi in the calf's meat that caused illness prior to the introduction of the home freezer, Lubna laughed: "Maybe then it was all fresh. The cows ate only herbs and not all the products that they are given now, so there weren't fungi." After a minute she adds, "Then, we ate lamb almost exclusively, so there was no need to worry about fungi. In lamb's meat there don't seem to be any fungi, but just to be certain, we also freeze it."

Understanding how the rules of purity and impurity operate is vital to the female culinary knowledge that is shared among the Palestinian citizens of Israel. As the one responsible for feeding the family, the woman composes the domestic menu by bringing together traditional cultural perceptions, a system of images connected to food, and practical considerations revolving around the supply available in the market. These factors encourage the woman to make the effort and devote the time needed for food preparation, while also avoiding the use of frozen products that are at odds with prevailing culinary and cultural attitudes.

The attitude toward meat in the Arab kitchen not only illustrates how daily culinary decisions take place within a matrix of cultural considerations but also reveals an additional central element in female culinary knowledge and the training women undergo—that is, how to cope with economic constraints. For example, the Palestinian woman learns how to make use of all parts of the animal, including internal parts and bones, in order to enrich dishes with protein. The internal parts of the chicken were usually fried and served for breakfast, and fresh goat liver was eaten raw with much black pepper and salt.

Palestinians developed numerous ways to use every part of the lamb, ensuring that none of this essential meat went to waste. In the past, lamb bones were usually cooked down to a gelatinous liquid, which could then be used to enrich *melukhiye* or other soups. *Fuareh* and *kirshe*— lamb intestines or stomach stuffed with rice—were widely eaten when poverty was pervasive and Palestinians' economic situation demanded frugality, even though the preparation of these dishes required much labor and great cooking skill. To make these dishes, tripe or intestines would be washed thoroughly and then disinfected with the help of spices. They would then be stuffed with rice and pine nuts along with pieces of meat or almonds, and then sewn and cooked in water with black pepper, *baharat*, and cinnamon.

Even the feet of the lamb were not thrown away. Skilled cooks prepared *karain* from them: After cleaning, the feet were boiled in water; at the same time, stuffed grape leaves and squash were prepared. When the feet became soft, a pot was filled with alternating layers of stuffed vegetables and lamb feet. When the dish was almost ready, dry bread *(fati)* was crumbled to thicken the soup and make it more satisfying. The fat from the tail of the lamb *(lia)* was used to prepare a spread for bread. *Mandil,* the fat covering the kidneys and heart, had another use—after being separated from the other internal parts and dried, it was kept for a long time and used in the preparation of stuffed vegetables, giving them the taste of meat without needing to use much meat.

Dishes using dough also answer the need for food that is satisfying and considered meaty without requiring much meat. *Sambusak, sfikhah,* and *shishbarak* are popular dough-based dishes. The shape of the *sambusak* resembles the Indian samosa and the South American empanada. They are triangles of short pastry dough stuffed with meat and baked in the oven. *Sfikhah* is made of phyllo dough filled with fried ground meat seasoned with salt, cinnamon, and pepper and baked in the oven. There are several versions of *sfikhah:* the dough may be cut in circles or squares, and it may be prepared with two layers of dough with meat in the middle or left open. There are many reasons for the variants. Triangle residents say that round *sfikhah* is typical of the Jaffa kitchen, where the women, according to Miriam from Acre, are seen as more modern:

> They don't have much time there: they work, they're busy; they're more modern and elegant than most of us. So they make shortcuts and cut circles, using a glass, and then they can bake it immediately.

Miriam explains that she has created her own version of *sfikhah.* She rolls out the dough, makes a rectangle, and puts a little lamb meat with onion, and sometimes pine nuts and spices, in the middle. She seasons the mixture with cinnamon, nutmeg, and pepper, and rolls out the dough like a blintze or Italian cannelloni. She freezes the *sfikhah* and warms them up as needed, serving them in what she sees as an "elegant fashion."

One of the most widely known dishes from the Arab kitchen is *kubeh,* in its various forms. *Kubeh,* combining dough made from bulgur and a meat filling, would seem to be simply a dish enabling a saving of meat, but it is more than just an ordinary dish: *kubeh* may be viewed as a gastronomic microcosm of the Arab kitchen. Its ingredients and methods of preparation reveal the differential importance of items in the Arab kitchen, the status of the woman and the system of her tasks in Palestinian society, and the use of ingredients as an indication of the economic situation of those doing the cooking: there is *kubeh* for the rich and *kubeh* for the poor; *kubeh* for those with time to spare and *kubeh* for the lazy or busy; and finally "mock *kubeh*," based on the principles of preparation of *kubeh* but not containing meat.

The distinction between *kubeh* made with meat and that made without reveals the special status of meat in the Palestinian kitchen: Meat *kubeh* is festive, and only those who can afford it will eat it on ordinary days. Vegetarian *kubeh*, conversely, is based on cheaper ingredients and takes less time to prepare. There is *kubeh* in the form of a chopped meat croquette or pie, resembling—in form only—meat pies from the European kitchen. *Kubeh* also mirrors the status of the woman in society and the level of domestic technology. Its preparation entails much work that is dependent on available and inexpensive labor by the woman. The *kubeh* served at the table is an indication of the woman's diligence and skill. Thus, the more meat the *kubeh* contains, the more festive the occasion, the better the family's economic situation, and the greater the skill of the cook. The only meat used for proper *kubeh* is lamb; in its absence, it is possible to compromise by using goat. Among the kinds of *kubeh* with meat there is also a scale of value: the fresher the meat, the more complicated the preparation, and the more immediate the eating—the higher the prestige of the dish.

We shall examine the various types of *kubeh*. The most esteemed is *kubeniyeh*—the festive version: bulgur with raw, very fresh lamb meat, spiced with hot red pepper, nutmeg, and cinnamon. Since it contains a large amount of meat, its preparation indicates a comfortable economic situation along with great cooking expertise and an important event. In the past, when a lamb was slaughtered, it was customary to prepare *kubeniyeh* from its meat: the meat was cut into small pieces which were then crushed by hand and mixed with very finely ground bulgur. The most elegant version mixed one kilo of meat with half a kilo of bulgur, while a more sparing version used equal quantities of the two. The most frugal version mixed one kilo of bulgur with half or even one-quarter kilo of meat. From the bulgur-meat mixture, patties were fashioned that were served uncooked alongside *khosi*—a dish of lamb meat and onion fried in olive oil. Because of the raw meat used in *kubeniyeh*, it had to be eaten immediately after being prepared. Diners would take from the *kubeniyeh*, mix it with the *khosi*, and eat them along with other dishes served at the meal, such as steak, stuffed vegetables, and rice. Olivia, who lives in Galilee, comments about *kubeniyeh:*

> The mountain people's *kubeniyeh* is the best. Once, before we had mixers, the bulgur and meat were ground with a mortar and pestle. The meat still had the muscles, which were then removed. That is the best flavor for *kubeniyeh*.

Many informants recall that during their childhood it was common to eat *kubeniyeh* regularly on Sundays after a lamb was slaughtered. An architect from the north whose childhood was spent in the village recalls how, at around ten o'clock in the morning, the men would bring his grandmother the slaughtered lamb and she would begin preparing it.

> I can still picture her sitting and crushing the meat by hand with a kind of hammer, mixing bulgur and meat. At around noon we would begin to eat. We would take the *kubeniyeh* and *khosi* with our hands and eat. It's been years since I ate *kubeniyeh* like my grandmother made.

What was left of the *kubeniyeh* would be rolled into round patties (*kora*) or elongated croquettes (*kawa'ir*) stuffed with *khosi,* and fried and eaten the next day. Some prepare *kobab,* which is roasted *kubeh;* others prefer *kubeh mashawiye*—round *kubeh* meatballs covered with lamb fat and baked in the oven that are typical of the region around Jerusalem; and yet others cook *kubeh* in soup flavored with sumac and nuts. In the north, *kubeh* with *laban*—patties of bulgur stuffed with meat and cooked in *laban* flavored with mint leaves—is popular.

Another popular version is *kubeh seniyeh*—often referred to by women either seriously or in fun as *kubeh* for the lazy. *Seniyeh* means "tray," and it is a general term for dishes served in baking pans after being baked in the oven or cooked in a metal tray on the stove. *Kubeh seniyeh* consists of two layers of bulgur with ground lamb (often left over from *khosi*) in between; it is baked in the oven until the top layer is brown and crusty. Women who do not use bulgur for various reasons prepare *kubeh batata,* a dish based on *kubeh seniyeh* in which the layers of bulgur are replaced by mashed potatoes with margarine and bread crumbs sprinkled on top.

Nonmeat dishes that mimic the form and texture of meat dishes are typical of ethnic and vegetarian cuisines. The use of meat substitutes enables the creation of meatless versions of familiar dishes, but it also allows the cook to vary the usual menu in response to economic, religious, or cultural needs.[12] This is the case for *kubeh:* when meat must be avoided for religious reasons (for example, during the fast before

Easter among Christian Palestinians), lack of time, or just out of a desire for a vegetarian dish, *kubeh* is prepared meatlessly, while preserving the principle of preparation of the classical *kubeh*: soft dough made only of bulgur and stuffing similar in texture to the meat stuffing. That is the nature of "mock *kubeh*," also known as *sarasira* or *kubeh kazabi* and defined as poor-man's *kubeh*. Very finely ground bulgur unused for other dishes is collected and cleaned of peels, washed and squeezed dry, and then mixed with grated onion, *baharat*, cumin, marjoram, dried mint, and salt. The mixture is allowed to dry until its texture resembles dough. Then small balls or elongated patties are fashioned; in each ball a hole is made with the thumb, and this hole is stuffed with small pieces of potatoes or garbanzo beans cooked with onions and spices. The patties are cooked in goat's-milk *laban* with water and salt until a thick mixture is formed; then garlic and mint are added and the mixture is stirred constantly to prevent lumps. The dish is ready when the patties stick to the bottom of the pot. Others cook bulgur balls in red lentil soup.

A different version of *kubeh* is *kubeh tehili bandora*: a dish made from uncooked bulgur mixed with onions and tomato and seasoned with *baharat*, marjoram, and mint and served without *khosi*. With the improvement in Palestinians' financial situation during the 1970s, people began to eat the classical version of meat *kubeh* more often. The few who eat the nonmeat versions now do so for the sake of nostalgia.

The ability to work with meat is critical to a Palestinian woman's sense of worth as a cook. Her ability to produce a meaty dish on a tight budget, and in the absence of a great deal of meat, is a highly valued skill. Many classic Palestinian dishes are built around using small amounts of meat to produce a meaty flavor. Thus, mastering these dishes is a way in which women reproduce their role—here as a thrifty nourisher—within the traditional family structure.

THE CULTURAL AND SOCIAL ASPECTS OF THE MEAL

In Palestinian society in Israel, the sociocultural world of the meal comes into being on three interwoven levels: the meal as a social event having distinct rules, the family meal, and the meal as a form of hospitality. The food served depends on a variety of factors: the structure of the meal, its place and time, the composition of the participants in the culinary event, and the economic situation.[13]

"For Whom Shall I Prepare, For Myself?"

In Palestinian society, the meal is a family gathering that functions to unify those present and demonstrate solidarity among the participants. The solidarity comes from reclining to eat together. In the traditional meal, diners use their hands to take food from a central plate. This custom indicates the very essence of propinquity and sharing among those eating. The culinary event also emphasizes and reinforces the system of power relations and authority in the family and in the community: between men and women, between parents and children, and between the various classes and groups. Arab culture obliges the host to humble himself in front of his guests and serve their needs. At the same time, the host always takes upon himself a certain measure of risk, since the guest can refuse the refreshments and, in so doing, challenge the status and power of the host.[14]

In terms of gender relations, the meal reflects male dominance both in the home and in society. In the past, men and women ate separately; women would serve men and eat only after the men had finished their meal. Today, in villages or among members of the lowest class, it is still possible to see women and children eating separately. The mealtime is still determined according to when the man returns from work, although today there is also consideration for the daily schedule of the children, and the dishes are determined according to tradition or according to the taste of the father of the family.

Although Palestinian women in Israel cook for the family, they do not consider their private needs as part of their culinary practice, and they don't see their own mouths as ones that need to be fed. When they are alone, women make do with leftovers (sometimes even without warming them) or a sandwich instead of a meal.[15] Women who are alone during the noon hours tend to "grab a bite of something," as they continue what they were doing. Without any connection to the food eaten, women's solitary eating would never be called a meal, because it has none of the ceremony of the meal. Amira from Jerusalem, for example, works half-time in a shop selling cosmetics. Her children are married and work, but they still come to her home every day to eat a hot meal after work. Amira arrives home around two, "grabs a bite to eat," and starts preparing a meal for six people. During the afternoon she will serve a hot meal to each one of her children separately, and when her husband arrives around six, she will eat with him. When I ask her whether she also prepares food for herself, she looks astonished and says there is no point in cooking for one. Women by themselves are to eat leftovers or grab whatever is in the house:

> When I came home I was hungry, so I took some bread, stuffed it with cold grape leaves, and ate the sandwich with olives, and I wasn't hungry anymore. Yesterday was the same. Sometimes I come home, have some *labaneh*, a little *dukkah*, olive oil, olives, and bread. It tastes best that way.

Maria, a Christian woman living in a Muslim neighborhood in Lod, describes a similar pattern. All her children except for one son have left the house. She became widowed at a young age and did something exceptional compared with other widows by refusing to live with her husband's parents. In recent years, she cooks only on weekends, when the children come to eat, because she does not care what she eats when she is by herself as long as she is no longer hungry:

> If someone comes, I cook. If no one comes, I have bread, hummus, cucumber, *labaneh*, and that's it. Tomorrow the children are coming, so in the evening, I'll prepare food.

Statements such as "That's not real food," "That's nothing special," or "I only have something in order not to be hungry" are heard from Palestinian women describing their eating habits when they are alone. Hadije, from a village in the Triangle, and her children only eat full meals when her husband returns home from his work as a chef at a cafeteria in the center of the country. Upon his arrival she prepares meat, chicken, *kubeh*, *maklubeh*, *melukhiye*, or whatever he wants. She serves the meal with rice, *laban*, and vegetables:

> When he doesn't come, his mother, the children, and I eat when we're hungry. There's bread, *labaneh*, white cheese, hummus. Sometimes we make *hubeizeh* or *olesh* or an omelet. When he comes, then sometimes the children ask for schnitzel, so he makes it for them, and I also eat a little.

On a cultural level, the meal is not simply food, but an event that requires effort and thought, created to present to the head of the household. When women are alone, they do not perceive themselves as being worthy of a cooked meal. They do not think of their rushed, unplanned, and unstructured eating as a meal because it is not an event that includes a gathering of family or friends, the women's labor, the masculine presence, the serving of several dishes, and the agreement of all present that what they are experiencing is a meal. When a woman eats alone, it is a spontaneous and instrumental act whose sole purpose is to satisfy the woman's physical hunger and enable her to continue her work.

The Palestinian kitchen in Israel distinguishes between the familial meal—either daily or festive—and an event during which food is served and yet is still not considered a meal. Food eaten outside the framework of the meal has no intractable culinary rules, and it is considered to be a spontaneous event, occurring when a guest arrives, when one of the members of the household feels hungry, or when only short notice is received concerning an expected visit. In the latter case, soft drinks, coffee, and refreshments will be served. Hishmi, an assistant to a kindergarten teacher in a Galilee village, tells me that when friends announce they are coming for a short visit:

> I send my daughter to buy nuts and almonds and I phone my husband's brother who works in Nahariya and ask him to buy a cream cake in the bakery near his workplace. I prepare *sfikhah*, and when the guests arrive, I serve it all. This is not considered a meal.

The case described above shows that the hostess is familiar with the ways of receiving guests by knowing how to have the food suit the event and how to make her guests feel comfortable. Refreshments served on such occasions are varied and likely to include *sfikhah*, almonds and nuts, and even snack foods like *bamba, bisli,* frosted wafers, sour candies, cake, and even cigarettes. The refreshments are eaten for the most part with the fingers, and only some items are eaten with the forks or dessert spoons that are used in large meals. What, then, would turn this culinary event that includes food and guests into a meal? For that we must first distinguish between the family meal and the festive one.

Family Meals and Festive Meals

A meal is a structured event with rules of behavior and a fairly stable repertoire of dishes. The traditional Arab meal, as opposed to the Western meal, does not have courses, and all the dishes are brought in at the same time and placed on the floor or on a low table. The food is eaten while reclining, and each diner takes it from the central plate, creating personally favored combinations. The food is eaten either with fingers or a spoon (as is used for soup). Only the fruits or sweets are kept for the end of the meal.

During the second half of the twentieth century, many members of Palestinian society replaced reclining with a set table and began to use spoons and forks, but they retained the practice of serving all dishes at once. The woman thus does not need to think about the suitability of the food and courses, but only about what dishes she is able to serve, on the assumption that all who are eating will fix themselves a meal as they see fit. Dina, a teacher in an elementary school in the Triangle, serves soup made from a potpourri of frozen vegetables made by a well-known food company (a strategy, she says, she "learned from the Jews"), store-bought hummus and olives, cucumbers she pickled herself, and chicken stuffed with rice and Arab cheese. Eating at her house, I begin with the hummus, continue with the soup, and only afterward start on the chicken. Yousuf, her brother-in-law, smiles:

> You eat like my Jewish colleagues at work. In the stomach it all gets mixed together. Why not eat soup after the meat? When I'm with Jews at work or in their homes, I eat the way they do, but I don't understand it.

Um George from Jaffa does not attach importance to the order of courses in the meal either. Every day she finishes cooking a few minutes before her older children return from work. She ladles vegetable soup with thin noodles into four individual bowls and places one in front of each child. She heats leftover macaroni from the day before and sets it in the center of the table alongside eggplant in tahini, slices of pickled turnips, dill pickles, olives, sliced radishes, and green onions. From the stove in the storeroom outside the house, she brings a pot with fried potatoes to the table. After setting out bread, she invites the members of her family to come to the table.

Nobody complains that the soup, macaroni, or potatoes are not hot enough; nobody wonders why, at the same meal, bread and two courses of noodles and potatoes are served together. The family eats from it all and without a set or definite order: a spoon of soup, slices of turnip pinched with fingers from the bowl, pita filled with potatoes and pickled vegetables, a bite of macaroni, another spoonful of soup, and the process is repeated again. Afterward, each person, at his or her own pace, washes their hands, a signal that they have finished eating. A few minutes after that, all members of the family sit down in the front yard and enjoy concluding their meal with oranges and coffee.

In the evening, Um George and her fifty-year-old daughter prepare stuffed vegetables. The next day around noon, Um George places in front of each diner a deep plate and a tablespoon. Slices of radish, pickled turnips with dill, pita, and stuffed squash, eggplant, and grape leaves are brought to the table. From the pot with the squash, Um George removes the remaining liquid. Each person takes stuffed vegetables, pours gravy over them, and takes more bread and pickled vegetables as desired.

These examples illustrate the characteristics of the Palestinian meal: First, contrary to the Western meal, in which a course receives its significance from those that precede or follow it, the courses in an Arab meal are part of a complex of dishes that are combined by the diner on the individual plate. Second, the Palestinian meal draws no distinction between ingredients perceived in Western culture as resembling one another and fulfilling identical functions.[16] Thus it is not inconceivable to serve potatoes stuffed with rice or potato salad alongside rice. Noodles are also the basis for meals with vegetables, fish, or meat, or the basis for another popular dish—rice mixed with noodles—which is considered a meal in itself.

Domestic meals also reflect the family's financial well-being. The number of times per week that women prepare meat is a major indicator. People report that since the establishment of the state of Israel, with the spread of a monetary economy and the decline in home slaughtering of livestock, the number of people who eat meat almost every day has grown. Alia from Sakhnin recounts:

> By the time I got married, we were already eating meat several times a week. Nowadays we eat meat every day, and sometimes my husband says to me: "Why did you make meat? I'm tired of having meat every day, why don't you make something else?"

There were exceptions for whom meat was always plentiful, though— the rich who had no need to budget their expenses and those whose work put them into close proximity with meat. Aisha, the daughter of one of the well-to-do families in Haifa from before 1948, speaks of the meals in her parents' house:

> Much of the land in this region once belonged to my family. For me, meat was just something we ate every day. Even now when I'm no longer wealthy, for me, a meal without meat seems incomplete.

As a result of the decline in home slaughtering, lamb has become more expensive than beef or poultry, so Palestinian women in Israel have cut down on eating lamb or have given it up entirely. Instead, they have increased their consumption of veal, beef, chicken, and turkey. Another reason for the lower consumption of lamb is the fear of cholesterol and putting on weight that gained traction when similar trends were becoming popular in the Jewish sector. Samir, a clinical dietician who works in a hospital and also runs a private clinic, reports an increasing awareness of the importance of healthy food. People have cut down on fat and reduced their consumption of meat for fear of high cholesterol and heart congestion. Therefore, he says:

> Women cook less lamb because it is very fatty, and they replace it with turkey because it is lean meat, and the same goes for chicken or beef. In recent years I have also seen a return to simple dishes, vegetarian food. It has become stylish. People have discovered that it's healthy.

Health awareness has caused women to remove lamb meat from the menu at the precise time when more families can afford it. In this way, lamb, which had played a central role in the traditional menu, has lost its dominance in favor of other meats, such as turkey and chicken, to which tradition had not assigned such prestige. But modernity and nutritional science have done well by these other meats. The change in habits of meat eating testifies to the general dynamics of change in the Palestinian kitchen in the wake of processes occurring outside it.

The structure of the meal also reflects cultural codes that channel familial and social relations. Eating while reclining by using fingers and bread transforms the bread into a kind of extension of the hand, bringing together the person and the food. Eating from communal platters is not only testimony to a lack of utensils or an attempt at thrift but also one expression, among many, of an entire cultural and social world. The idea at the heart of this custom is that all are hungry together, share whatever is available together, and are satiated together. Tawfik, a teacher of Arabic living in Jaffa but originally from a Galilee village, thinks that it was not by chance that food was eaten with the fingers and people were seated shoulder to shoulder above a common bowl:

> It symbolized closeness, the absence of barriers. We are all satiated or hungry together. The bread serves as a spoon, or rather a kind of food shovel. We put the food onto it and bring it to the mouth.

A key tenet of Palestinian hospitality is that whoever enters the home during mealtime is invited to join. Beyond demonstrating good manners and honor, an invitation to the meal shows that members of the household have opened up their home to their guest, thereby disclosing their economic situation and the eating customs in their home. In turn, the guest is expected to accept the invitation and enjoy the food. Enjoyment is not necessarily conveyed by the quantity of food eaten, but more through words of praise for the food and the cook. Naama, a social worker from southern Israel, asserts that participation in the meal is built around gestures such as leaning in the direction of the food, tasting, and putting food into the mouth. Guests are not expected to finish all the food. On the contrary, it is even good manners to leave some food on the plate:

> In that way, they will see that you've eaten all you wanted. The diners eat together but not at the same pace. Everyone has his or her own speed and his or her own hunger. Whoever is finished goes to wash their hands, as if to say, "I've finished eating, thanks."

In spite of the changes in eating habits that have occurred as a result of women joining the workforce, especially the decrease in the number of family meals eaten together, the preparation of a meal is still a daily task of the woman, symbolizing family unity, belonging, and closeness. Fuad, a member of the local council in Arrabe, recalls that during his childhood women worked on the family land. Because most families did not have many utensils, they all ate from the same plate, sitting shoulder to shoulder. Eating was a purely instrumental activity that provided nourishment for the body. But times have changed:

> Today, sometimes you eat alone, but meals still mean family gatherings. When we eat together, I ask my children what they learned today at school. I ask my wife how she is; we speak about what happened at work.[17]

The contact between Palestinians and Jews in Israel initiated patterns of imitation, including the institutionalization of trends that found expression in table manners and the culture of eating. Even though sometimes men and children brought the new trends home, women were the ones required to implement them. In most homes, the collective platter gave way to the individual dish, and the spoon and fork replaced the fingers and bread. In the center of the table stands the serving platter, and from it, the woman serves each of the diners a personal portion. A'adel, a trainer of male and female nurses who has a master's degree in social work, reports that eating utensils and beautiful dishware are becoming essential for young brides. Older people like his parents still eat with their fingers, using bread as a food shovel, especially when eating dishes that are complicated to eat with a knife and a fork, like *mansaf:*

> This is why we often eat with a tablespoon; it's simpler. Do you know how good it feels to eat *mansaf* with the fingers or to tear off from the thin pita with the meat and rice? But what can we do—using utensils is more

hygienic. It took time before we managed to convey to the women more awareness about hygiene.

The chair of the board of education in a town in the Triangle, who is married to a biologist, explains that he and his wife foster in their three children the habit of eating with utensils as a means of developing the children's individualism. He claims that eating with personal utensils does not harm family unity. On the contrary, it encourages the growth of close-knit families consisting of individuals with their own identities, each having their own small, personal space. Just as people want each of their children to have a room of their own, and they decide not to have more children if they lack the economic means to give them a good education, all family members should have their own plates:

> Today, young couples live in separate houses with separate kitchens. We even look for special names for our children. We don't name our children automatically after parents or use traditional names anymore, especially for our daughters. If you ask me, these are some of the good things we learned from you Jews.

The family meal serves more than just food. It is a profound reflection on the cultural and economic context of Palestinian society. The abandonment of the collective platter, the replacement of fingers with a spoon, the introduction of solitary eating, and the choice of menu are all culinary practices that demonstrate the institutionalization of individualism, improvement in the economic situation, and the adoption of customs from outside the Arab sector.

Meals for Guests

Hospitality, which is the responsibility of the woman, draws upon female cultural knowledge and serves as an indication of the way she manages her own home. Hospitality among Palestinians in Israel differs from that of Jews in Israel in its attitude toward food in general and in the type of dishes served in particular. In the Jewish sector, the central idea is to vary and offer guests a unique repertoire that is not served in other homes. In the Arab sector, by contrast, hospitality is based on the quantity and quality of familiar foods and on a menu that includes much food, generally, and a great deal of meat, specifically. The focus on preparation of set foods relieves Palestinian women of the need to surprise guests with original dishes the likes of which they have not yet tasted yet still enables women to show that they are aware of social expectations. Attention shifts to the type of ingredients (such as the use of canned foods, margarine, mayonnaise, and commercial cereals) and planning the quantities. But entertaining also offers Palestinian women an opportunity to demonstrate familiarity with new dishes, and traditional menus are often enhanced with modern nuances. Serving a new dish is mostly intended as a kind of decoration, a public statement that modernity has penetrated the residence of the host family. The new dish would be one that had been tasted at a wedding in a restaurant, in the home of friends, or in a Jewish home. Neutralization of the element of surprise and originality keeps the visit from becoming a competition between women. The dishes constituting the menu for entertaining are characteristic of various population groups—highly educated and less so, urban and rural. For example, when Hadiga from Kafar Yasif has guests, she makes *kubeh seniyeh* or *kubeh* in the form of patties, depending on what she feels like, as people like *kubeh* and it always looks good. *M'khamar* is another option:

> It is red-colored chicken, put on the large flat bread that you call Iraqi pita. On it I put onion, pine nuts, and sumac or red pepper, which gives the chicken its red color. I put it into the oven and it turns red.

M'khamar is considered festive because it is a meat dish that takes a long time to prepare, demonstrating both female skill and an investment in the satisfaction of the guests. A plate of *m'khamar* always looks impressive because of its size and the red color of the chicken, and it arouses much wonder and appreciation. At large family gatherings, the tendency is to serve skewers of chicken kebab and *shishlik,* potatoes, and salads. Contact with the Jewish population has enriched the list of dishes that women prepare for guests: schnitzel, goulash, salads with mayonnaise, and cakes. The result is a culturally varied guest menu, including traditional festive foods alongside foods considered modern. A special-education teacher from the northern part of the country testifies that traditional Palestinian dishes such as *kubeh*, open or closed *sfikhah,* and tabbouleh are now served with potato salad with mayonnaise, corn salad, and mushroom salad next to them:

> I have guests tomorrow and I'll also make a mayonnaise potato salad to go with the *sfikhah.* That way, the guests will know that I know how to prepare it and that I'm modern. With the coffee, I serve sweets and cream cake.

On holidays, women are expected to prepare large meals with many courses to feed and impress guests. Olivia from Shefar'am, for instance, hosts fifty people every Christmas in her home. Even though she works eight to ten hours a day in her beauty shop, she prepares the meal without any help from her family. On Christmas eve, around noon, she starts decorating the house and setting the tables, which requires clearing the entire living room. After all the guests have arrived, she puts the salads on the table. These include tabbouleh to be eaten with lettuce, three kinds of eggplant, tahini, garbanzo beans, red pepper, balls of *kubeh,* closed *sfikhah,* potato salad, cabbage both with and without mayonnaise, artichoke hearts, two kinds of mushrooms, and a vegetable salad. It is only then that:

> We serve meats, stuffed chickens, *uzi* [dough filled with rice], and next to this, rice with almonds, pine nuts, and *laban.* At the end I serve sweets— *ma'amul* that I make and baklava that I buy.

The greater the hospitality shown during the party or the holiday meal, the more prestigious it is considered to be. Those whose financial situations allow it host generously, with the wife preparing many meat dishes and a variety of salads and desserts for the guests, not limiting herself to just one meat dish. The absence of a set structure for the meal, in Western fashion, is apparent. As in Europe during the Middle Ages, the difference between the first course and the second is the order in which they are brought to the table—an order determined according to the taste of the hostess and not according to set and generally accepted criteria. Sandra, whose family owns two restaurants in Acre (one in the old city and the other in the new city), and who lives in a penthouse in a new building there, tells me that she wanted her daughter to have a memorable wedding. Therefore, the meal was even "more elegant" than a Christmas meal:

> For the first course we served *kubeh* and kebab. The second course was grilled lamb, chicken *shishlik,* and lamb ribs with potatoes. On the tables there were ten salads—hummus, tahini, tabbouleh, *labaneh,* pickles, vegetables, fava beans, grilled eggplant, and Greek salad made from eggplant. For dessert there were fruits, ice cream, and coffee.

The fact that both the first and second courses contained meat and that each of them could have been the main course of the meal is of no significance. The hostess claims that the principle that guided her was to demonstrate wealth and generosity and to provide a lot of food. The order of the courses was arbitrary; it would have been possible to serve the ribs first and then the *shishlik.* Amal from Abu S'nan is not surprised by this menu and tries to explain the logic behind it. The salads, according to her, are considered dishes in themselves, not only to be eaten with other foods. Moreover, while Jews would not serve two meat dishes in the same meal, she says, it is not considered inappropriate for a Palestinian meal to include a variety of meats:

> That way guests can see that we're not stingy at their expense. It's not important what comes first and what afterward because maybe there wasn't room on the table for all the food. Maybe I too would have started the meal with *kubeh* and kebab, because they're smaller, and then I would have served the ribs, which are larger.

Simon Charsley, Sara Delamont, and Leslie Prosterman, who analyzed wedding meals in English and American societies, emphasize the involvement of the family in shaping the menu.[18] The bride's mother has a central role to play: she coordinates the dishes and components within the family budget, the time of the event, and the place. Delamont argues that through the choice of menu, the family of the bride informs the intended groom that she is ready for marriage and that her culinary knowledge is sufficiently extensive. A tasty meal that meets all the ceremonial norms signals that the bride has been taught to be a devoted wife and will know how to prepare good meals for her husband. If the meal does not meet the standards, it is a sign that the bride is not yet ready to take charge of a household.

In the traditional Palestinian Muslim society, men and women celebrate their marriage separately. The women in each of the families are in charge of deciding on the menu and cooking the food. The bride celebrates her wedding with her family, allowing the women of her family to enjoy themselves. Unlike an American or English bride, she is not considered responsible for her wedding ceremony. The location of the event is of major importance for Palestinians in choosing the wedding menu. If the wedding takes place in the home, the menu will be limited, and the food, despite the extensive preparations, will play a secondary role in comparison with the dancing or the henna ceremony for the bride. Azam, a teacher from Kafar Qara, says that in traditional wedding celebrations the groom rides a horse through the village and then goes through a traditional shaving ritual as everyone sings and dances to music:

> The women prepared food and the guests were invited to enter in small groups. Each one was given a plate with lamb meat, rice with pine nuts and *laban*, and a few salads. Everyone danced and enjoyed the occasion.

Nobody would serve a meal with a number of dishes because it would be difficult for the women to prepare.

A Muslim female social worker from Galilee claims that only in recent years has food begun to appear at the home wedding receptions of brides. Although more and more women choose to get married in wedding halls, there is still a lot of work left for women to do should the bride want a traditional village marriage ceremony:

> Tables are brought into the house, and guests are invited to enter in groups and are given their food on paper plates. They don't sit beside the table all evening and eat as is the case in a wedding reception in a hall, but rather, they enter, eat, and go back outside to dance.

Compared with a home wedding, with its traditional menu including only a limited number of dishes, the menu at a wedding reception in a hall is extensive and varied, and the food is the element that determines whether the event is imprinted in memory as successful or not. The choice of menu does not reflect the bride's or her mother's competence in cookery or hospitality; the menu testifies instead to the celebrating family's financial means and its commitment to customary norms of hospitality. A menu that is not suitable will not be considered a demonstration of lack of domestic knowledge but rather a lack of cash or a lack of respect for the guests. Sylvia, a nurse in a hospital in the center of the country, says she thinks of a wedding as being neither an indication of women's domestic knowledge nor an occasion in which mothers of brides are tested, as no one doubts their culinary knowledge. Regardless of how modern her generation is:

> Today as well, when a man takes a woman for his wife, he first finds out whether she can cook, and he makes sure she learns before the wedding. It doesn't matter how liberal they say they are; the men still want their wives to cook, even if they are ready to help in the house.

Although women internalize and practice a system of female knowledge, part of which implies planning the wedding menu and cultivating familiarity with the rules of hospitality, a wedding does not testify to the culinary expertise of the young bride or of her mother. Palestinian female knowledge and the ability to plan the menu—be it traditional in a home wedding or rich and varied in a wedding in a hall—are taken for granted, and there is no need to put them to the test. The older women have been engaged in cooking for many years, and their experience is self-evident. A similar argument can be set forth about the younger generation of Palestinian women. Although some are better educated than their mothers and develop professional careers, their work outside the home is not undertaken at the expense of their traditional role but, rather, in addition to it—a matter that I discuss extensively in the next chapter. Moreover, when a young woman is about to marry, her cooking skills are a subject of conversation between her family and that of the groom. It is clear to both families that the task of cooking will be hers, even if she intends to study and to work outside the home. An agreement must be reached on the level of culinary skill the young woman is expected to acquire prior to her wedding. Since in most cases the period of time between the engagement and the wedding is long, the young bride has enough time to learn to cook and many opportunities to demonstrate her knowledge.

Today, the bride who seeks to demonstrate her familiarity with the art of entertaining and cooking has other possibilities. When she arrives at the home of her husband, she treats him and her in-laws to food and drink that she has brought with her from home. These are special dishes, such as stuffed partridges, prepared only for special occasions. On the one hand, this demonstrates her familiarity with the art of receiving guests; while on the other hand, she will be free, on the day of her wedding ceremony, from cooking and caring for the needs of her husband. Akhmed, a doctoral student in biology, explains that the young bride enters a new home where there is no food. In order to be free to join her husband and not to need to cook, it is customary to give her food that has already been prepared by her mother:

> My mother gave my sister stuffed young partridges with rice and pine nuts. Why? Perhaps because it is a special dish or because the bones are fresh and can be chewed.

Female knowledge of daily meals and ceremonial meals, then, is manifested by the choice of dishes, their manner of cooking, and women's willingness to help other women in their cooking on special occasions. This chapter has examined the content of female knowledge in Arab society in Israel, its culinary and cultural boundaries, and the ways in which it is put into practice. The level of domestic technology influences female knowledge in several ways and in several spheres: it institutionalizes work practices, illuminates the division of labor between men and women, and classifies the type of dishes and the modes of their preparation. We have seen that technological means determine the methods of preserving and storing food, the methods of relating to food, and often, also, how variants are created. At the same time, technological development on the domestic level has not freed the Palestinian woman in Israel from her work in the kitchen, but has only lightened her physical burden.

Women bear the brunt of responsibility for feeding their families and are therefore the actors who bring and translate cultural and social norms into the kitchen on a daily basis. As part of their role, women respect and carry on norms of entertaining that characterize Palestinian society and local power relationships. A woman's social expertise is revealed in her culinary repertoire.

CHAPTER 2

The Social Sphere

The Culinary Scene as Constructing and Reinforcing Power Relations

This chapter addresses three aspects of culinary practice in the Palestinian kitchen in Israel. First, I look at the connection between culinary practice and familial stratification, examining how women carry out their domestic duties in ways that express the preferences of the person who wields authority in the family. Even though cooking enables women to exercise authority in the home, it has not become a lever for redefining their roles or the system of family power relations. Changes to women's domestic responsibilities have not, on a fundamental level, challenged the division between women's and men's traditional roles.

Second, I discuss how relationships among women emerge in the course of everyday culinary activity. Women not only exchange culinary information within their communities but also offer one another mutual assistance when preparing dishes that require considerable work or cooperation, such as those for special events like weddings, engagements, or holidays. Culinary activity is at the center of community relationships among women, and it provides a reason for women to gather and share work and ideas. Although collaboration in the kitchen advances the public role of women, it has not drastically changed the power structures in the male-centric society. Rather, women have gained autonomy in certain aspects of life as long as they do not challenge the male authority in the household.

Third, cooking is vital to the social role of Palestinian women in Israel. Culinary tradition is perceived as a stock of practical informa-

72

tion to be handed down from older women to the younger generations. The ability to cook is an essential asset for women who wish to marry and establish a family. By passing on cooking knowledge from one generation to the next, women both participate in a gender hierarchy that confines them to the domestic sphere and challenge prevailing norms by acting as agents of innovation and change in the home and kitchen.

innovation is a relative concept here - not the same as Western culinary innovation

IS FEMALE KNOWLEDGE ALSO FEMALE POWER? DOMESTIC COOKERY AS EMPOWERING WOMEN

The study of food enables us to learn about power structures within families and communities. From a practical point of view, food serves as a strategic means of achieving goals and desires in the domestic arena. Today, the culinary sphere affords Palestinian women in Israel the opportunity to make decisions that their mothers did not enjoy, such as whether to purchase electrical appliances for the home or to add new dishes to the domestic repertoire. Socially, women's preoccupation with food not only enhances the authority of the husband, who enjoys food prepared for him by his wife or another woman in the household, but also strengthens the grip of the traditional division of labor. Culinary decision making testifies to the Palestinian woman's overall acquiescence to her place in society as a cook and as the one in charge of the domestic sphere. Unlike a Jewish woman in a neighboring community, whose idea of "liberation" might be focused on the sharing of labor between the sexes, a Palestinian woman might view social change as the opportunity to seek out and take advantage of technologies that would alleviate some of her domestic responsibilities, and she might expect her husband to occasionally help with shopping or washing dishes.[1]

Palestinian culinary practices in Israel are an expression of this society's gendered division of labor and familial stratification. Traditionally, a bride moves into the home of her husband's parents and becomes part of the labor force charged with feeding the extended family in general and its male members in particular. The bride is subject to the directions of her mother-in-law, who supervises her cooking and the maintenance of the home. Hanan, a thirty-five-year-old medical secretary from Deir Hanna, married at age twenty and came to live with her husband and his mother. Even though Hanan had studied to be a medical secretary, she had to work with her mother-in-law and sisters-in-law in the kitchen.

Her mother-in-law instructed her on how to serve her husband coffee and tea and how to cook in a manner that would please him:

> All the men needed to be pleased with my food, and I needed to cook for them. My husband at first was afraid to say to his father that he wanted to live alone with me but when his father died, things became easier for us. His mother tells me much less what I should do. Nowadays, women cook only for their own family.

Fahima lives in Lod with her husband, her two sons with their wives and children, the second wife of her husband, and her unmarried sons. The daughters of the second wife have moved to live with the families of their husbands. In the mornings, Fahima supervises her daughters-in-law as they prepare food and care for the children. The second wife goes out on errands. The elder daughter-in-law is twenty-three years old, six years married, already the mother of two and expecting her third child. The younger daughter-in-law is eighteen, married only a few months ago. When she married, she stopped studying at the teachers' college. Since she is new in the household, she stays close by her sister-in-law and learns from her.

When I arrived, I found the two young women kneading dough in the yard. Then they washed spinach leaves and fried them lightly with onions and spices. They made squares of dough and placed spinach filling in the center of each square. They folded the dough into pockets and put them into the wooden oven in the yard. The elder daughter-in-law checked the dough pockets as she explained to the younger one how to grind chickpeas. When the pregnant daughter-in-law complained that she was hot and the work was difficult, the younger one took over for her. Later the two daughters-in-law cut vegetables, put *labaneh* on a plate, served coffee for the neighbors who had stopped by, and then returned home to prepare cake. In between it all, they hung laundry and changed the young child's diaper. Their mother-in-law came over every few minutes to check on things and give instructions.

A description of the daily life of Hanan and Fahima illustrates a basic feature of Palestinian Arab society in which, after marriage, women become the primary laborers of the family, often feeling taken for granted by the families of their husbands. After a short period of domestic training led by an older woman in the family, they are expected to know how to provide food for everyone. They learn not only cooking skills but also their social place in the family.

The power structure in the Arab family, along with economic and cultural factors, influences women's culinary choices. When women decide the menu they walk a narrow path: they are able express creativity and control, but they must not overstep the bounds of their culturally defined roles. Most do so successfully because they choose to cater the menu to the tastes of their husbands and grown sons, sometimes suppressing their own desires and preferences. An architect living in the north who spent his childhood in a village notes that today, in contrast to his childhood, many women are liberated from budgetary limitations and can satisfy the desires of their husbands more easily:

> When I was a boy, in season, we didn't ask what we would be eating that day, but what kind of eggplant our mother would be making that day. There was also a season of tomatoes and a season of okra, and a season of *hubeizeh*. Who thought then that it was possible to eat what one wanted? My mother tried to prepare what my father liked.

[handwritten margin note: most food only just making inroads into the Mid East ↓ much more seasonal]

The need to take into consideration both economic constraints and their husbands' desires led women, until the time of the First Intifada and then between the First and Second Intifadas, to travel to markets in the Occupied Territories to buy products that were hard to find within the borders of the state of Israel. Purchases in the Territories proved to be economical. Ayda from Lod, who bases her kitchen on seasonal products due to her difficult economic situation, travels to Gaza on a weekly basis. She even traveled during the first Intifada. In order to make sure nothing happened to her, she dressed up like a Gaza woman, refrained from speaking so that no one would recognize her Palestinian accent, and rushed through the counters so that she would get back in time to meet her children when they came home from school:

> The prices here leave me no choice. Everything is cheaper there. For sixty shekels I buy food for a week. Our husbands are also pleased, because they are served the food they like and for not much money.

We see, therefore, that financial constraints and the tastes of the husband are the main factors that the wife takes into consideration when planning the menu. In educated or well-off families, children also play a central role in shaping the menu. Women report that they suit the menu to both the husband's wishes and those of the children; in some cases they may prepare different dishes for the husband and for the children. Mahmud, who runs a cafeteria in the business district of Ramat Gan, and who comes home only on weekends, knows that when he arrives, a meal that is to his taste will await him. He admits that he has no idea what his children or wife like to eat or what they eat when he is gone:

> My wife knows that I love *maklubeh* with eggplant and chickpeas. So when I get home on Thursday evening she always makes *maklubeh*, and we all eat it. On Saturday I grill meat. I don't know what she and the children eat when I am not home.

The husband's status in the Arab family in Israel enables him to dictate the culinary repertoire of the family and to add new dishes without any consideration for the preferences of his wife. Suna, a special-education teacher, learned to prepare Chinese food for her husband, even though she is far from enthusiastic about it. He had eaten it several times in restaurants with his colleagues, loved it, and bought her a Chinese cookbook so that she could prepare him Chinese dishes at home:

> It's like eating uncooked food, so I cook everything longer. I actually was afraid for him to eat it. I make small amounts because only he eats it. The children and I eat the rice and other things.

typical Arab attitude toward foreign food

Suhad, a housewife from Jaffa, navigates between what her children want and what her husband wants:

> My husband doesn't like modern dishes, only traditional foods. My children only want rolls, cornflakes, pizza, and macaroni with tomato sauce. I make my husband food according to our ways and eat with him when he comes home. The children eat rolls with pastrami, pizza, and macaroni.

When the husband isn't home on a daily basis or when he gives his wife a free hand, she prepares whatever she chooses. Ma'aruf, who works in the center of the country, tells me he does not interfere with his wife's cooking because he trusts she will never neglect her domestic duties. Moreover, his only chance to eat traditional Arab dishes is when he is at home:

> Yesterday I came home and found my wife outside picking *hubeizeh*, which she was going to cook for lunch. I love it; at work I don't eat *hubeizeh*. There are some things we eat only at home. If a man were to eat *hubeizeh* outside his home, what would people think of him?

Along with fulfilling the desires of those with authority at home while ignoring their own personal tastes, Palestinian women in Israel are careful to consider religious doctrines. Most Palestinians in Israel are Muslim, and a smaller number of them are Christian. At the same time, they try to ensure that the culinary preferences of the men in the family will not be harmed because of religious constraints. The holiday menu is determined in part by tradition and in part by the tastes and customs that each family has developed. Among Christians, for example, abstinence from meat before Easter has encouraged the traditional vegetarian menu to persist. Seventy-year-old Sonia, from Jaffa, is careful not to eat meat for the forty-eight days preceding Easter. Some of her family members join her, while others shorten the meatless period. Sandra, her fifty-two-year-old daughter, explains that her mother observes the religious prohibition without restricting the men in the family, who will not forgo meat for such a long time. For example, Sonia's husband avoids meat for only twenty-four days, and her brothers follow a meatless diet for only a few days prior to the holiday. Sonia respects the needs of every individual in the family, says Sandra:

> My daughter is pregnant, so I told her not to stay meatless, because it's not good for her. So now she remains meatless for only five days before the holiday. My mother prepares meat for all of them, but she herself doesn't eat it.

During this time, Sonia mobilizes the traditional repertoire: *frike*, bulgur croquettes cooked in *laban*, *shulbato*, *hubeizeh*, *hindbah* with tahini, and *bsara*. In the days leading up to Easter, she prepares for the holiday meal, sends food gifts to others, and cooks simple daily meals for her family. The food gifts are cookies made of semolina dough filled with nuts or dates. The two types taste the same and differ only in shape: *ma'amul* takes the form of an elongated ball, and *ka'ek* looks like a small bagel—round with a hole in the middle, symbolizing the wreath of thorns on the head of the crucified. Preparation of the cookies demands time and skill. Sonia is considered the greatest expert on preparation of dough in her community. Women come to her with the mixture they have prepared so she can evaluate the softness of the dough and the flavor it will have after baking. When I visited her during her preparations for the holiday, she and her older daughter were busy preparing the dough. In a tub large enough to bathe a baby they mixed semolina with soft margarine, and at the same time they heated water until it was lukewarm. When I asked how they knew that the water was warm enough, they answered: "We put our little finger into the water and count to ten. If you can hold your little finger there, it's a sign that the water is okay." Very slowly they added the water to soften the dough. They prepared a large quantity of cookies, and the kneading continued for several hours. Sonia supervised her daughter, and when it seemed as if her daughter had been neglecting a part of the dough, she called it to her attention.

When the kneading was finished, the two women mixed dates with corn oil and cinnamon. To prepare the *ma'amul,* the daughter flattened little pieces of the dough and added teaspoonfuls of the date filling at intervals. She created balls around each bit of filling, and then pinched each ball with delicate tongs to form a small striped pattern, scattered powdered sugar on the cookies, and baked them in the oven. For *ka'ek,* Sonia and her daughter made strips of dough about ten centimeters long. They flattened the strips and placed the filling along the length of the strips. Then they rolled the dough over the filling, creating a round, pinched it with the tongs to create stripes, sprinkled sugar on top, and baked it in the oven. They packed the *ma'amul* and *ka'ek* into packages and presented them to guests who came to the holiday meal. The cookies would also serve as the dessert course of this meal.

Despite the fasting, or perhaps also because of it, the Muslim holiday of Ramadan obliges Muslim women to undertake varied and extensive culinary activity. Unlike the menu during Christian fasting, the Ramadan menu is rich and built more around spur-of-the-moment tastes and desires than upon dictates of tradition. Fatkhi, a doctoral student of political science who works in the local council in a village in the Triangle, says that Ramadan allows people to fulfill their culinary fantasies every evening:

> During Ramadan we're preoccupied with food all the time. How many times has my wife phoned while we've been sitting here? The first time she wanted me to bring chocolate, the second time she wanted me to buy a fresh chicken at the store. You'll see that soon she'll let me know that the child wants an avocado.

He was right: the next phone call included instructions to buy avocados. Fatkhi returned home after fulfilling all of his wife's requests and waited while she prepared chicken and avocado salad for the meal.

Still, there is another trend, hinting at a possible change in the family relationship system and in the definition of women's roles; many women are beginning to reshape their role as cooks without revolting against the traditional division of labor. For instance, women started applying modern technological devices that significantly shorten cooking time and cut down on kitchen labor. Moreover, as a result of their participation in the labor force, fewer women today engage in the preparation of laborious dishes. Rather, they choose to prepare dishes that require less time and labor investment. Furthermore, professional women turn to their mothers for help with their domestic duties. This arrangement works to their benefit because it does not challenge the position of the men in the house. In sum, most women, especially those who work outside the home, choose dishes that make use of modern technologies or do not entail a great deal of labor, or they are helped by their mothers with cooking for the extended family even after the children have already left home.

Take the case of Sana, a political activist from Abu S'nan and the mother of four married daughters and one daughter still living at home. Sana defines herself, first and foremost, as a housewife, and only second as a public figure. On the other hand, her daughters are careerists who depend on their mother's willingness to continue to shoulder the traditional tasks, even though tradition is already willing to release her from them. During the afternoon, her married daughters arrive, along with their husbands and children, and sometimes also her sister's grandchildren, to eat in her home—each of them at their own convenience. Sana reports that she goes through an average of 1.5 kilos of rice each day. No one goes hungry. Sana justifies her endless support to her extended family by saying that her daughters are busier than she is. One is a dentist, the second is an artist, and the third is a pediatrician—all very demanding careers. The daughters all work full time and enjoy their husbands' full support. Sana believes that, in addition to helping her daughters, cooking for her family helps sustain familial relationships:

> I'm happy that they come and that the children come. They respect me. They sit with their grandfather, eat with him, hear what he has to say, honor him. That's how I preserve the family, and my daughters can go to work.

Sana's words demonstrate a gradual change occurring today, especially among educated and well-to-do Palestinian families, that recognizes the right of women to develop independent careers. The change is generational, and Sana herself, even if she wanted it, could not both have a career and maintain a traditional role in her society. Because the status of the man in the family is maintained and the services he expects to receive from his wife are provided by another woman, the Palestinian woman in Israel today can go outside her home and pursue a career.

Increasingly, women see themselves not as a default source of domestic labor, but rather as the glue uniting the family, the ones who maintain hierarchy and traditional power relations. Women who work outside the home still fulfill the traditional array of women's domestic responsibilities. Even today, women wishing to have careers outside the home often find that they must contend with criticism and bitterness on the part of their husbands, who don't like the idea of their wives developing their own independent lives. Tawfik, a teacher from the Triangle, believes it is impossible for women to work and also manage a household. Therefore, he decided to marry an uneducated woman who has no desire to work out of the house:

> When a woman works, there is no home, no food, no clean clothes; the children don't feel they are being looked after. In my family, we eat together when I arrive home. The children set and clear the table and I wash the dishes. When the wife works, you eat separately.

A different situation—one that no doubt is an anomaly but also informs us about commonly held expectations—is that of George, a technician living in Ramla. His story indicates both the formal power of the head of the family and the rising power of women. George was an employee for many years. He held a respected, high-salaried position that brought him status and honor in the community. Several years ago George decided to open his own business, to be a competitor of the business that had employed him. He resigned from his job and invested his severance pay and the savings he had accumulated in opening an independent business. After the first investments in a building, he was left without start-up capital for production and had to rely on advance money from orders. George couldn't keep up with the pace of the orders and went into debt. The banks refused to approve loans for him to continue production, and he was forced to sell the business. His wife, who worked as a teacher in a local school, complained that he couldn't provide for her livelihood or for the future needs of their growing children. She was angry that he had left his well-paying job for an "adventure," while the family was forced to manage on less and live from her salary alone. George eventually left his wife and went to live with his mother. His two sons, aged twenty-five and twenty-eight and both unmarried, chose to follow him. He gave up his wife's services for his mother's cooking. The older son explains his father's actions and the support he received from them in terms of the differential power men and women have in the family:

> My mother laughs at my father. Things didn't go well for my father, but he's the head of the family, and he deserves respect. We eat with him at noon, talk with him, sleep with him in the same house, ask him what to do, and in that way, we show our respect for him.

The case of George is exceptional because he chose to leave home, as do many Jewish men whose marriages encounter difficulties, instead of exploiting his authority and sending his wife away. In so doing, he took a risk in forfeiting his honor and paid a heavy price; he ate at his mother's table, and he found himself dependent upon her financial support. He was mocked for his actions, but his sons continued to respect him without regard for his achievements or failures. For them, the honor of the father was not a subject for negotiation but rather a way of life that they needed to live by.

Even though the male supervision of female culinary practices reinforces the traditional division of labor between men and women in Palestinian society in Israel, since the late 1980s women have begun to expand their traditional roles in order to improve their positions in the home. For example, women have taken more control over decisions regarding purchases for the home. Women have always maintained responsibility for buying the food—except, at times, for the meat—but in recent years, more and more women have also assumed responsibility for larger home purchases, such as electrical appliances. Ostensibly, women consult with their husbands before making these purchases, but in fact, they generally inform their husbands of their decisions as they request money for the purchase. Advertisers are aware of this phenomenon and reinforce it with their advertisements. An advertiser from Jaffa working with the Arab sector plans his campaigns under the assumption that women decide what to buy and when to bring home appliances. Therefore he directs his words to women:

> The man comes with her, takes out the checks or the credit card, speaks to the shopkeeper, but she has told him to come, what to ask, and she knows what refrigerator or washing machine she wants.

This is not to say that women are freed from their domestic responsibilities by controlling domestic purchases, but rather that they are capable of influencing how their domestic duties are fulfilled. A new, well-equipped kitchen, a spacious home, a large refrigerator, and a modern bathroom are not only a reflection of the family's economic situation; they are also tools that allow the housewife to be more efficient in implementing the traditional division of labor. Eventually, all parties are rewarded—the home, the children, and the husband.

In the same way, women decide which after-school program to register their children in, which high school the daughter will be enrolled in, and whether or not to buy a computer for a child. They also make daily food choices that influence the health and well-being of the family. Sylvia, for example, thought her husband's back was becoming bent over the years, and she decided to take action to improve his situation. She figured it was because their diet was too low in calcium:

> So each morning we drink instant coffee with milk and eat cornflakes with milk. I also buy white cheese and Prili and Dani [yogurt] which we eat. When the grandchildren come, we drink chocolate milk. So we get some calcium into our bodies.

Basmeh, an English teacher, decided that her family needed to go on a diet. Her own high blood pressure was taken as a good opportunity to change the family's eating habits:

> I came home and told my family: look at us, a bunch of fat people. My husband and our older son are very heavy; they eat all the time. Our daughter, too, even though she's small, she's fat. So I decided that from today on, we're finished with cakes, *labaneh*, and fried foods.

As we have seen, the subject of food sheds light on power relations in the family and in society. The kitchen has become a social space in which women exert control over their families and their domestic roles. Unlike in Western society, where women's liberation is focused on renegotiating the gendered division of labor, Palestinian women accept their traditional roles, but they gain a certain autonomy and work to reduce their burden through access to modern technology.

IN THE COMPANY OF WOMEN: COOKING AS CREATING BONDS AMONG WOMEN

The exchange of gastronomic information and the mutual help that goes along with daily culinary activity create a unique female experience and sisterhood among Palestinian women in Israel. The latter is most evident in the preparation of meals for special occasions, such as weddings, engagements, holidays, and other religious ceremonies, or in the preparation of dishes requiring a great deal of labor and planning. This is not to say that women in the kitchen are always cooking in public. On the contrary, women are not paid for their work in the kitchen, and they do not receive professional recognition or advancement for their culinary skills. Their public culinary practices remain limited to the community event alone.

Joint labor in the kitchen is an integral part of Palestinian community life in Israel, and it is supported by exchange relations: women who need to organize a large event turn to relatives, neighbors, and friends in order to borrow kitchen utensils and request their help in cooking. Receiving help creates relations of friendship and obligation between women and ensures that, in times of need, every woman can depend upon help from the community.[2]

Older women, who possess much culinary knowledge, are highly respected in Palestinian society. It is as an expression of this respect that they are invited to cook for weddings. The most honored cooks do not do the ordinary work: their job is one of supervising, adding seasonings, tasting, and preparing the special dishes. In Shefar'am, for example, there is an excellent cook who is eighty-seven years old. Even though she has passed on the supervisory role in her home to her oldest son's wife, many community members continue to invite her to cook for weddings that take place in their homes. As chief supervisor, she asks the women of the celebrating family to take responsibility for utensils and products and to act according to her instructions. She instructs them on choosing vegetables for stuffing, but she empties out the insides herself, saying that the way the vegetables are cut is what determines their taste. At the same time, she instructs the women in how to prepare the filling, but she herself places the vegetables in the pot, seasons the dish, and makes certain that it does not overcook.

Nabia from Kafar Yasif, who cooks for her married daughters, has gained a reputation in the community as an expert cook. She is frequently requested by one of her relatives, neighbors, or friends from the town to help cook for a wedding. Her help takes the form of organization and supervision, as she asks women whose culinary skills she trusts to help. The women borrow pots and pans from members of the community and, under Nabia's direction:

> We prepare the hot red peppers that we want to use in the *kubeh*. We wash them, clean them thoroughly, and grind and mix them with meat and bulgur into *kubeniyeh*. From what is left, we prepare *kubeh*. We then prepare rice with pine nuts and spices.

The possession of female culinary knowledge in Palestinian society does not provide grounds for challenging the system of power relations at the level of the home and the community. The translation of culinary knowledge into prestige is individual and does not overstep narrow limits. The social and political conditions in which Palestinian women in Israel live are such that the reward of honor and respect accompanying their extensive culinary knowledge simply means that more work and responsibility fall upon their shoulders. The women participating in the cooking do so out of obligation to their families and communities, and they do not use their participation as a means of expanding their authority. They report being satisfied with a symbolic reward, with the thanks of the community and their recognition as good cooks; in spite of the burden and responsibility, supervision of wedding preparations are not interpreted as work but rather as a mark of honor. The women do not complain in public about their status, and they usually do not ask to be relieved of cooking for the community. In this way, assuming the public role of the community cook only reinforces the system of power relations between men and women.

Until the 1960s, a vibrant social life revolved around cooking as well. Women cooked together in the home of the extended family, exchanging experiences, conversing, joking, and releasing tension. In the community, women made a habit of meeting to help each other prepare a reserve of food for winter: a supply of bulgur or *sha'ariya*—small, thin noodles. Preparation of *sha'ariya* was not part of the regular daily routine but rather an activity that took place after working hours. With the approach of winter, neighbors, friends, and female family members would gather, and in one night, they would prepare noodles for four or five families. The morning before, the woman would prepare a supply of dough, and in the evening, the house would fill up with neighbors and friends. Each woman was given a tray and a piece of dough, which she kneaded into a long, thin strip. Then she would wind the dough onto one hand and use the other hand to pinch the dough into small noodles, which she stacked onto the tray. The *sha'ariya* were dried in the sun, fried in oil to prevent sticking, and stored in sacks. The gathering enabled women to use and develop techniques that would increase their female skills while enjoying an opportunity to be away from home and chat. Samira, from Abu S'nan, remembers these gatherings from her childhood. Every night the women would go to another house to help the homemaker. Girls and young women joined older women with the aim of learning how to make the noodles. If their results didn't pass muster, they rekneaded the dough and tried again. Some old women, she recalls, were so tired after the day's work that they fell asleep while pulling pinches of dough. Others would use the time to joke, drink coffee leisurely, and gossip:

> Every woman would bring her candle with her, because there was no light on the street, and she would be wearing house slippers. Each woman was given a rope of dough about a meter long, which she coiled onto her hand, each time pulling off a little of the rope, with two fingers. The length and

thinness of the rope were a measure of each woman's skill. The next day all the women would look for their missing shoes because with the lack of electricity they would walk home with the wrong shoes.

Now there is less communal culinary activity because many women have limited time for cooking and industrial products have largely replaced the items whose preparation required cooperation among women. The culinary social experience has become limited to the exchange of information among neighbors meeting for a morning conversation. Women share recipes, chat about the children, drink coffee, and then go home around eleven in the morning to cook separately. Alham, a housewife from Jaffa, is visited by her neighbors every day. Not only is she considered an expert in all matters related to food, but she is a beloved source of advice, known for helping to resolve arguments and problems with husbands or children. Her next-door neighbor says she learned from Alham to add cumin to the cooking water to prevent cooked vegetables from causing a bloated stomach. Another young woman brought her friends Moroccan pastry "cigars," filled with spiced ground meat, that she learned to make from her Jewish neighbor, and she explained how to prepare them. The neighbors tasted the dish and decided that they, too, would prepare "cigars" at home.

The social ambience that develops around cooking and the cooperation among women do not jeopardize the traditional family structure or bring men's power into question. On the contrary, transforming cooking into a social club and institutionalizing collective work patterns strengthens women's traditional role as cooks and their sense that they are destined to be the domestic workforce. The social activity and the traditional female sphere of activity are thus mutually supportive. Moreover, women know that helping other women guarantees that they, too, will have help and support when they need it. Their interactions enable them to improve their cooking skills and increase their daily working capacities while providing them with social support that expands their domestic space. Activity in the communal domain replicates domestic tasks in a setting outside the home, and in so doing, it leaves women little time to ask questions about their lives as women and about the possibility of changing the system of family roles and power relations.

WOMEN'S SELF-PERCEPTION OF COOKING

Women's perception of themselves as cooks is fundamental to how women see themselves in Palestinian society in Israel. Few women are able to consider the possibility of a family life free of the obligation to cook or to demand an egalitarian division of the domestic burden. Culinary knowledge does not translate into financial reward or a professional identity. Rather, it is essential to how women value themselves within the family. To pursue an education or career would be to limit the time a woman has to master home cooking. The higher the level of the woman's education, the later and shorter her culinary training will be. While less-educated women may sometimes begin learning to cook when they are as young as twelve years of age, educated women often do not begin until they are married, when their mothers or their husbands' mothers help them with the cooking tasks or they learn by trial and error.

Nadia has a master's degree in education and is a special-education teacher. She grew up in Jerusalem in a well-to-do family. Her husband is a successful businessman, and they live in a large, new apartment building in the upper-class neighborhood on top of Mount Carmel in Haifa. They have two cars and employ a cleaning woman—something very rare in the Arab sector in Israel. Even though Nadia leaves the house at 7:30 every morning and comes home around 4:00 p.m., she clearly understands her responsibility as a cook, as do her husband and the rest of the community. It is the same for other women, even if they work full-time outside the home. Cooking, for Nadia, is something Palestinian women learn throughout their childhood. She explains that women would call their growing daughters to the kitchen to watch the older women cook:

> If we work, that's our problem. We still need to clean, cook, and care for the children. Today the men help, not like my father, but I make sure there's food and plan what to eat so my husband and children are satisfied. My husband sometimes does the shopping and washes the dishes, but I can't depend on it.

Despite her economic security and the financial stability that could free her of some of the household tasks, Nadia perceives her role in the home as not very different from that of a housewife, a worker in the service industry, or a woman of the older generation.

According to Marwa, a housewife and high school graduate who is married to the head of a local council in Galilee, the woman carries a great deal of responsibility. This extends beyond cooking to finding food for her family—both when there is enough money and when there is not—to receiving guests, to managing the household:

> If there's no food, that's our problem, and we'll look outside in nature to find enough to feed the family. My husband sometimes phones and tells

me, "I'm bringing guests," and sometimes he brings them without telling me. So I need to know how to cook and need to be sure there is always something in the house.

In spite of the difference in education between Nadia and Marwa, the two share the opinion that the woman is obligated to prepare food for her family, regardless of her profession. Aisha, from the village of Barta'a, holds a similar view. She married at seventeen and failed to complete her high school education. She never thought about higher education or working outside the home. When she reached the age of forty, she traveled for the first time in her life, spending two days with her husband in Eilat. Even though her village is near the town of Hadera, she rarely goes to town, and then only with her husband. She has only been in Tel Aviv once. During the day I spent with her, she asked me how I cook squash, eggplant, and chicken. When she heard that I did not cook every day but only now and then, and even then with the help of cookbooks, she burst out laughing in wonder:

> I cook every day, there is no other option. Now it's easier because there are preserves and a wonder pot and an oven. That's how he likes it. Doesn't your husband get angry at you for not cooking?

The three women, despite their differences in education, lifestyle, and economic situation, agree that the woman must do the cooking. A higher education, a profession, and other activities do not release a woman from the task of cooking or from other domestic responsibilities. Even when the husband cooks outside the home, as is the case with Abir, a secretary from Jerusalem whose husband owns a pizzeria, the domestic kitchen is the woman's territory where the man is not allowed:

> At the most, he may wash the dishes, but he won't tell anyone he's doing that, so they won't think he isn't respected at home. I get up at 6:00 a.m. to cook so before 8:30 a.m. when I arrive at work, I've cooked and cleaned. I often cook in the evening, and then at noon I only cut up a salad and warm up the food.

Women doing the cooking is therefore something taken for granted; it is an essential part of the daily scheme of things and of the socialization of women, and there is no disagreement about it. In the past, culinary training began at a young age: girls were called into the kitchen to observe their mothers or grandmothers cooking, and they gradually learned to take part—first preparing vegetables for cooking, then watching the pot and stirring. Learning to season was the last stage in a young woman's culinary education: only someone sufficiently experienced would be privileged to season the food and have the right to serve food to one's father.

After her marriage, a bride needs to get used to the tastes of her husband and her in-laws, something that often requires more learning and training under her mother-in-law's tutelage. Fahima, living in Jaffa, married at age sixteen. Her husband opened a small store that eventually became a supermarket. Fahima arrives at the store during the early morning hours to help her husband and returns home before 11:00 a.m. to cook and clean. At 2:00 p.m. her husband closes the store and comes home to eat and rest. At 4:00 p.m. they both go back to the store and work there until evening, and then they return home and eat a light meal. In the evening, Fahima's husband rests, watches television, or chats with the neighbors, while Fahima starts preparing the meal for the following day. Her training as a housewife began at a very early age:

> When I was fourteen, my mother started teaching me to cook so I'd be ready for marriage. She taught me step by step until I was ready for the seasoning. When I got married, my mother-in-law insisted I learn to cook her way. She said her son only loved her food.

Fatma, who lives in Ramla and grew up in the Negev, remembers cooking as a central part of her childhood activity. When she married, she already knew how to cook well, and she expanded her existing repertoire during her married life with suggestions from her neighbors, her daughters, and television shows. She acquired her original set of domestic skills by observing and training under the supervision of her mother:

> Girls didn't usually go to school but stayed home and learned to cook. When I married at fifteen, I knew how to cook. My mother cooked over an open fire of twigs, which was burning all day long. My daughters and my sons' wives learn from me. It's the woman's job to take care of the home.

The formal socialization of the young Palestinian woman ends when she is sufficiently skilled to take upon herself the management of a household. Older women want to gradually turn over responsibility to their daughters even before they marry, so that they will gain experience in managing a household, or to the oldest daughter-in-law, who will be expected to manage the household of the extended family when the father dies. When Nadia, from the village of Makrem, became widowed, she passed responsibility for the household to her daughter-in-law Hishmi and narrowed her own role to preparing special dishes. Hishmi and her husband housed Fatma in a small apartment next to theirs, and Fatma started to eat with them. When Hishmi's sixteen-year-old daughter became engaged to the owner of an automobile garage, the young woman left school at her fiancé's behest, and she now spends her time in the kitchen practicing cooking and receiving guests. Hishmi guides her and is proud of the fact that she neither needs to tell her how to treat the houseguests nor when and how to set the table and serve the meal:

> In the morning, when I'm at work, she cooks. When I come back I eat and tell her "You need to do this and you need to do that for it to be good." That's how she practices. Her fiancé wants her to be ready for him, and I know he'll be satisfied.

A scientist from the Triangle reports that his sister—a woman in her twenties about to marry—is undergoing a similar training process. The presence of an engaged woman in the household, he argues, is of benefit to all because the bride keeps practicing and trying new dishes:

> Every time I come, there is special food that she prepares. My father says that whenever a daughter gets married, there is interesting food at home. Her husband can rest assured that she knows how to cook and also loves doing it.

Unmarried women can avoid cooking: they eat at their parents' table until the latter pass away. Then they will manage an independent household under the supervision of the eldest brother or else they may move in with the brother and sometimes become the "mother of the household." Some don't know how to cook and don't take part in maintaining the household, since they were never on the way to marriage. Forty-nine-year old Alice, for example, works in a textile factory and lives with her eighty-five-year-old mother. Despite her age and the fact that she supports the family, Alice is considered to be the youngest daughter at home and one who needs to be taken care of. Her mother awakens her every morning at 5:45 a.m. and warms up milk for her. She prepares a sandwich for her daughter to take to work, and when Alice returns home, a warm meal awaits her. Alice takes this treatment for granted, and her attitude toward her mother's food resembles that of a young child. On her way home, Alice wonders what her mother has prepared for her, hoping she did not cook a dish she is not fond of. Moreover, she takes it for granted that only women engaged to be married need to learn to cook:

> I never married, so my mom never taught me to cook. My oldest sister [who is only three years older than Alice] teaches all her daughters to cook so they are ready for marriage. I can clean the house and warm up food. It's not good that I don't know how to cook because my mother is old and it's hard for her.

On the other hand, Maria, an elementary school teacher and social worker in the Triangle, chose not to marry and rejected those who asked for her hand. Like Alice, her culinary skills are minimal, but she admits that cooking doesn't interest her. In her view, being a single woman justifies her avoiding work she doesn't like:

> I live with my parents, and my mom is an excellent cook. I like having food ready for me when I come home. I have a car, so I do the shopping and help them out with money if they need it. When my mom was in the hospital, I cooked for my dad, and he suffered my food for a whole week.

Single women who choose to cook take upon themselves the role of family cook. Some women do not marry because their parents expect them to care for them when they get old. Mary, a single woman in her sixties, lives in a very large house in a mixed city. She is the only one of eight siblings who did not marry. After her parents died, Mary continued to live in the large house where she had grown up, and she inherited the task of the mother as family cook. Her brother, sister, and a large number of cousins come to her house every day to eat their main meal, to bring her supplies, and to take food home. As her nieces grow up, they are sent to Mary to learn to cook before they marry. Every day her older brother arrives at around 1:00 p.m. for a meal. His wife, she says, works too hard to cook on a daily basis. Her niece comes when her classes at university finish. Mary loves her niece's company because "she tells me what she's learning, and I learn from her." Mary sees herself as freeing the women in her family from cooking by taking upon herself the role of the family cook who makes sure everybody in the family gets a daily homemade meal.

Aysha, in her thirties, has also remained unmarried because of a decision by her parents. She belongs to a group of Arab women who were the first to be trained as tour guides, and she lives in a Galilee village

[handwritten marginal note: that's awfully self-sacrificing]

with her parents. Aysha says that she has always loved to cook and collect recipes. She has chosen to cook for her parents, and she cooks almost every day: Palestinian, Chinese, and Italian food. She draws from the knack she has for cooking and sometimes uses recipes she has cut out of women's magazines:

unusual

> It's fun for me. I always read recipes, see what suits me, and try new things. My parents got used to me cooking, and they eat all kinds of new things. My mom also cooks—when I'm traveling or when I'm tired.

Women who pursue education and careers often do not take on the responsibility to cook for the extended family, and sometimes do not or are not able to pass along culinary knowledge to their daughters. As a result, the number of educated women who marry without earlier culinary training is growing. This change is not met without resistance. Many feel that women's education conflicts with their traditional female roles. Some, like Ali, complain that:

> Today young women don't have time to learn to cook. They go to the university, and they learn to cook only after they get married.

Others, like Ziyad, a teacher in his fifties, regard young, educated women as lazy and spoiled. He complains that, in contrast to women of his generation, younger women insist on getting married only after their house is built, the living room is furnished, and all electrical appliances have been acquired. Moreover, modern young women are unwilling to invest time and work in preparing laborious dishes:

the dowry problem

> My mother and wife used to make *kirshe*, but my daughter finds it disgusting. My wife makes *couscouson* and bakes bread but my daughter wants to be modern and buy everything. Did you see the house she's building? An Italian living room, marble, a fireplace with bricks from heaven knows where. It makes me laugh, even though I know it's not funny at all.

Some young women work to make their social existences more flexible. Ibtisam, age twenty-three, grew up in Ramla, double-majored in education and Middle Eastern studies, and after completing her studies, took a course for senior secretaries and began working in the Arab section of the Ministry of Education. She is about to marry a social worker from Kafar Qara. Her supervisor says that she and other young women have no respect toward the Palestinian tradition and culture that honors the woman who stays at home. Ibtisam, the most radical among the Palestinian women I met, tries to redefine the role of the woman—without much success. The conversation between Ibtisam and her supervisor is presented verbatim:

Supervisor: She doesn't want to cook. She wants to eat only in restaurants. Why should she stand on her feet in the kitchen for six hours just for a man?

Ibtisam: That's right. I don't want to spend all day in the kitchen, just to have all the food disappear in one moment. I don't even know how to make myself an omelet.

Supervisor: I tell you, it's all for show. What do you want to tell your lady friends? That today you stood in the kitchen and prepared stuffed vegetables or that you went to a restaurant?

Ibtisam: That I went to a restaurant.

Supervisor: You see? She doesn't understand how much respect there is for a Palestinian woman. A woman's honor is to manage a home. Do you know how much I respect my wife? How much I appreciate her? Am proud of her? Because of women like you, our traditions will be lost. Do you know what Ibtisam is proud of? That nobody believes she's a Palestinian. Is it a disgrace to be an Arab woman? How far will things go if even we believe that we have horns?

Ibtisam: Don't you understand that I don't want your respect for serving you food when you come home from work? I want respect for who I am. I don't want to cook, don't want to be stuck in the house with the children, don't want to sit all day with my mother-in-law. I want to work and buy clothes and be beautiful, to travel and go to restaurants.

Supervisor: Do you know how much money it costs? You know, even though my wife doesn't work, I have more money than friends whose wives work. They spend a lot of money on kindergarten for their children, ready-to-eat food, laundry; I don't spend any of that money.

Ibtisam: You don't understand at all. What is money for if not to be spent?

Supervisor: I know your future in-laws don't want you to work, and they want you to learn to cook, and I know there are problems. You'll learn to cook and to be a good wife. You'll see; they'll respect you and you'll enjoy it.

The conversation between Ibtisam and her boss reveals the cultural and gender gaps between generations of Palestinian women in Israel. Ibtisam sees her supervisor as one who fails to comprehend the changes that have taken place in the definition of a woman's tasks. To her, he represents Palestinian men in general and the older generation in particular, which feels threatened by the personal freedom she and her female friends demand. The man, for his part, attaches lesser importance to the generation gap; Ibtisam, in his eyes, is an agent of change who has aligned with a Jewish-Western lifestyle, helping to erode Palestinian society from its traditions. He accuses her of lacking a basic understanding of the culture from which she has sprung.

Amir cooks in a restaurant in Acre. His daughter studies social work at the university and is not considering getting married. Unlike Ibtisam's supervisor, Amir is not concerned about the loss of tradition, knowledge, or women's honor. Instead, he worries about the personal and concrete: Will his daughter show enough wisdom, when the day comes, to be a good wife to her husband, even though cooking doesn't interest her? Is she aware of the fact that her husband will be dissatisfied and that she will not have a good life?

> She has other things on her mind besides cooking, but she must know how to prepare food. Today, the girls don't try. They learn in theory, but you have to burn the food once to learn when to lower the flame. One must learn when to add spices; one must learn to feel the food.

Adults in general and men in particular are concerned about two aspects of the decline in women's cooking skills: one is the fear of losing tradition and of changes in the system of family relations, and the other has to do with the practical—the concern that women will lose their culinary expertise. Both Palestinian men and women say that training needs to be carried out one-on-one, not only to supervise young women but because of the character of the culinary domain and the type of skill it requires, which is primarily acquired through daily work and experience. An experienced woman is capable of judging a dish by its scent, color, and consistency. The idea of writing down traditional recipes—a process necessitating exact measurements of quantities and cooking times—is not a substitute for experience. Here's how Nabiha, from Majd al-Kurum, expresses it:

> Food is something that's felt. I feel the food. I put a spice in my hand and see if it's enough. I mix the food and feel whether it's ready. You can see by its color, its odor; I don't even need to taste it to know if it's good.

Older Palestinian women and men recognize the loss of female cooking expertise and fear the consequences of that loss on women's personal lives as well as on Palestinian culinary culture in general. Female culinary knowledge has played a major role in the constitution of Palestinian culture in Israel. In the first part of this book, I have analyzed the content of that female knowledge. I have explored its culinary and cultural boundaries, and the ways in which culinary knowledge is put into practice. Domestic technology influences female knowledge in several ways and in several spheres: it institutionalizes work practices, illuminates the division of labor between men and women, and classifies the type of dishes served and the modes of their preparation. Technological means determine methods of food preservation and storage, methods of relating to food, and often how variants are created. At the same time, technological development on the domestic level has not freed Palestinian women in Israel from their work in the kitchen, but has only lightened their physical burden.

As we have seen, the analysis of female culinary knowledge in Palestinian society in Israel is an interesting case study of the relationship between food, gender roles, ethnicity, and identity. It shows the role food plays in the formation of a distinctive ethnic and national culture and the informal role women play in sustaining a national culture whose legitimacy is constantly challenged by political authorities. The study shows that women voluntarily turn into active social agents who mobilize what is perceived as a taken-for-granted female culinary knowledge as a means of constituting and perpetuating a distinctive female and ethnic identity.

In addition to analyzing the ways in which culinary knowledge is put into practice, I have shown in this chapter the extent to which housework is an essential part of Palestinian women's self-perception, regardless of their work outside the home. In addition to constituting a communal feminine identity, these practices also enable women to position themselves as social agents who sustain Palestinian culinary tradition and take it upon themselves to introduce the younger generation to its food culture.

Although cooking and feeding can provide women with means of gaining certain autonomy, the case of Palestinian women in Israel shows the limitations of women's use of food practices in reversing power relations and improving women's position in the household. Men's tastes, along with seasonality and financial abilities, govern women's decisions regarding the menu, and their own particular food needs are ignored.

Finally, I have emphasized in this chapter the extent to which food becomes a significant means for establishing a cultural reservoir of knowledge that constitutes shared cultural assumptions and historical perspectives, all of which form a national narrative to preserve their social distinctiveness. In the second part of the book, I look at the ways in which these narratives change to incorporate modernization and political recognition.

PART TWO

The Public Dimension

The Encounter with Jewish Society

Laila lives in a seventy-two-square-meter apartment in a public housing project in a mixed city. She is forty-five years old, a mother of five and grandmother of two. Her husband, who is also her cousin, is a hired metalworker. Laila works for a Jewish family as a babysitter. Moving from an "Arab house" to an apartment in a long block of public housing was her greatest dream. She felt fortunate to leave her old stone house—a structure with high ceilings and six spacious rooms—and take up residence in an apartment the size of two of the rooms in her previous home, whose ceilings constantly felt as if they were landing on her head. She brought with her only a few possessions, those that would testify to her separation from tradition and the move to modern society. Laila sold her Arab house for a large sum of money and was now living her dream.

One morning a truck arrived and loaded all the modern equipment that was in Laila's old house, leaving the rest behind for the new tenants. Only the old-style wooden furniture, the buffet with its collection of decorated coffee cups, a Formica dining table, and the electric appliances that filled the modern kitchen made the move to the new apartment. Three of Laila's children, those who still lived at home, exchanged their large wooden beds for bunk beds and were delighted with their new contemporary room.

Laila laughs when she tells of the dozens of Jews who wanted to buy her large house and were struck by its high decorated ceilings, spacious rooms, large windows, and the natural coolness it maintained during the oppressive heat of August. She watched in amazement as potential buyers planned the split-level arrangements they would make in the high-ceilinged rooms, the new bathrooms they would construct, and the decorated windows that would replace the present large ones. Some even hired contractors to see if it was possible to install an air conditioner or convert the patio into a two-car garage. Laila wondered why you would need air conditioning in the cool house, or why you would want to destroy the patio—the heart of the house, which was used for idle female conversation, family gatherings, sitting under the winter sun, and growing mint plants and a glorious lemon tree. Laila says she does not regret selling her old home, and experiences only joy in her new one. She addresses me defiantly:

> You Jews taught us to be modern; you built public housing for yourselves, and when you moved out, you sold the apartments to us. You told us that public housing is cleaner and more beautiful, and now, you ask me if it doesn't hurt me to leave the house that belonged to my husband's grandfather? The pain has already passed. You wanted us modern—okay, you have us modern. After so many years, I don't know how to live the way they lived in the past; I know how to live like my Jewish neighbor.

Leaving a house with a yard in favor of a small public housing apartment unit is a typical practice among Palestinia n citizens living in mixed cities in Israel today. Laila lives a modern life to the fullest, as if to say that whoever wanted to modernize the Palestinian citizens of Israel should not expect the flame of tradition to remain lit within them or lament its disappearance or its transformation into an exotic fragrance within the consciousness of the majority group. The pain at abandoning the house to a wealthy Jew she accepts with equanimity as a trade-off for her welcome into the warm embrace of modernity. Laila has fulfilled an imperative that had permeated her being over many years until she finally believed that the way of life customary among her forefathers had become outmoded. Instead, she longed to adopt a modern lifestyle, even at the price of leaving the land, transferring it to others, and accepting a public housing apartment, something that is no longer desirable to her Jewish neighbors. The ember of modernity is handed over to her and her generation thanks to alternative lifestyles adopted by the Jewish public, and not necessarily out of a willingness to accept Palestinians into the national, social, and cultural collective that defines the state of Israel.

By contrast, Nadia—who lives within walking distance of Laila—remains in the large old house that had belonged to her husband's parents, and she hopes that one of her sons will come to live in it when she dies. Nadia is keeping the promise she made to her mother-in-law, who often said that one should never leave a house, and that a person who leaves his house is not worthy of it, being devoid of respect for the land and for his roots. Instead, Nadia brought modernity home by combining national motifs and modern technology, creating an interesting synthesis of Palestinianness and Israeliness. Nadia renovated her kitchen a few years ago. She is proud of her wooden kitchen cupboards, huge refrigerator, freezer, microwave, two-compartment oven, and set of pots and pans, just as she is proud of the traditional dishes in her culinary repertoire. The walls of the kitchen and the two bathrooms are covered with ceramic tiles. In two of the bedrooms, which resemble lofts, Nadia has divided the space in creative ways so that her children have privacy and their own rooms.

In the living room, alongside embroidered goblins and landscape paintings, are three portraits of equal size: one of Abdel Nasser, the president of Egypt prior to Sadat; the second of Chaim Herzog, a former president of Israel; and the third of Nadia's deceased husband. "This is the president," she says of Nasser, adding that the painting has been hanging in the house ever since the 1960s. "He made us proud when we didn't have very much pride." "Why don't you hang up a painting of Arafat?" I ask. Nadia doesn't dare go that far. A picture of Arafat, the founder of the PLO, in the living room might, in her opinion, be considered antagonistic toward the state of Israel and jeopardize her right to live there. In another few years, when the situation becomes clearer, she might hang his picture. She hung the painting of Herzog as a symbol of her coexistence with and recognition of the state of Israel. "Why Herzog and not Ben-Gurion or Ezer Weizman?" I press. She gives me a penetrating look. Ben-Gurion was the person who transformed her and her family into refugees in their own land, into third-class citizens. He separated them from their families and regarded them as enemies. Herzog symbolizes the beginning of coexistence, of respect. And as for Ezer Weizman, she didn't find an appropriate photograph of him.

The weaving of "modern" motifs into daily life and the attempt to construct a distinct national identity through food are aspects of the meeting between the Jewish and Palestinian populations in Israel—a meeting revolving around two axes. One axis, illustrated by Laila's story, is the attempt to integrate into the Jewish way of life. Many

Palestinian citizens believe that access and exposure to Jewish community has raised their own standard of living. It has enriched their kitchen with new dishes, advanced cooking technologies, and novel ingredients, even if at the price of abandoning traditions. The other axis, reflected in Nadia's story, is the meeting of the personal dimension with the political one, which makes its mark upon private life down to the choice of pictures to hang on the walls of the home.

Living as a group defined as a hostile minority imparts political significance to what would otherwise be merely private experiences. Ordinary acts—such as riding on a bus, entering a movie theater, buying an apartment, or registering children for after-school activities in the municipal community center—sometimes become so difficult and humiliating for Palestinians that they make an effort to avoid contact with the Jewish population. The blurring of boundaries between the personal and the political has culinary implications as well. Questions about the Palestinian kitchen are interwoven in the Israeli political structure, in the processes of creating a national identity, and in the web of relations between the Jewish and Palestinian sectors.

The second part of the book focuses upon the imperative of modernity in the Arab kitchen in Israel and the link between the development of this kitchen and the processes of constructing a distinct national identity. Chapter 3 explores how modernity is perceived and expressed in the Palestinian kitchen in Israel. It examines the circumstances that have enabled culinary modernization and the ways by which women adapt new culinary knowledge to suit the needs of their families. Chapter 4 looks at how the Arab kitchen has become marginal in Israeli society and how it is connected to a broader system of political and community relations. The marginality of and distaste for Arab cuisine deters Palestinians from opening restaurants and developing other entrepreneurial food projects in Israel.

CHAPTER 3

Labaneh with Light Bread and *Knafeh* from White Cheese

Tradition and Modernity Meet

Modernity is a key word for Palestinian citizens of Israel.[1] The modern lifestyle encourages mobility and gradual detachment from the past. For Palestinians, modernization entails a rise in educational level, greater professional opportunity, gradual entry into the middle class, recognition of their equal rights in Israel, consumption of new products, and adoption of life patterns perceived as more Western and more suited to the specific demands and needs of the Palestinian public.

During the final decades of the twentieth century, social stratification reshaped the face of Palestinian society in Israel. On the fringes of the Israeli bourgeoisie arose a Palestinian bourgeoisie, which aimed to exist within the Israeli economy. During the same period, the intelligentsia, whose numbers had grown, began to organize. Academics sought to have an impact on life in the villages to which they had returned. Institutions that acted outside the parliamentary framework arose.[2] Exposure to democratic political apparatuses raised political awareness among Palestinians in Israel and stimulated organization to achieve civil rights, raise the level of education, and thus promote social mobility.

Contrary to the Western perception, which advocates exchanging the old for the new, modernity for Palestinians in Israel does not constitute a break with tradition but rather an attempt to add to and complement tradition while improving the quality of life and assigning new meanings to their lives and traditions. Modern life includes better housing conditions, good education for children, access to privacy, improved health and medical care, a gradual change in patterns of dress, and a change in conceptions of marriage. In the realm of cuisine, it includes the buying power to purchase new appliances for the home and kitchen and the enrichment of the culinary repertoire, both of which lead to improved living conditions for women. One also finds religious revival or national awakening among some members of the Palestinian public in Israel. The adoption of ways identified as modern is perceived not as antithetical to such developments, but, on the contrary, may be seen as complementary.

In the domestic sphere, and especially in the culinary domain, women are the agents of modernization. Wives prepare dishes that they have encountered outside the home for their husbands and children. They use new electric appliances and gradually abandon complicated dishes for those that are easier to prepare. The desire to adopt technologies that are perceived as useful creates patterns of imitation, implementation, and transformation of culinary knowledge in the Palestinian kitchen in Israel.

These patterns find expression in four complementary ways. First, culinary modernity emerges from the replacement of traditional dishes prepared in the home with versions that are easier to prepare, thanks to advances in domestic technology or ingredients now purchased in stores. The purchase of ready-made dishes is considered both a status symbol and an indication of economic well-being that saves women hours of work. It is also an attempt to blur the differences in lifestyle between Palestinian and Jewish citizens of Israel. But paradoxically, the modernity that might be expected to replace tradition actually enables some traditional dishes to remain in the daily culinary repertoire.

Second, in addition to their desire to bring modernity into the kitchen, Palestinians exhibit an aversion to new products and new methods of cooking antithetical to the traditional Arab kitchen. The desire for innovation and variation is not reason enough to adopt a new product or unfamiliar recipe; the new product must also be perceived as making the kitchen healthier and fulfilling functions beyond those of the product it replaces.

Third, innovation is introduced into the Arab kitchen by the media, the food industry, and Jewish neighbors. I argue that the Arab media promotes innovations as long as they are suited to the needs of the Palestinian public, while the Jewish media often adopts a patronizing position and seeks to educate the Palestinian public. The food industry, on the other hand, tries to adapt to the special demands of the

Palestinian sector and to win it over as a permanent customer. Jewish women who make friends with their Palestinian neighbors create a web of exchange relations by means of which the latter learn of new dishes that are considered modern. Jewish society has only limited access to the Palestinian domestic kitchen, but Palestinians in Israel have been able to cross the boundaries of Jewish society and adopt certain customs while also preserving a distinct separation between the two societies.

Fourth, modernity enables the reestablishment of culinary tradition in the Arab kitchen in Israel by transforming everyday dishes formerly associated with poverty and scarcity into nostalgic dishes that symbolize ethnic culture. In this way, modernity has become central to the ongoing process through which the Palestinian public in Israel redefines its identity and place in Israeli society.

"THERE IS *SHISHBARAK* IN THE SUPERMARKET": THE ARRIVAL OF READY-MADE FOOD

Abir, a thirty-nine-year-old kindergarten teacher from Arrabe, invited me to her home to see how she prepared *mugrabiya,* the Palestinian version of couscous. She precooked garbanzo beans and chicken broth in the morning, before my arrival. Around noon she invited me to come into the kitchen with her so that she could finish preparing the meal. To prepare the *couscouson* that accompanies the chicken broth and garbanzo beans in the traditional way, one mixes bulgur with flour and a little water in a strainer, using circular rubbing movements to create tiny, round grains about the size of the pasta-like squares known to the Jewish public as *ptitim.* The grains are steamed on top of the boiling soup pot. I expected to see Abir bending over the strainer, working small grains with her fingers, separating them from one another, and steaming them over the boiling soup, but instead she boiled water in the electric kettle, poured it into a pot, and waited for it to come to a boil again. Then she poured the contents of a bag of *ptitim* into the pot, and when the grains were ready, she distributed them among the individual plates and ladled soup and garbanzo beans over them. Abir tells me that her mother and her grandmother prepared *couscouson* every winter, and that by the time she was seventeen, she was already a participant in the preparation. Her mother and grandmother would spend hours making *mugrabiya,* but in her modern version, it is almost fast food. The pressure cooker in which she cooks the garbanzo beans

and the chicken broth saves her most of the work and frees her from
working the grains.

> Today almost nobody makes *mugrabiya* the way the older women used to
> make it. I know how to make it with bulgur and flour, but I won't make
> it that way. If there's ready-made *couscouson*, there's no need to make it.
> That's why we eat lots of *mugrabiya* in the winter.

Replacing a domestic product with a store-bought industrial one is
typical of young women of Abir's generation, especially those who are
better educated, who are in no hurry to spend hours preparing dishes
in their kitchens and can afford to buy commercial products. Preserving the original taste is less important than the convenience, speed,
and prestige of modern status symbols. The substitute *couscouson* that
Abir and her friends use indicates detachment from traditional dishes
whose preparation requires expertise, time, and much labor in favor
of innovations and shortcuts made possible by modernity. Abir has no
regrets about the gradual disappearance of the traditional *couscouson;* she does not want to contribute to its survival in the Palestinian
Arab kitchen by preparing it. However, by making a modern version
of it, she contributes to its remaining an integral part of the current
kitchen. Without this shortcut, *mugrabiya* would disappear entirely.
Ptitim are an excellent substitute, in her opinion, since they symbolize
modernity yet also make it possible to retain the traditional character
of the kitchen. Hishmi, a nursery school teacher from Kafar Yasif who
is married to a butcher, also praises modernity, which has reduced the
time she spends in the kitchen and made it possible for her to take on
other female functions:

> You [Jews] brought us several good things that make me cook faster.
> I have an oven, a food processor, a toaster, a dishwasher. My mother
> would work eight hours a day preparing food; I work about one and a
> half hours.

The arrival of electric appliances in Palestinian households in Israel,
which Hishmi and Abir take for granted, necessitated coping with innovations that did not always accord with traditional women's work in
the kitchen. Like industrial products, technological innovations were
seen as improving that which already existed, not negating it. In order
for electric appliances to win acceptance, it was essential for women
to see them as new versions of old technological devices, rather than

as a break from them, as a lecturer in an academic college in the north explained to me:

> When my father bought a gas stove, every morning my mother or my aunt would light it with a match and lower the flame. It stayed lit all day. Every time they needed a burner, they would take a piece of paper, light it from the burning flame, and use it to light another burner.

This example shows how the prevailing culture may use a particular appliance in its own unique way. Palestinian women regarded the stove as an appliance that fulfilled the traditional functions of the *taboun,* a kind of elevated *taboun.* The fact that there is no need to keep the flame lit and that one simply turns the knob in order to ignite it was irrelevant for them: they continued to light the fire every morning and leave it burning all day. Choosing the traditional form made it possible to accept the stove as an efficient appliance that did not undermine existing cultural perceptions, but rather fed off them and improved them. The rationale of leaving the flame going all day needs to be understood in this cultural context.

Palestinians' zealous consumption of canned foods also illustrates how contemporary technologies are adopted in an Israeli context. Canned goods are more popular among Palestinian families than the Jewish public. A Jaffa advertiser says that Palestinians identify canned food with modernity, hygiene, and availability of fruits and vegetables out of season. Even though in some ways canned food is arguably the antithesis of freshness, canned goods have certain health connotations for Palestinian citizens of Israel. In the past, food that was in season, free of chemical sprays, and cooked daily was considered fresh, healthy, and clean. But experience has taught that fresh foods can be the cause of illnesses: unpasteurized goat's milk caused intestinal diseases, lamb was defined by the medical authorities as rich in cholesterol and therefore harmful, and vegetables that had not been disinfected were afflicted with pests. Canned foods, by contrast, are considered healthy and clean because they are hermetically sealed and subject to strict examination. As a result, they are now popular in the Palestinian kitchen in Israel.

And yet Palestinians home cooks tend to be suspicious of foods preserved in other ways that are commonly available in Jewish Israeli supermarkets, including frozen meat, vegetables and fruits, and beans and lentils. According to a Jaffa copywriter, cold cuts, hot dogs, hamburgers, and schnitzel are new products for Palestinians that were introduced in their frozen form and therefore are accepted as such. It helps that they do not look natural and that there is no knowledge in the community about how they look in their natural state. Moreover, he argues, Palestinians are fascinated by the fact that machines make food; they think less about the distance machines impose between humans and nature because machines connote cleanliness and sterility. Palestinians are also suspicious about vegetables and fruits sold at supermarkets in Jewish areas. According to the Jaffa copywriter:

> Some think the vegetables sold in local stores are better and cheaper than those from the supermarket. They will also not always purchase lentils and garbanzo beans because not every type of lentil is suitable. We use small lentils. Red lentils are bought but not green ones, because we need to have unpeeled ones.

Thus, canned foods evoke hygienic connotations that fit with modern lifestyles; they distance the individual from the fruit of the earth in exchange for hermetically sealed food untouched by a human hand and without strange odors clinging to it, which allays the mantle of suspicion that accompanies Jewish food. The same principle applies to popular breakfast cereals, sweets, and snacks: because these are products untouched by human hands, they symbolize a break between nature and human food and are insulated from the odors and tastes associated with the Jewish kitchen. The Palestinian public sees consumption of these products as an entry into the heart of modernity and happily accepts their industrialized taste. Packaged cereal has become a popular breakfast food, and cookies, chocolate, chocolate spreads, snacks, crackers, and candies, considered to be primarily children's food, are found in every pantry.

The arrival of industrial products along with the improved economic situation of Palestinian citizens of Israel intensified the tendency to seek out modern versions of traditional dishes, such as *labaneh*. Some women still prepare *labaneh* at home, but most young, educated women prefer to buy ready-to-eat *labaneh*. Fatma, a resident of Jaffa who lives on welfare payments, still makes *labaneh* at home by boiling cow's milk with a tablespoon of *laban*. After it cools, she pours the liquid into a pot, covers it, and lets it stand:

> The next day it's sour, so I put it into a cloth bag until all the liquid has dripped out. I add salt and olive oil, and I have *labaneh*. It's also possible to add a little chicken soup [bouillon powder] to improve the taste.

Fatma has combined modern industrial food with homemade *labaneh* by adding bouillon powder. Her daughters don't prepare *labaneh* at all.

They buy the *labaneh* made by Raja Dairies from Tamra. The young-est daughter sometimes even buys *labaneh* in the supermarket, but only when she doesn't find Raja's *labaneh* in the neighborhood store. Modern life has taught that goat's milk is dangerous to one's health and that an industrial product is preferable to the natural one. Palestinian women who continue to prepare *labaneh* at home do it for its unique taste, but instead of using goat's milk, they use store-bought cow's milk or the containers of *laban* that food companies pack especially for the Arab sector. Hiba, a housewife from Acre, agrees that the *labaneh* her grandmother used to make out of goat's milk tasted the best. However, she and other women have been scared by nurses from the pediatric clinic who claim that goat's milk causes stomachaches:

> It worried us, so we began using cow's milk, and it didn't taste as good. So our neighbor said that she makes it from *laban* that they sell in the store. She buys five liters of *laban* and puts it in bags until all the liquid drips out; then she adds salt, and she has *labaneh*. My mother started doing that too.

The shift to commercially pasteurized milk also influences the con-sumption of *laban* for cooking and for preparation of dairy dishes. More and more women buy commercial *laban* instead of using home-made *laban* from goat's milk. Before cooking, they mix the *laban* with an egg to prevent lumps from forming. Homemade *knafeh* has under-gone a similar change. Originally *knafeh* was made out of Arab cheese, which was soaked in water to remove its saltiness and then worked into a flexible texture. Now, homemade *knafeh* has been abandoned in favor of store-bought or quickly prepared *knafeh*. Ayda, a fifty-two-year-old from Jaffa who works as a babysitter, admits that she no longer prepares *knafeh* at home because it takes a lot of work to make it well. Still, she says:

> Sometimes I make *knafeh* at home, but not often. I make *knafeh* out of soft white cheese that contains 9 percent fat.[3] I put the cheese on the dough and then place it in the oven. It tastes very good that way.

Homemade hummus is also on the decline. Most Palestinian women buy ready-made hummus that comes from factories near Nazareth or Baka al-Gharbiya or from local restaurants. Some even buy industrial hummus and season it with olive oil and lemon. That's how Mari from Ramla makes it. When we come home from the market, she suggests that I have lunch with her. She slices tomatoes, red pepper, and cucum-bers, and adds salt. Alongside the fresh vegetables she places canned olives and corn. She takes out a container of commercially prepared hummus from the refrigerator and seasons it with olive oil. She also brings to the table slices of yellow cheese, white cheese, commercially prepared red cabbage salad, and a Turkish salad she has purchased. Mari believes that with the passing years, there are more resemblances than differences between Jewish and Palestinian eating habits:

> We've also begun to buy whatever it's possible to buy. I don't make hummus, because it's a lot of work, and I don't have time. I buy hummus—whatever kind I find in the store. I add olive oil, lemon, a little seasoning.

Replacing a domestic product with an industrial one also characterizes the consumption of dough-based dishes. Palestinian women today prefer to buy noodles or phyllo dough for *sfikhah* rather than preparing them at home. Those who still prepare the noodle dough at home are gradually abandoning kneading it by hand and turn instead to the mixer or food processor. The ceremony of preparing *sha'ariya,* as described in the previous chapter, is now seen as unnecessary: noodles shaped like long grains of rice replace traditional *sha'ariya.* These noodles are used in preparing the traditional dish of rice with *sha'ariya.* Hal'am, a fifty-year-old from Shefar'am, tells me she hasn't made noodles for at least fifteen years because the preparation takes too long and no longer pays off:

> The financial situation has improved, and noodles don't cost a lot of money. It's always possible to go to the store and buy them; it's not necessary to prepare enough to last for the whole year. My children and grandchildren are used to the *sha'ariya* from the store.

Hal'am notes the connection between modernity and the financial situation. Modernity reflects not only economic means but also the potential for acquiring status symbols. When economic well-being permits, there is less need to invest hours in food preparation, and it's possible to find alternatives in the stores. These substitutes are dishes of convenience, signifying that a family's economic situation is strong enough to spare the wife hours of work in the kitchen. Hal'am represents the younger generation: the generation that has grown up since the establishment of the state of Israel and has acted as a harbinger of modernity. This generation prefers ready-made products to domestic ones, thereby blurring the cultural differences from its Jewish neighbors. The older generation is also adapting and learning to accept modern innovations.

Does the changeover from homemade noodles to ready-made ones, from hummus made by hand by the housewife to store-bought hummus, or from goat's-milk *laban* to that of commercial dairies indicate the demise of traditional dishes, or are these dishes merely changing their form and the way they are used? Will the next generation not use noodles in their traditional form—that is, fried and cooked with rice—but instead find other uses for them? The juncture between modernity and tradition breaks off at frozen meat: the faith in the new and the industrialized fails to include frozen meat, which, as discussed in chapter 1, is considered taboo among most of the Palestinian population, even though it saves money and effort. Still, individuals do make attempts to break this taboo as well. Walid, who lives in Umm al-Fahm and works for the Ministry of Education, often drives with his wife to a supermarket in Hadera, a nearby town, because it is cheaper than the stores in their village:

> About a year ago we were in the supermarket and we looked for the dough my wife buys for *sfikhah*. All of a sudden I see ready-made *shishbarak*. I said to my wife, "Look, here's *shishbarak* ready made."

When I asked in wonder whether it was really *shishbarak* that he saw, Walid replied: "Yes. Frozen and packed in Styrofoam trays and wrapped in plastic. They were filled with meat or with potatoes." But when I asked him if they were actually called *shishbarak,* he admits they had a different name, which he could not remember. It was only after I wondered whether they were Chinese dumplings, ravioli, or *kreplach* that he recalled:

> Yes, *kreplach*. I didn't know how to pronounce it. And now you are telling me it's an Ashkenazi dish? It's a little bigger than *shishbarak*, but sometimes we buy it and my wife thaws it and cooks it in *laban* with mint and spices, because the meat isn't seasoned like we do it.

The arrival of prepared and preserved food signals a paradox, wherein the process by which the new replaces the traditional also enables traditional dishes to survive in the daily repertoire as part of the menu that the younger generation will recognize as part of their cultural heritage. The purchase of *kreplach* and *ptitim*, for example, and their preparation as though they were *shishbarak* and *couscouson,* enables them to keep their place in the Palestinian kitchen in Israel and at the same time permits the adoption of a modern lifestyle. Forgoing the traditional flavor of the dish is considered a worthwhile compromise because of the saved labor. Rather than disappearing, traditional foods that had ensured a nourishing meal have become modern dishes reflecting not only purchasing ability but also awareness that use of industrial food lightens the burden of domestic tasks.

The impulse to modernize includes an additional new element—the desire to enrich the menu with healthy food. For example, Palestinians started replacing lamb, which is rich in cholesterol, with turkey or chicken. At the same time, the decline of agriculture and the disappearance of the family as a production unit made the raising of sheep unprofitable, and the price of lamb rose to the point where many families could not afford to buy it for daily use. But some argue that the effort to avoid foods rich in cholesterol is precisely what made cholesterol into a widespread health problem among the Palestinian public. According to a politician from the Triangle area, the incorporation of modern food items into the Palestinian diet resulted in the abandonment of its healthy components, such as olive oil, which was given up in favor of margarine:

> Now, you tell us it's not healthy, that it has cholesterol. You brought us cholesterol, high blood pressure, sugar. You told us to eat turkey and chicken, but we used to eat lamb, and we were healthy. Today we eat chicken and we're sick.

The apprehensions about the cholesterol content of lamb have helped turkey and beef win a place of honor in the Palestinian kitchen in Israel. As part of the modernization process, *shawarma, kofta,* and stuffed vegetables are now prepared mainly from turkey or a combination of turkey and beef. *Kubeh,* the last bastion of lamb meat, is made more and more from veal. The meat is seasoned as if it were lamb, with cinnamon, *baharat,* black pepper, and nutmeg. Lamb symbolizes, for the most part, the kitchen of the past; it evokes a sense of longing for a disappearing world, one in which domesticated animals were part of the household. Replacement of lamb with turkey or beef is part of a contemporary health-conscious diet. The gradual disappearance of lamb from the kitchen does not contradict the hierarchy of foods in the Palestinian kitchen but rather its greater depth. True, lamb has lost its status as the meat most in use, but its cultural superiority has remained. It is now a festive food rather than an everyday food, and other meats are seasoned and cooked as if they were lamb. In this way the Palestinian public in Israel has created a meat hierarchy of its own, with lamb at the top of the ladder. Palestinians regard lamb similarly to the way in which the Jewish public regards beef.

LASAGNA WITH CINNAMON: THE "ARABIZATION" OF WESTERN FOOD

Ayda from Jaffa invites me for breakfast. She spreads a tablecloth on the coffee table and brings in *labaneh* from the Tamra commercial dairy to which she has added olive oil, *zaatar* with olive oil, green and black olives from Reine in Galilee, slices of tomato and cucumber, Arab cheese that she buys from villagers in Galilee, commercial jam, and low-calorie bread from the grocery next to her house. "It's good for my diet," she says as she sets down the bread. "I need to watch my weight, so I stopped eating pita bread and began to eat low-calorie bread. It's not as tasty, but it has fewer calories." After Ayda has eaten six slices of low-calorie bread with *labaneh,* she prepares instant coffee using milk instead of water and asks how many artificial-sweetener tablets I would like.

This story sums up what is happening today in the kitchens of many Palestinian citizens of Israel: low-calorie bread is replacing traditional bread, not only liberating Ayda from what she perceives as superfluous calories but also presenting her as modern, as one who adopts innovations and is in step with the spirit of the times. Ayda does not refrain from eating *labaneh,* olives, or high-fat cheese, but she chooses to cut down on bread and sugar. Breakfast at Ayda's shows us the means by which the traditional character of the kitchen is preserved, while new elements are adopted. These are seasoned in the traditional manner and classified according to traditional categories of thought.

As Ayda's breakfast illustrates, culinary boundaries have become more flexible and now allow for the inclusion of new products. This is not to say that the Palestinian kitchen readily adopts all new and modern techniques and products. A new product is not adopted for its innovative qualities, but for its compatibility with or function in the traditional palate. In other words, modern foods and technologies must replace something familiar. The "Arabization" of food allows one to remove traditional dishes from the daily repertoire and change the status of others. In this way the daily repertoire is enriched without contradicting traditional principles. New products find their way into the culinary repertoire through adaptations and changes to suit the Palestinian public, involving tastes that suit the traditional spirit and at the same time symbolize modernity.

Ascribing traditional qualities to modern dishes is not perceived as a negation of the modern products' innovation, but rather as presentation of the new and different in terms of improving the old. For example, the new products are perceived as healthier, cheaper, and less time-consuming to prepare. New dishes whose tastes are too foreign to the palate, whose prices are too dear, or whose ingredients and cooking methods are very far from the traditional Palestinian kitchen are generally not accepted.

Take the case of the potato. Many home cooks now use potatoes—which are common and inexpensive in Israel—as if they were pumpkin, eggplant, or squash. Potatoes have begun to play a central role as a starchy addition to traditional ingredients in other familiar dishes as well, such as *maklubeh,* a dish of rice with sliced or cubed vegetables. The vegetables are placed on the bottom of the pot, rice is placed on top, and water is added. When the cooking is finished, the pot is turned over onto a wide plate and the result is a main course resembling a cake. Possible ingredients for *maklubeh* are garbanzo beans, eggplant, cauliflower, tomatoes, and now potatoes. The use of potatoes has thus enriched the repertoire without fundamentally changing the dish.

Margarine is also very popular in the Palestinian sector, and its extensive use now is an example of the integration of a product with modern connotations in a traditional kitchen. Some of the qualities and functions attributed to various oils have been transferred to margarine, and at the same time, margarine has been assigned new meanings and uses. Margarine has been accorded a connotation of healthfulness because it is perceived as being less fattening than olive oil. Gradually, many have abandoned olive oil in favor of margarine, even though nutritionists do not recommend it.

Umm Muhammad is eighty years old. A number of years ago she was found to have a high level of cholesterol, and her doctor advised her to avoid foods rich in fats. She chose to avoid olive oil and corn oil, using margarine instead, and to eat more vegetable salads. During the week I spent with her, she used twelve packages of margarine while cooking for eighteen people. Margarine, besides being a "cure" for the problem of high cholesterol, is thought to improve the taste of food and provide gravy and a pleasant aroma. One day Umm Muhammad prepared two pots of stuffed squash and a pot of stuffed eggplant. She cooked the stuffed vegetables in a pot of water with a lemon, tomato, seasonings, and a package of margarine. When I ask her why she includes margarine, she explains:

> It's for the taste and for good health. I put a package on the stuffed vegetables when I cook and it gives the food a pleasant aroma. I watch what I eat because of the cholesterol.

Sandra, age fifty, uses margarine instead of *samneh* (clarified butter)[4]:

> In our store we have *samneh* that comes from the Occupied Territories, but people don't tend to buy it much because they have stopped eating it. *Samneh* has a strong odor and taste. Today margarine is used on rice or meat and it tastes better.

Sandra also sees how modern products can push traditional production aside. Since the 1960s, bouillon powder has become the dominant material for making gravy. Since soup is not a dish in its own right but rather serves as gravy, women use the powder as a seasoning for meat dishes, vegetables, or stuffing. The use of powder is so widespread that even women in their forties insist that they cannot imagine preparing food without bouillon powder. As they see it, the powder gives the food a special flavor. Alham from Jaffa, who has been married for the past twenty years, says:

> Chicken soup is magic that gives flavor to the food. I put bouillon powder in everything: meat, vegetable pies, and macaroni. My mother does too and she cannot think of what she used before there was bouillon powder.

Alham's neighbor reveals how she prepares gravy for meat and vegetable dishes from bouillon powders of various flavors:

> I make potatoes stuffed with meat and onions with gravy. For the gravy, I take mushrooms, mushroom soup powder, bouillon powder, and water, pour it onto the potatoes, and put them into the oven.

Abir, who lives in the Triangle, learned to prepare vegetable soup from her sister-in-law, who is married to a chef. She is aware that for Jews, soup is the first course, but in order to make it part of the domestic repertoire, she preserves the soup's original function in the Palestinian kitchen as gravy. She describes the preparation process:

> I take a bag of frozen mixed vegetables and cook them in water with bouillon powder. I cook that way for about half an hour until I see that the soup is ready. My children love it with soup mandels, but we eat it with rice and meat.

Thus, bouillon powder and frozen vegetables are used to prepare dishes that play a traditional role in the meal. Abir and other women create interpretations anchored in their culture, enabling these dishes to become part of a culinary repertoire in the Arab home.

The modern Palestinian palate is no longer accustomed to the traditional dishes, and the taste of those dishes is considered unusual and ill-suited to the modern lifestyle. People prefer to buy commercial products when they are reasonable substitutes for traditional products, yet have contemporary aromas and tastes.

In addition to Jewish products and convenience foods, Hungarian, Chinese, French, and Italian dishes can all be found in Palestinian kitchens today. These new cuisines have been introduced by young people exposed to new dishes while traveling to study abroad or by watching international cooking shows on TV. Perhaps the most popular foreign dish in Palestinian homes is goulash. Unlike Hungarian goulash, which is made of meat spiced with paprika and cooked in tomatoes and sour cream, the local Palestinian version eliminates the sour cream and replaces the paprika with more familiar spices. One of the reasons that goulash became popular is that its preparation and serving are consistent with the accepted practices for cooking and serving meat in the Palestinian kitchen. The meat is cooked in liquid, which creates a large volume of food, and the dish is served with rice. Dina, a counselor in the Taibe community center, learned to prepare goulash from her Hungarian sister-in-law, whom her brother met while attending medical school in Budapest. It was at her sister-in-law's house that Dina first tasted goulash. However, the goulash they ate was not the version her brother had tasted in Hungary but a modified version:

> My brother wasn't so fond of her [his wife's] goulash because it didn't have the same aroma as our food had. She used paprika and sour cream, and he didn't care for the taste. So he told her to use *baharat* and pepper and not to use sour cream. Many in the village eat it that way.

Families whose children did not study in Eastern Europe discovered goulash at weddings or in the homes of friends or relatives, and later reproduced the dish at home. Some of the cooks were surprised when I asked if they added sour cream to the dish. They reported that they hadn't even known that sour cream was one of the ingredients in goulash. For them, goulash meant beef lightly fried with onion and cooked slowly in tomato paste, seasoned the way meat is seasoned in the Palestinian kitchen. Zohir, a chef who works both in Ramat Gan and in the Triangle, tells me that there is a constant demand for goulash, adapted to local tastes, for wedding receptions. Women who take his cooking classes also ask for it because they see it as en elegant and modern dish. However, he admits, the local women will not prepare goulash the Hungarian way because of the different seasoning.

Likewise, students who studied in Italy reproduce Italian food when they return home. But their parents or relatives, who never knew the original Italian dishes, change the recipes and adapt them to local customs and flavors. Sana and Makroum discovered Italian food in Genoa, where they studied medicine. Since their return home, they prepare Italian food when they don't have time to prepare a more complicated meal. Upon returning from Italy, Sana became aware of the differences between her pasta and that of her mother. While her mother uses macaroni, cooks it until soft, mixes it with canned tomato paste, margarine, and plain yellow cheese, and cooks it again, Sana cooks it half as long as her mother does. Sana prepares sauces from tomatoes with anchovies, tuna, broccoli, or peas, or makes white sauce. On her visits to Italy she buys Parmesan, and if she is out of it she substitutes the Turkish *kashkaval,* as the taste seems similar to her:

> For me, pasta is fast food. While the water is boiling, I prepare a large amount of sauce and freeze it. That way I have it ready for several meals. It closely resembles what my husband and I ate in Italy.

Pasta dishes are not foreign to the Palestinian kitchen, which makes widespread use of noodles in tomato sauce. On the other hand, lasagna and pizza had to be adapted before being completely accepted into the Israeli Palestinian kitchen. In the case of lasagna, the principle of noodles layered with meat and sauce was retained, but the seasonings added to each of the ingredients were different from those in the original dish. Basmeh, the owner of a Haifa cosmetics shop, learned how to prepare lasagna by watching her Jewish neighbor make it. She realized she could produce what she considered to be a "tastier version" by adjusting the spices and certain ingredients so that the dish would have a familiar fragrance and flavor. For instance, while her neighbor stir-fried turkey meat seasoned with thyme, black pepper, and garlic, Basmeh used lamb or turkey and seasoned it with cinnamon and *baharat.* While her neighbor used large noodles that did not need to be cooked, Basmeh used whatever noodles she had in the house:

> Sometimes I use tomato paste, but the result is very tasty even without it. I spread meat on the noodles and cover it with sour cream and slices of cooked tomato. And again noodles, meat, and sour cream until it's all

finished. On top I put plain yellow cheese and a little mozzarella and put it in the oven.

Other women gave me similar recipes for lasagna as well. Some of them didn't include mozzarella, and others didn't include plain yellow cheese. Some used canned tomato sauce or paste, others used fresh tomatoes, and still others used no tomatoes at all. What was common to all the recipes was the arrangement of the ingredients in layers, as in the case of *kubeh seniyeh,* and the traditional seasoning. Lasagna thus symbolizes both the new and the familiar.

Pizza, a dish particularly popular among children, has also been adapted to the common Palestinian repertoire. Laila from Haifa told me that when her son started asking for pizza, her husband insisted that she make it for him so he would not eat it at a pizza counter, "where one cannot be sure whether it is clean":

> So sometimes I make dough as if for bread and spread tomato paste on it along with yellow cheese, *zaatar,* and olives. Sometimes, if I'm short on time, I take bread [pita] and put on it cheese and olive oil and *zaatar* and put that in the oven.

Nadia, secretary of the workers' council in Jerusalem, is married to the owner of a pizzeria. Her husband worked for many years at a pizzeria in Jaffa. Since many of the clients were Palestinians, he learned how to prepare "pizza for Jews and other kinds of pizza for Arabs." After a number of years, his brother-in-law suggested that they open a pizzeria of their own. According to Nadia:

> We have pizza for Jews and pizza for Arabs. We have pizza with ordinary cheese, with tuna, with olives, with salami, and with mushrooms. And we have pizza with *zaatar* and pizza like *sfikhah,* with ground meat.

Like lasagna, pizza was only incorporated within the culinary boundaries of the Palestinian kitchen after being adapted to the tastes and needs of the Palestinian community. The adaptation was mainly a matter of ingredients and seasoning. The combination of bread baked in the oven with *zaatar* changed pizza from an unappealing, foreign dish into one that felt familiar, yet new.

The incorporation of Chinese food into the Palestinian kitchen however, has been more problematic. Chinese food arouses aversion in Palestinians for several reasons: first, the cooking time is short; second, the combinations characteristic of the Chinese kitchen do not fit with prevailing tastes in the Arab kitchen; and third, the dominant ingredients and seasonings in the Chinese kitchen are foreign to the Arab kitchen.

The Palestinian kitchen emphasizes lengthy cooking, especially of meat and fish, while one of the principles of the Chinese kitchen is quick and minimal frying of meat, fish, and vegetables. This discrepancy in cooking method leads many Palestinians to refuse to eat Chinese food on the grounds that it has not been sufficiently cooked. The only way to bring Chinese food closer to the Palestinian kitchen is to lengthen its cooking time. Sausan from Akko describes her version of a Chinese dish that she sometimes prepares for guests:

> I take a can of carrots and peas and strips of veal or schnitzel or chicken. I cook them in a pot with half a cup of water, oil, and a little soy sauce and sharp pepper for about three-quarters of an hour.

Olivia from Acre, who is considered to be the oracle of traditional Arab cooking in her city, provides another example of the "Arabization" of Chinese food. When I ask her if she cooks Chinese food, she laughs and says it is not Chinese food she cooks but Chinese-Arab food, as there is an Arab spirit in her supposedly Chinese dishes.

> They [the Chinese] put in a lot of soy sauce; it's very dominant, and I choke from the smell, so I dilute it with water. I also don't use sugar or fruit, only nuts. It's disgusting to eat meat with sugar. I take lamb or veal with vegetables and a small amount of nuts and cook them quickly, about twenty minutes, with a little oil.

Olivia has no delusions about cooking authentic Chinese food. She adopts its form and infuses it with her own content, drawn from Arab culinary culture. She lengthens the cooking time and shunts aside the seasoning characteristic of the Chinese kitchen.

Chinese food remains unpopular among some Palestinians because it combines ingredients from categories of food that are deemed unmixable. The combinations of sour with sweet, sweet with salty, or meat with fruit are inconceivable for many of those with whom I spoke. Turkiya, a Christian living in Galilee, tells me that the Chinese food offends the principles of creation, destroying the categories that were formed in the act of creation, and therefore should not be eaten in its original form:

> I can't eat meat with fruit. Why did God put fruit there and meat in another place [gesturing with her head in the opposite direction]?

So that they wouldn't come together. How would you prepare fruit with meat?

And Tawfik from the Triangle area complains about his "modern wife," who insisted on preparing chicken with cherries and pineapple for his birthday:

> She worked all afternoon on the chicken and killed it with cherries and pineapple, and what was the result? Who eats chicken with jam? I asked her if she was trying to tell me that the Chinese eat that.

The main principles that govern the acceptance of new dishes into the Palestinian culinary repertoire are the desire to add variety to the kitchen and the need to preserve the accepted categories and basic rules of cooking. The ingredients that are popular in the Chinese kitchen make it difficult to include Chinese dishes on the Palestinian menu. Octopus, crab, tofu, and soy sauce are alien to the culinary norms of this kitchen. When there is nevertheless a desire to vary the traditional menu and experience new dishes, suitable substitutes will be found that enable the inclusion of "Chinese" or other modified dishes in the meal.

AGENTS OF INNOVATION

The media are also agents of innovation encouraging the entry of new products and styles of cooking into the Palestinian kitchen. Periodicals such as *Abir* and *Sinara*, published in Arabic and owned by Palestinian businessmen who are citizens of the state of Israel, include recipe sections. The Arabic radio show anchored by Violette Batat (who passed away while I was writing this book) on the Voice of Israel always had a recipe corner, where there was even a recipe competition sponsored by large food companies. And cooking shows in Arabic appear regularly on public television. These media share a preference for modern recipes over traditional Palestinian ones; the latter attract attention only around the holidays. A nutritionist who wrote a cooking column in a paper published in Arabic explains that this is a consequence of the fact that traditional gastronomic knowledge is well known among Palestinian women, even the young and well-educated ones, so it would be offensive to provide written recipes. Therefore:

> I write about things I think will be attractive for the Palestinian woman. For example, meat or vegetable patties; cannelloni is also suitable, because it can be filled with meat. I wrote about vegetable pies because

people asked. And especially many kinds of cakes—they have the most demand.

A director of family programming on Israeli television confirms these trends and notes that of the numerous letters that she has received, many requested specific recipes such as grilled chicken, various kinds of soup, vegetable pies, "Jewish-style" *kubeh,* pizza and other foods made with dough, and salads. The program commentators try to respond to the demands of the public.

The nutrition expert and the program director mentioned above present recipes in response to public demand. But Violette Batat, director and presenter of an Arabic radio program on Kol Yisrael, saw herself as educating the Arab public "without harming them or their tradition." Ms. Batat, a Hebrew University graduate with a degree in psychology and English literature who was born in Iraq, told me that she had reached the Arabic department of the Kol Yisrael broadcasting authority in 1957 as part of the "takeover" by Jews from Iraq of Arabic radio. Starting in 1965, she presented her own program. She also worked in Naamat (the International Movement of Zionist Women) and served as chairperson of the Arab women's department in Israel. The strength of her radio program, in her view, was its ability to educate an entire community, including Arabs living in neighboring countries, about modern living, hygiene, family planning, and a style of eating more suited to the twentieth century. According to her, many women heard her program and implemented her suggestions. She used to ask her listeners to send her recipes and selected those that would suit the Palestinian tradition while according with their budget. For instance, she did not recommend a cake recipe that called for fourteen eggs because she thought it would be too expensive and unhealthy. Moreover, she believes her listeners prefer recipes sent by Jews, such as eggs and rice or jelly with fruit, because they are taken as "modern":

> They don't want something from Arabs. Every time I bring an Arab specialist to the program—for example, an Arab doctor to speak about a bypass operation—they write and ask why I didn't bring a Jewish person. For them, a Jew is an expert. It's the same with food.

The belief that the Palestinian public desires change is one of the main reasons that the food industry invests in marketing itself to the Palestinian sector in Israel. Consumer market forces, in fact, drive culinary change. Because of the way in which the commercial life of the Palestinian community is organized, this public is less exposed to new products than the Jewish public. Much of the trade in the Arab sector takes place in small stores with limited selections, rather than in the large shopping centers characteristic of the Jewish sector. Consumer awareness among the Palestinian public is more limited, and there is less interest in the marketing campaigns of the chains. Often, even though the prices of food products sold in the villages are higher than their prices in the city, the Palestinian public prefers to conduct its transactions in the villages. A researcher who carried out surveys in the Arab sector argues that this public also tends to believe advertisements more than the Jewish public does:

> People relate to advertisements as if they were information and not an attempt to sell them something. Almost no critical thought takes place about the advertisements. Despite the status of the male, in practice, it is the woman who decides what to buy. The advertisers understand that and direct their ads to the women.

Perception of the Arab market as a unique segment with its own needs has given birth to extensive marketing campaigns, special packaging, and advertising offices specializing in sales techniques and promotion to the Arab market. The entry of many dairy products for daily home use is an example of this direct marketing. A marketing person working for a large dairy company says that the company's products were slow to sell in the Arab sector. The company had to learn the market's needs:

> For example, we learned that *laban* is used in the Arab sector for cooking, sauce, preparing *labaneh,* and as a popular accompaniment for meat and vegetable dishes, so we began to market *laban* in containers of five liters in the Arab sector.

Marketing large containers of *laban* was seen as a practical solution, but in general, the entry of new dairy products into the Palestinian kitchen in Israel was mostly a matter of convenience and symbolized familiarity with modern products. Specialty dairy products were presented as a handy solution for snacks, especially as a means to ensure increased consumption of calcium. Kher, who lives in Jaffa, says that her children were the first in the house to ask for daily treats, and she and her husband complied with their wishes:

> My children want only [brand-name dairy treats] just like Jewish children. They eat cornflakes with milk and a lot of yellow cheese. My

son—if you give him bread with yellow cheese, he's happy. But *laban* he doesn't eat.

Fuad, a teacher of Arabic and Hebrew from the Triangle, describes the reciprocal relations between his children and the dairy industry in these words:

> If you were to open my refrigerator at home, you would think that I am at least the assistant general manager of Tnuva [Israel's largest dairy producer and distributor]. The whole refrigerator is full of cheeses, bags of chocolate milk, and other dairy products!

The increasing consumption of commercial dairy products is based on the principle of enabling entry of foreign dishes into the Palestinian kitchen in Israel. The item must be new, but not too new compared with what is already accepted. Adults buy dairy treats for their children even when they themselves do not eat many of them, and the variety of cheeses is limited to cottage cheese and white cheese for spreading. Fatty cheeses, low-fat cheeses, and those with an unusual texture or taste are not popular. The difficulty in placing them in one of the recognized food categories makes it hard for Palestinians to accept them. For that reason, these cheeses are sometimes a source of amusement. Bassam, a social worker from Haifa, says:

> Cheeses with 0.01 percent fat make me laugh. You want to hear something funny? Once, my wife decided to go on a diet, so she bought that kind of cheese. She tasted it and said it tasted like sand.

Makram, a registered nurse, adds:

> I was at the circumcision of someone's son from where I work. There was a large platter of French cheeses and everybody suggested I taste them. It was sickening. What an odor!

Strong cheeses like Roquefort and Gorgonzola are unpopular among Palestinians in Israel not only because they are very different in flavor from traditional Arab cheeses, but also because of the different role that cheese occupies in the Palestinian kitchen. For Palestinians, cheese is mostly consumed as part of a light meal, and big cheese plates in the European tradition are rare.

Two additional products that have become popular in the Palestinian kitchen, perhaps because they appear modern, are instant coffee and cakes, especially cream cakes. Jewish grocers commonly sell these goods, which are enjoyed by Palestinians because they do not contradict basic principles accepted in the Palestinian kitchen. Instant coffee does not take the place of black boiled coffee, but is an addition to it. Especially when made entirely of milk and sweetened with an artificial sweetener, it is one of the refreshments served to guests arriving for evening visits. This coffee is considered a modern, Jewish-style refreshment, and a beverage that enables the use of less sugar and more milk. Amal, a beautician from Galilee, tells me that she and her husband switched to instant coffee because she believed black coffee caused calcium loss, whereas instant coffee requires the addition of milk, thus providing a source of the calcium that is lacking in the traditional Palestinian diet:

> Look at all our older people, how bent over they are. It's because we don't get enough calcium. So I said to my husband that we weren't drinking enough milk. Now every morning my husband and I drink hot instant coffee made from warm milk and honey.

When Fahima from Akko moved to an apartment building in which most the tenants were Jewish, she started drinking instant coffee with her neighbors. When Tova, her neighbor, first asked her how she liked her coffee, she did not know what to say. After a while she realized that all the other neighbors drank their coffee with two sweeteners and a little bit of milk:

> So I began to say that too, and I found out that it tasted great. One evening I made that kind of coffee for my husband. He said he liked it. Now I serve instant coffees to my guests like the Jews because it's more festive and prestigious.

The arrival of instant coffee in the Arab sector had two complementary effects: from a nutritional standpoint, it was considered healthier because it lessened the consumption of sugar and increased that of milk; and socially, its use was an indication of modernity because it was a copy of a custom popular with the Jews among whom the Palestinians lived. The role played by instant coffee among Jewish women—that of a drink consumed during a short rest period or while conversing with other women—continues to be played among Palestinian women by the traditional boiled coffee.

From their Jewish neighbors, Palestinian women also learned to prepare a variety of cakes that until then had not been part of the traditional kitchen. During the 1950s, Arab women learned to prepare an orange-flavored sponge cake from their Jewish neighbors. Since then the culinary repertoire has expanded, and along with dry cakes, more cream cakes are made.

Despite the love of cakes, there are some recipes that remain outside the culinary reservoir for reasons of tradition or budget or because the ingredients are not suitable. Arabiya, a speech therapist, received as a gift a German cookbook that has been translated into Arabic and published in Lebanon. She immediately knew that the cookbook was not written by an Arab woman because Arab women would not use kiwis at all, let alone in cakes. First, kiwis were not that popular among Palestinians. Second, kiwis were expensive and therefore would not be used for baking but for eating fresh. When I asked her what kind of fruit would be suitable for making cakes she said:

> An apple cake or an orange cake could be suitable. They're fruits that we know, and we have a lot of them. Cakes with whipped cream or cakes that are decorated and colorful would do very well, especially for festive occasions.

Cake preparation also symbolizes modernity because it requires precise measurements. This method of cooking, dependent on written material, became a central pattern in transmitting culinary knowledge in the West starting at the end of the nineteenth century. As explained in earlier chapters, Palestinian women cook according to feel. But they prepare cakes from exact recipes and follow the instructions precisely, as is the rule in the modern kitchen. Only after gaining experience in cake preparation do they abandon the written recipe and depend on their intuition. In other words, learning about cakes enabled Palestinian women to practice modernity not only because cakes added new dishes to the Palestinian kitchen but also because they popularized a new cooking style that favored exactness and measurement over personal intuition.

TRADITION AND MODERNIZATION

The contemporary additions to the Palestinian kitchen in Israel have imparted a new dimension to its traditional dishes. Some of the dishes that required a great deal of labor became much easier to prepare; others were transformed from everyday dishes to rare ones boasting nostalgic aromas. Modernization, which might have been expected to detach the Palestinian kitchen from the past, instead fostered in it the very qualities that might have been neutralized: nostalgia and a longing for the past and for simplicity. Instead of limiting the past to the collective culinary memory, modernity infused food with a historical dimension and set it along the continuum of premodern, modern, and postmodern culinary periods. Even though the line between the periods is unclear, it is certainly possible to speak of the characteristics of each category. As we saw in the first part of this book, the food consumed during the premodern period was simple, seasonal, and based upon the fruit of the earth. The modern kitchen, on the other hand, is characterized by admiration of the new and gradual abandonment of traditional dishes in favor of an expanding culinary repertoire; and the postmodern dimension is expressed in the increasing tendency of the Palestinian kitchen to attach a nostalgic value to traditional dishes, to bestow on them a festive status, and to integrate current trends into traditional dishes, such as using modern technology for their preparation and eating them alongside modern dishes.

The yearning for traditional food in general characterizes minority groups that are exposed to the culinary influences of a dominant culture. Members of the first generation of the meeting between the minority group and the dominant one tend to preserve their dishes, whereas members of the absorbed group tend to see the kitchen of their ancestors as inferior. Members of the second and third generations gradually adopt the tastes of the dominant group. The more accepted the members of the minority group feel, the more they tend to separate themselves from their culinary heritage in favor of new dishes. At the same time, members of the dominant group include more and more ethnic dishes in their meals, imparting to their everyday food an exotic touch.[5]

Globalization is a process that facilitates the transfer of cultural knowledge. New dishes penetrate traditional kitchens, and ethnic minorities influence the dominant group as well. Gastronomic tourism is widespread, and people throughout the world can travel, visit restaurants, or read articles and books that introduce them to foreign dishes. This access contributes to a homogenization of national kitchens as they try to attract a wide and varied public while emphasizing the similar more than the different. This homogenization also helps revive traditional dishes and create a culinary mythology, with each culture emphasizing its unique dishes while it defines them as resembling traditional dishes of other kitchens.[6]

In the Palestinian kitchen in Israel, modernization led to two opposing trends: on the one hand, traditional dishes whose preparation was laborious gradually disappeared. On the other hand, traditional dishes reentered the kitchen in a measured way and with new status: what previously had been everyday dishes, connected with poverty and want, became prestigious foods and ethnic and cultural symbols. Both these trends were assisted by improved economic well-being and contact with Jewish society. The better economic situation not only improved the menu; it also enabled a return to traditional food without the stigma of poverty. This return, undertaken through free choice, has had the effect of redefining culinary difference between the Jewish kitchen and the Palestinian one.[7]

Shortened food preparation time and an increasing standard of living make life for Palestinian women much easier. Very few in the Arab sector regret the disappearance of some of the traditional dishes, because this phenomenon signifies the entry of the Palestinian kitchen into the modern era. Among the traditional dishes that are disappearing from the Palestinian culinary repertoire in Israel are foods based upon the internal organs of the animals, such as *fuareh* (stuffed intestines) or *kirshe* (stuffed tripe). Palestinian women are no longer willing to take the trouble to prepare these dishes, since most of the effort involves cleaning the stomach or intestines—difficult and prolonged labor for which there are no shortcuts. Neither Nadia from Jerusalem nor her mother prepare *fuareh* or *kirshe* anymore, because they can afford to eat meat on a daily basis and no longer need to use every part of the animal:

> If we don't eat it, the reason isn't a lack of money but rather that we don't want to eat meat that day. I don't mind my kids not knowing these foods. They are familiar with other foods. We have enough food, and we are also learning about new foods all the time.

Unlike Nadia, Mahmoud, a chef in an Acre restaurant, broods over the loss of traditional dishes such as *afshi*, in which a cow's head, feet, and intestines are stuffed with rice, cooked in soup, and served with crumbled bread, providing a lot of food:

> Today we have food, and even if the economic situation is difficult, nobody will make *afshi*. My daughters want only grilled chicken or steak. All the internal parts they find disgusting. They don't understand that because of those internal parts, we always had food to eat.

Most Palestinian women have abandoned cooking internal organs in favor of more neutral parts, whose connection to the animal is more abstract.[8] Preparation of the internal organs of the animal suited a society that lived near animals, but proximity to animals is not part of the daily experience of the Palestinian population today. With the new definition of human–animal relations in modern times, the internal organs of animals signify an outdated way of life and arouse aversion.

The influence of modern life on the Palestinian kitchen is also to be found in the appearance of the private dimension in eating habits. According to Fatkhi, a doctoral student in the humanities from the Triangle, Palestinians express a growing concern for their children's education and more respect for children's privacy. Therefore parents want each of their children to have a room of their own and to go to university.

> We no longer eat reclining on the floor but give each of the diners a plate, table spoon, and fork. We've stopped eating from a common plate, and we don't put our hands into the food. It's as if we had placed some distance between ourselves and the food—as though there were mediators between us and our plates.

Modernization therefore has not only brought new dishes, products, and cooking technologies into the Palestinian kitchen; it has also redefined the woman's perception of time and the cultural perception of the human–animal continuum. It is true that modernization has liberated women of some of their difficult domestic tasks, thereby creating some newly available time for their use. But at the same time, Palestinian women also began to work away from home, and their greatly increased involvement in outside activities took up much of that free time; time has become dearer. Because of the new situation, culinary dispositions have also changed, and dishes demanding lengthy preparation have been removed from the daily domestic repertoire. Modern substitutes have been found for some dishes, and other have disappeared entirely.

As previously noted, after the minority group adopts modern eating patterns, it tends to return to the traditional foods in order to distinguish itself from the dominant culture and also to invite other nearby minority groups to share their cultures and expand their own repertoires.[9]

It should be observed that the first signs of a return of Palestinians in Israel to the traditional kitchen, in evidence during the 1990s, do not testify to their feeling at home and integrating into "Israeli" culture. On the contrary: Palestinians' outsiderness is what enables the culinary sphere to be an arena in which they enjoy mastery, one in which Jewish Israeli society has only limited access and control.

Among Palestinians in Israel, the return to traditional dishes mirrors a similar trend that has taken place for a number of years in the Jewish sector. In both cases, the phenomenon is not characteristic of the working class but occurs for the most part among members of the middle class.

Many third- and fourth-generation Jewish descendants of European origin are now returning to the traditional dishes of their ancestors. This is a phenomenon of nostalgia, with individuals and groups attempting to define themselves in ethnic terms. The younger generation of Ashkenazi origin are searching for a political identity, reclaiming Yiddish language, and their return to such dishes as *chamin* (stew), stuffed fish, jellied calf's foot, chicken soup, *tzimmes* (sweet carrots), and *kreplach* (pockets of meat-filled dough) may be seen in this context.[10] With many new cookbooks published by Mizrahi kitchens in Israel, covering foods of Moroccan, Kurdish, Yemenite, or Iraqi origin, Ashkenazi groups are also seeking culinary roots that can serve as cultural bases upon which to define themselves and distinguish themselves from all the other groups. Nostalgia for traditional dishes among the Palestinian middle class in Israel is part of the same process. As more and more Palestinian families in Israel become part of the middle class, they take part in similar processes experienced in the Jewish middle class.

Walid, an academic living in Galilee, connects the return to traditional dishes in general, and to dishes based upon wild plants in particular, to the influence of similar processes that have occurred in the Jewish sector. He asserts that the Palestinian public received symbolic sanction from the Jewish public to follow this path. He claims that in the same way that Jews imitate Americans, Palestinians imitate Jews:

> Just as we abandoned wild plants and moved over to canned foods, because of you, we are also returning. As if after industrialization, we discovered nature all over again. We, too, started preparing special dishes on the weekends, just like you. Women work and can't actually do much cooking during the week so traditional and time-consuming dishes have become special foods.

Ahmad, a senior-level educator in Jerusalem who works for the Ministry of Education, confirms that the return to traditional food is done as a part of leisure activities. As in the Jewish sector, people have started baking bread or cooking dishes their grandparents used to make. The return to these traditional dishes, he assesses, is not due to financial hardship but rather as part of a hobby. For instance, he says:

> We've begun going out to pick *akub*, just for the fun of it. The whole family goes together; we have a picnic, and also pick the *akub*. Today, when someone makes *frike*, or *frike* with meat, or *kubeh* with *labaneh*, the whole village comes and enjoys it.

Imitating Jewish society contributes to the sense of integrating into the society, and that integration enables a return to tradition without fear of stigmatization of the Palestinian community and its dishes. As for the Jewish sector, there is great nostalgia for dishes that have all but disappeared from the traditional Palestinian menu, and this nostalgia bestows on such dishes a special status in the Palestinian kitchen—no longer everyday and simple as they were in the past, they have now become symbols of the economic and cultural changes that the Palestinians are undergoing.

To conclude, modernization in the domain of food has caused Palestinians to imitate the culinary practices of the Jewish public while adapting new culinary practices to their own needs and customs. Innovation and gastronomic modernization shed new light on Palestinian culinary traditions, allowing the Palestinian kitchen to become more modern. Culinary cultural exchange and change take place within the unending broader process in which the identity and place of the Palestinian in Israeli society is defined. Preserving Palestinian food in the home, including the changes it has undergone, has been a means to institutionalize a unique sphere of knowledge that has not been appropriated in full by Jewish society. Thus, food has become a domain in which boundaries are gradually crossed, with Palestinians adopting customs and imitating to a certain extent the patterns of eating practiced in Jewish society. At the same time, this activity has enabled Palestinian citizens of Israel to continue to delineate the cultural boundaries that separate them from Jewish Israelis, thus articulating a unique cultural identity and heritage.

CHAPTER 4

Encountering Israeli Jews

*"When There Is No Pride, Cookbooks
Are Not Written"*

Every morning Fathi arrives at his restaurant, checks the fresh produce, gives instructions to the kitchen staff, and begins to prepare the day's food. Fathi graduated from the Tadmor Culinary Institute, did his internship at a hotel in the center of Israel, and worked in Acre as a sous chef at a restaurant owned by a Mizrahi Jew that served Mizrahi food.[1] After a year as a sous chef, he opened his own restaurant in Nazareth, serving Arab food mostly to people living in and around Nazareth. "I have about two hundred Jewish customers a year," Fathi reports. "All my other customers are Palestinians."

Yousef inherited a restaurant from his father in the center of the country. He opens his restaurant early in the morning and closes it when the food is all gone. He says he knows fourteen different ways to prepare hummus, so each day he serves hummus with a different flavor. Most of his customers are Jews. While Fathi's and Yousef's restaurants attract different clientele, their menus are similar: they both offer hummus, *labaneh,* tahini, several dishes with eggplant, *kubeh,* stuffed grape leaves, hummus with meat, and broiled meats and fish. How can the similarity in the menus of the two restaurants be explained in light of their different locations and clienteles? To understand how the menu has been set in Palestinian restaurants in Israel, one must understand how culinary culture is political, and how business entrepreneurs capitalize on the social understanding of ethnic food.

In Israel, there are few Arab cookbooks and few upscale Arab restaurants, though some Mizrahi Jewish restaurants offer Arab foods. The dearth of Arab cookbooks and restaurants is part of a broader phenomenon in Western society: cultural colonialism. Cultural colonialism occurs when the dominant group monopolizes the cultural and culinary assets of minorities and sees them as its own. The adapted cultural products are returned to the minority group in a way that presents the dominant group as being open to foreign cultures and acting to bring cultures together. This process of appropriation occurs in many spheres—from the arts to cuisine.

Restaurants and cookbooks are social texts by which dominant and minority groups write, rewrite, and construct their pasts and their public images. At the same time, these social texts open a door to ethnic enterprise that liberates the minority group from dependency on the local labor market. Such texts illuminate the connection between culinary processes and political ones and provide a glimpse into the prevailing web of power relations. When restaurant menus and cookbooks are viewed as texts, they reveal the relations of trust, suspicion, and exchange between two cultures. As menus and cookbooks change, we see how a dominant, majority culture begins to accept a minority culture.[2] An analysis of the menu in Arab restaurants in the state of Israel may also provide answers to such questions as: When does the minority group write its history and culture and when does the dominant group do so? How do the texts present the minority group? Finally, how, and under what circumstances, do their images and history change?[3]

The Western practice of eating at so-called ethnic restaurants is a rising trend and phenomenon in Israel. However, many Jewish Israelis are reluctant to eat at restaurants located in Palestinian towns and villages. This is primarily because of the unique political situation of the Palestinian minority population in Israel. Palestinians in Israel are a minority group with a profound sense of displacement, even in their native land, a place enmeshed in political and territorial conflict. They also constitute a diasporic minority that seeks to define and institutionalize a distinct ethnic identity in connection to the Palestinian national identity. Keeping a tight hold on the traditional kitchen becomes a collective strategy to resist the cultural appropriation of Palestinian food. Food, along with land, ethnic pride, and national identity, could be described as safeguarded by Palestinian citizens of the state of Israel. However, as in the case of immigrants, and because of a strong sense of displacement and exclusion from Israeli society, the first generation of Palestinian citizens in Israel has clung to its kitchen as if it were the last remnant of its culture. The second generation, meanwhile, is more willing to give up traditional foods in favor of adapting to the dominant culinary culture—perhaps because the right to belong to Israeli society was not presented to them as an option.

Immigration literature provides useful models for understanding how cultural adaptation can take place between an ethnic minority group and a dominant culture. Generally, members of the third and fourth generations of an immigrant society develop political loyalty to the dominant, absorbing society. Their cultural and national identities are clear, and they realize their right to independent textualization and ethnic character through symbolic ethnicity.[4] This is the case in Israel, where members of later generations of Palestinian citizens identify not as a minority group, but as a distinct and unique ethnic group.[5]

Entrepreneurial enterprises—such as ethnic restaurants, language schools, travel agencies that organize tours to the homeland, and stores that sell merchandise from the country of origin—provide avenues by which ethnic or minority groups may institutionalize partial control over the character of the cultural texts that they create for the general public. Such business ventures also provide alternative sources of income for immigrants or minorities with limited labor opportunities.[6] An ethnic restaurateur who strives to make a living from a reservoir of unique culinary knowledge must first determine a target clientele. Will the restaurant serve patrons from the restaurateur's own community? If so, its food might be "authentic" and affordable. The restaurant might become a meeting place for the local community, a familiar and comfortable place to converse in one's native language and maintain autonomy from the dominant culture.[7] Entrepreneurs seeking a clientele beyond the boundaries of their own group, however, do so only when they recognize a mainstream demand for their unique culture, and, of course, when their economic situation allows them to make a start-up investment.[8]

Deciding about the character of a restaurant and its target public forces Palestinian entrepreneurs in the state of Israel to consider the political relationship between Palestinians and Jews, as well as the place of the restaurant in Palestinian culture. Even though Palestinians in Israel did not migrate, they have experienced feelings of exile and uprooting, and therefore share many cultural and economic patterns familiar to immigrant populations.[9]

Unlike many ethnic restaurants in the West, which either appeal to the restaurateur's own group or adapt menus to appeal to the dominant group, Palestinian restaurants in Israel have the same menu, regardless of whether the intended customers are Jewish or Palestinian. Despite this, Palestinian and Jewish diners have different relationships to Palestinian restaurants. A Palestinian entrepreneur, directing his efforts toward his own people, knows that his clientele comes for the purpose of enjoying a meal outside the home and giving the woman of the house a day off from preparing a meal for the family. Eating in a restaurant, in this case, is a festive occasion, and diners will order meat or dishes they might prepare only infrequently at home. At a Palestinian restaurant, as at a Palestinian home, dishes are all served simultaneously, and diners assemble the components of their individual plates. Entrepreneurs turning outside their community compete for the Israeli customer, who eats his noon meal at a restaurant and hurries back to his office. The commercial success of these entrepreneurs depends on the status of the Palestinians in the broader society and on their ability to use culture as a way to mediate a long history of Jewish public hostility toward Palestinian citizens of Israel.

Cookbooks are an additional means for developing an ethnic economy, as they enable not only the creation, preservation, and conveyance of culinary knowledge but also its adaptation to changing conditions and the different population groups consuming the food.[10] Writing and revising a Palestinian cookbook, therefore, would be a process by which "authentic" Palestinian recipes would be adapted for a Jewish public, thereby introducing minority recipes into a dominant culture. These recipes would be adapted to the taste of the dominant group and integrated into its culinary history and culture, while presenting the host culture as open to the food of the immigrants in the country. [11]

The market for Palestinian cookbooks in Israel has until recently been quite small. Most Palestinian cookbooks have been private initiatives, such as pamphlets or other self-published projects. Palestinian cookbooks in Arabic have not been published in Israel because there is little demand for a translation. Bookstores in the Arab sector offer cookbooks that have been published in other Arab countries, especially Lebanon. Most are expensive and offer European recipes in translation; only a few are sources of Arab recipes. The decision to publish Arab cookbooks—in Arabic or Hebrew—is an economic decision made by publishers (who are Jewish, for the most part). From the stock of cookbooks in the bookshops, we learn that the Jewish public has hardly been exposed to Arabic cookbooks written by Arabs. Because of the popularity of Kurdish, Tunisian, Moroccan, and Indian cookbooks, the absence of Arabic cookbooks raises questions as to the status of Palestinians in Israeli society. Keter Publishing House has published two Arab cookbooks. The first one, written by Nawal Abu-Ghoch in 1996, approached Arab food with a paternalistic palate and eyes. The second cookbook was written by Miriam Hinnawi in 2006 with the aim of sharing recipes for Palestinian dishes many Israelis are already familiar with, such as hummus, tahini, *ful,* cauliflower with tahini, tabbouleh, stuffed vegetables, and roasted chicken with sumac. Also in 2006, Husam Abbas, a famous restaurateur from Umm al-Fahm, and Nira Rousso, a well-known Jewish food writer, published a cookbook of recipes from Abbas's restaurant. It was the first and only Arab cookbook to become a best seller. Interestingly, all three cookbooks provided only kosher recipes.

The struggle for cultural respect and recognition has left Palestinian citizens of Israel ambivalent about whether to expose their cuisine to Jewish Israelis and doubtful about the extent to which Jews would be willing to eat authentic Palestinian food. Exposing one's culture to those previously unfamiliar with it requires the minority group to win recognition and social respect in the host culture, a status not yet fully accorded by Israel to its Palestinian citizens. Palestinians encounter an ambivalent and suspicious attitude on the part of the Jewish population in Israel; furthermore, the possibility that Palestinians might institutionalize a distinct ethnic identity enjoying recognition from the political establishment is dismissed as illegitimate. At the same time, thanks to the advance in Palestinians' level of education and income, political awareness has grown, as has a desire to be involved in public life and become a part of Israeli society as a group with equal rights whose unique culture would receive official recognition.[12]

Palestinians in Israel maintain a distinct relationship to their culinary heritage: first, they feel that the possession of unique culinary knowledge enables them to entrench themselves within their culture and prevent Jews from appropriating and adapting a culture that is not theirs; second, they feel that the time has not yet come to share the secrets of their kitchen with the Jewish public. While in recent years Palestinians have opened successful "ethnic" restaurants for the Jewish sector, Palestinian cooks have not yet succeeded in promoting a distinctly Arab haute cuisine. In other words, there are few elite Palestinian contemporary restaurants and even fewer that serve domestic dishes.

In discussing Palestinians in Israel, pundits have asked too few questions about the content of Arab culture and its adaptations within Jewish society. The culinary tradition of Palestinian citizens of Israel has never been a subject for consideration. Partial appropriation of their culinary knowledge and its transfer to Jewish "ownership" has been interpreted as a willingness on the part of Palestinians to hand over their knowledge. But in practice, there is an inclination among Palestinians in Israel to preserve culinary knowledge in the private sphere as an act of control over culture and an attempt to establish a sphere in which domination by Jewish society is limited. This chapter offers a textual analysis of Palestinian culinary knowledge as it finds expression in the public sector, focusing on the tension between the representation of Palestinian culture by the Israeli establishment and Palestinians' own culinary narrative. We shall examine how power relations and inequality are negotiated by the unique character of Palestinian restaurants, and by the absence of culinary texts.

The marginalization of the Arab kitchen in the Israeli culinary scene has several related explanations. First, the absence of respect toward Palestinian citizens in Israel makes the emergence of culinary curiosity toward them more difficult. At the same time, Palestinians are repelled by the Jewish Israeli kitchen. Second, Palestinians feel that their culinary culture exists in the private sphere and thus that there is no need to put recipes into writing, especially since written knowledge will not contribute an additional layer to the one that already exists. Third, directing a written body of culinary knowledge outside the boundaries of the community would require a redefinition of the relations between the Palestinian minority in the state of Israel and the dominant Jewish society, a definition that does not entail cultural colonization. To appeal to Jewish customers would require a culinary reorganization to suit the structure of the Jewish meal, something that might increase the appropriation of Arab dishes by the Israeli kitchen. Fourth, the fear of such appropriation is accompanied by a renegotiation of the boundary between personal and public-political space, with implications for the ability of the Palestinian public in Israel to separate personal experiences from political ones.

Finally, this chapter examines under what conditions culinary tradition is mobilized to cope with a difficult economic situation or for purposes of marketing, and what makes it possible for Palestinian citizens of Israel to use food as a marketable ethnic commodity, as other ethnic groups do throughout the world.

"IF I'M NOT ACCEPTED, WHY WOULD MY FOOD BE ACCEPTED?"

The Jewish public is selectively open to eating Arab food. The Jewish kitchen's adoption of some Arab dishes has been made possible mostly because of geographical proximity. At the same time, Palestinians' political conditions—such as living under a military regime until 1966, having limited integration into the labor market, and being ghettoized into certain neighborhoods—has contributed to mutual suspicion between the two groups and the stigmatization of Arab food. The Palestinian citizens of Israel sense that the time has not yet come to introduce the Jewish public to the secrets of their kitchen, because relations between the two groups are still fraught with tension. Mahmud, who lives in Abu S'nan and cooks in a Mizrahi restaurant owned by Jews in Acre, believes that Arab cooking will continue to be perceived as marginal in the Jewish sector because Palestinians in Israel cannot afford to think about the preservation of their culture:

> When you're under pressure, there is no time to preserve the culture. We worry about living conditions and wonder whether we will be able to provide for our families. One needs to be proud to wish to preserve tradition. When there is no pride, cookbooks are not written.

Susu, a teacher and youth leader from the Triangle, adds that Jewish society's ignorance of everything connected to Palestinian society also influences its attitude toward the Palestinian kitchen. This ignorance is nourished by and in turn nourishes enmity and arrogance, which also find expression in the attitude toward other dishes. The Jews, she argues, neither wish to learn about Palestinians nor to let go of the stereotypes they have of them. Susu says that one day, as she was shopping in a store in Kafar Saba, a woman came in and asked for a head scarf. The salesperson showed her a colored and ugly kerchief, which the customer referred to as an "Arab kerchief." To Susu's question about what an Arab kerchief was, as most kerchiefs Palestinian women wear are white, the woman responded that Susu did not have to defend Arabs:

> I told her, "I'm not defending anyone; I'm Palestinian, and I think that you don't know what you're talking about." And then she said to me, "You

don't look Arab." People don't understand that it's not a compliment to hear such a thing but rather very insulting. So do you want the Jews to eat the food of those they think of as dirty or find disgusting?

Varda, a history and social science teacher from Baka al-Gharbiya, frequently attends extension courses for teachers. After listening to her speak, her fellow students often say that she neither looks nor sounds Arab, a comment they may intend as a compliment but that Varda finds insulting. Varda believes the comment about her looks is part of a general Jewish attitude toward the Palestinian population, whose food and homes Jews think of as dirty and whose style of dress they consider tasteless:

> The sentence "This is something Arabs eat" often implies that it's not worth tasting because it might be dangerous. I think you are open to food from the entire world except the food of your neighbors. There's no mutual trust between us. If you haven't eaten in my home, you haven't yet gotten to know me and don't want to know us.

Many of those I spoke with believed that the Palestinian public would share its culinary knowledge with the Jewish public if the latter were ready to receive it. Basmeh, a speech therapist from Galilee, claimed that until Palestinians are accepted as different yet equal and included within the social boundaries of Israeli society, the likelihood of Jews buying a Palestinian cookbook was low:

> At home I try out Western recipes, but how can I expect that you'll try what I cook? When you do accept me and include me, I'll come with my entire being, my character, my apparel, my religion, my tradition—my entire heritage.

George, a civil servant from Shefar'am, believes that Jewish Israelis are unwilling to try Arab food because they hold a stereotypical view of Palestinians. In other words, they view Palestinians first as members of the Arab nation and only afterward as human beings or trained professionals. It is complicated to be an Arab in Israel, according to George, because Arabs are at best invisible. Jews, he claims, ignore the possibility that Arabs could be excellent doctors, pilots, or engineers, or charming lovers. This psychological block, George claims, prevents Jews from expanding their knowledge about Palestinians:

> When people see my young daughter, they see how blond she is and how pretty and what enchanting green eyes she has, and they say, "She can't be an Arab." And that's how it is with our food. What you've stolen from us,

you like; and you like to come to our parties and be served lamb; but to try eating our regular everyday food—never.

The prevailing perception that Jews are afraid of Palestinians is so deeply rooted that Palestinians themselves sometimes reinforce it. In five of the interviews I conducted for this book, the hosts promised that no harm would come to me in their homes, because they were "good Arabs." For example, when I visited Abir in her home in a Galilee village, a friend of hers arrived for a visit. This friend was introduced to me first as a distant cousin of Arafat's wife and only afterward as an educator who was running a special college program for Bedouin women. Throughout the woman's visit, Abir kept checking in with me, every few minutes, to make sure I was not afraid or uncomfortable in her friend's presence. When I asked whether there was a particular reason to be afraid, Abir reassured me there wasn't, but she insisted that I phone my family and notify them that I was in no danger, as they were all "good Arabs."

Another explanation for Jews' lack of openness to Arab food is the difference in meal structure and table manners in the two cultures. Arab customs, such as simultaneously serving courses and eating with fingers or a spoon while reclining around the table, arouse apprehension that Jews may feel uncomfortable. Sometimes this fear can even overcome Palestinian pride about their traditions. Wajdi, a doctoral student in history who is the chair of the board of education in one of the cities in the Triangle, speaks of cultural difficulties stemming from the different eating habits and admits that when he entertains his Jewish friends or colleagues he always thinks about how he appears in their eyes. To save his children this embarrassment he is teaching them to eat with utensils:

> I tell them it's more elegant and respected. I don't want them to feel uncomfortable when they eat with Jews.

This aversion is mutual. Interviewees report their discomfort with Jewish dishes and customs. Palestinian intellectuals do not ignore the fact that some Palestinians reject Jewish dishes, and they admit that this does not contribute to dispelling the mutual apprehension. In Western society, a willingness to eat together is testimony of close relations; while acquaintances or colleagues at work will be invited for a drink, an invitation to a meal is a declaration of friendship.[13] This social mapping, linking a culinary event with interpersonal closeness, is foreign to Palestinians, who tend to invite anyone who happens by at mealtime to join them. My hosts informed me that a number of times they had invited Jewish friends from work for a meal. These friends came, ate, and enjoyed the visit, but they didn't return the invitation. Fatkhi, a supervisor in the Ministry of Education, tells me that his Jewish colleagues were curious about coming to his house but only one reciprocated his invitation:

> I came with my wife and our older daughter, who is the same age as his daughter. At the beginning my wife was a bit shy, but later she and my friend's wife, who is also a teacher, talked, speaking about discipline, school curricula, and the physical conditions in the school.

When I asked Fatkhi why the others did not invite him, he said:

> Someone once told me that Jews invite only their close friends to a meal. Not like we do, where anyone who comes by is invited to sit and eat with us. So maybe I'm not their friend. I really don't know.

Fatkhi interprets an invitation for a meal as an act of good manners, openness, and respect for others. His invitation to his work colleagues was an attempt to establish good work relations, but instead it emphasized the difference between them. According to Fatkhi, his colleagues understood the invitation to eat in his home as an attempt to create relations of friendship, which is why only one man reciprocated and invited Fatkhi to his home.

Eating in the home of a Jew is also perceived as problematic. The Jewish meal consists of foreign dishes and is steeped in different aromas and seasonings, all of which sometimes make eating difficult. Food aromas and the perception of cleanliness play a central role in a Palestinian's willingness to sit down at the table of a Jew. Ziyad, a teacher of Hebrew and Arabic literature at a Jewish school in Haifa, says he judges food first by its smell:

> If the smell doesn't seem right to me, I don't eat. I have Jewish friends from school whom I visit only after first eating at home. I am not able to touch their food. Something in its odor does not agree with me.

Sonia, a chemistry teacher from Shefar'am, adds:

> There's something about the odor of Jewish dishes that sometimes upsets me; sometimes it even makes me nauseous. I miss the aroma of

our spices. It's not so nice of me to say this but it's hard for me to eat your food.

The mutual aversion, on a social as well as on a gastronomic level, among other factors, also explain the absence of Arab cookbooks from the Israeli cookbook market—either in Hebrew or in Arabic.

WHO NEEDS A COOKBOOK?

When ethnic communities and minority groups remain closed within themselves, the culinary knowledge at their disposal is self-sustaining. Daughters learn from their mothers, and women expand their individual repertoires by adopting recipes from their neighbors. There is a sense that the kitchen is alive and developing. The traditional division of tasks that still characterizes the Palestinian family in Israel, as well as Jews' avoidance of Arab food, also encourage preservation of culinary knowledge within the home and discourage its written documentation. Only in cases where culinary knowledge becomes watered down through separation from the mother culture, or because of a diminishing number of new immigrants from the land of origin, will the need to preserve it more formally in writing become pressing. Even though the founding of the state of Israel divided many Palestinian families, Palestinian citizens in Israel were not severed from their culinary culture. Living in Israel exposed them to new culinary knowledge, but it did not compel them to discard their existing eating habits. Shukri, a geographer from the north, believes that Palestinians who argue that they have experienced cultural severance are just trying to complicate a simple issue:

> We were able to continue with our culture, and at home we could keep eating as we had been accustomed. The food was there all the time and there was no longing for something that was missing. What we miss now is our own fault; we wanted to be modern and eat new foods.

Unlike the Palestinian citizens of Israel, the third and fourth generations of Jewish Israelis, whose origins are from North Africa or Europe, willingly gave up part of their culinary heritage in favor of modernity. Lacking a sense that their traditional food was disappearing, they felt no need to commit their culinary heritage to writing. Some Palestinians now dissociate the longing for home from the longing for food, while others use food to express their yearning for a homeland. Palestinian refugees who continue to visit the sites of their obliterated villages also carry out a set of food practices. They pay attention to the fruits and herbs that grow in these sites and see these plants as enhancing a temporary re-creation of the pre-1948 life.[14] By continuing to cook traditional Palestinian foods, women introduce their children to collective Palestinian culinary knowledge and instill Palestinian culinary tradition in the younger generation.[15] "Arab food has not disappeared," declares Hishmi from Ramla:

> It has only improved and developed over time. I'm not worried. We prepare the same food in the same way with only small changes, to make preparation faster, healthier, more modern.

Yasmin, a social worker from Lod, confirms this analysis, supporting it with concrete examples:

> My mother worked with her hands. She made *kubeh* with her hands, bread with her hands, *kofta* with her hands. I make the very same dishes but work with the food processor.

Because domestic culinary knowledge is preserved from generation to generation, there is no motive for writing recipes for the wider public. Transforming culinary knowledge into a cookbook is unnecessary as far as the Palestinian public is concerned and, moreover, lacks commercial potential. According to my informants, the production of a canonic written body of knowledge also requires a recognized central culinary authority who would take responsibility for assembling, transcribing, and disseminating that knowledge. Even if there is agreement on the general nature of a dish—its central ingredients, texture, and aroma—there are always disagreements about the small details that would obstruct the recording of culinary knowledge. Furthermore, women express concern that written recipes would not represent the full community of Palestinian women in Israel. Munira, a political activist from the north, expresses this concern:

> Writing a cookbook is complicated because each woman has her own way of cooking. If I write, I'll write my way, and then, what about the others? Is my food the only Palestinian food? How can I succeed in presenting a total picture of Palestinian society?

I became aware of the maze of opinions and recipes and of my informants' desire to present a unified voice, at least in the presence of a Jew, when Aysha and Samira, two sisters-in-law who live in Ramla, tried to explain to me how *seniyeh* is prepared. The disagreements between them on this subject caused amazement and bursts of laughter until it seemed they were speaking of entirely different dishes, with their only agreement being the name. According to Aysha, one makes *seniyeh* by mixing ground meat with parsley, garlic, salt, *baharat,* and cinnamon in a pan. When Samira reminded Aysha that she forgot to mention the eggs, Aysha was surprised to hear that Samira used eggs and insisted that they were not an integral part of the recipe. Samira insisted that she always used eggs, as they held all the ingredients together. Similarly, when Aysha explained that one needed to pour water on top of the mixture, cook it over a flame until the water evaporated, and then add tahini, Samira was surprised:

> What do you mean over a flame? I put it straight into the oven and add the tahini immediately.

Palestinian women say that Palestinian cuisine, by nature, includes a great deal of variation. Ingredients and cooking techniques are so particular to the individual family that it would be nearly impossible to create an essential Palestinian cookbook. Because their culinary culture is transmitted orally, Palestinian women have little sense of what cookbooks have come to mean in Western societies. They see cookbooks as representing some kind of "true" culinary knowledge rather than as individual aggregations of recipes that represent only the author. The fact that a Palestinian cookbook would be directed primarily to non-Palestinians—since there would be no need for it within the community—is what creates the need to find uniformity and agreement about representative knowledge that would bridge the differences among the individual versions. Nawal, a teacher of English from Gush Halav in Galilee, explains:

> We can't allow ourselves to exhibit our disagreements about food to you. As it is, you don't think the best of us, so we need to demonstrate unity and agreement in your presence.

Nawal says that every woman, home, and region in Palestinian society in Israel possesses its own complex and unique culinary knowledge, which makes it difficult to provide authentic recipes that represent the entire Palestinian population. There is great apprehension that instead of creating an organized body of knowledge, written recipes would cause division and disagreement. Before committing Palestinian culinary knowledge to writing, therefore, it is necessary to reach agreement about what that knowledge is, how to disseminate it, which categories will constitute it, and who is authorized to write the book and pass it on. This dilemma is unique to Palestinians who are citizens of Israel but unable to penetrate the social boundaries of Jewish Israeli society. In Western countries, immigrants who have integrated into the dominant middle class do not necessarily feel the need to adopt a united stance vis-à-vis culinary knowledge, but simply assume that a larger variety of versions of ethnic food would contribute to a more varied market and would enable as many individuals as possible to express themselves.[16]

Along with the desire to present a united front and to reach agreement on the content and boundaries of culinary knowledge, additional difficulties appear regarding the scope of the project. The culinary knowledge of the traditional Palestinian home is acquired and accumulated through observation and trial and error. Committing recipes to paper suggests that an oral and practical tradition, with its great richness and variety, can be reduced to standard cookbook form. The need to measure quantities and cooking times does not lend itself to a process largely dependent upon the senses and an individual "feel" for the dish. For that, the cook would need to depart from her familiar daily activity and adopt work patterns that are not natural to the cooking she knows.[17]

The fact that Palestinian women in Israel cook more than Jewish women do and that their pantry contains more basic commodities is one reason why Palestinian women find little need for cookbooks. Jihan, a speech therapist from Kabul, contends that Palestinian women encounter difficulties when they try to cook according to recipes from existing cookbooks because many of the books are translated into Arabic from English or European languages and many of the recipes are inappropriate for local conditions and tastes or do not accord with existing culinary knowledge:

> There was this book that told us what to do with pomegranates. It made me laugh; I saw that they hadn't a clue about pomegranates. You follow? The book needs to be appropriate.

Existing ethnic cookbooks fall into two main categories. The first collects traditional culinary knowledge to prevent it from disappearing along with the first generation of immigrants. The second is intended to broaden and enrich the culinary knowledge of the dominant group, and includes books written both by members of the minority group and by members of the dominant one.

Cookbooks of the first type contend with problems of precision, translation of sense and feel to exact measurements, and faithful presentation of all strata of culinary knowledge. These cookbooks are useless in the Palestinian community because knowledge still travels from one generation to the next and most women still learn to cook under the supervision of a family member. Committing culinary knowledge to writing for the dominant group raises questions as to the suitability of certain authentic tastes to a public that is unaccustomed to them and that has learned to view members of the ethnic group as inferior. The identity of the cookbook writer and the substance of the adapted knowledge is another issue raised by my interviewees, who question the ability of a foreigner to their culture to transcribe its culinary knowledge. Therefore, Palestinians are reluctant to disseminate their culinary knowledge or let a Jewish culinary agent be in charge of the documentation of their food practices. Jamal, an employee of the Ministry of Education, believes that Palestinian cookbooks written by Jewish authors extend political oppression to the gastronomic sphere:

> Why do I need you to preserve my food? We do a very good job of preserving it, because by us it is transmitted spontaneously. So we don't need the Jews to preserve our heritage. And why should they be the ones to profit from it?

IS HUMMUS ISRAELI FOOD? APPROPRIATION OR PARTNERSHIP?

The organization of a body of written culinary knowledge intended for use outside the boundaries of the community involves a redefinition of the relationship between the minority group and the dominant one. Does transmission of knowledge from the minority group to the majority take place as part of a culinary exchange between equals, or is it part of a process of cultural colonization? In Israel, for a cookbook to be profitable, it must arouse interest among the Jewish public, overcome obstacles of foreignness and suspicion, and present possibilities for varying the daily menu. Addressing the Jewish public requires organizing knowledge in a way that is appropriate for the structure of the meal to which the Jewish public is accustomed. At the same time, the organization of a body of culinary knowledge written for the Jewish public reinforces the appropriation of Palestinian dishes, which gradually become identified with the Jewish Israeli kitchen.

One of the main difficulties in translating culinary knowledge from the Palestinian kitchen to the Jewish one stems from the structure of the traditional Palestinian meal, in which courses are served simultaneously. In order to adapt Palestinian dishes for the Jewish public, they need to be classified according to the function they fulfill in the "typical Israeli meal." For example, should the soup be redefined as a first course or should it remain the basis of the meal along with bread and salad? This suggests further questions, such as how to present *melukhiye*, which resembles stew but is served in the Palestinian kitchen as a sort of gravy to accompany rice or meat. Similarly, in the Palestinian kitchen, soup symbolizes thrift, since its cooking water is usually used to prepare an additional dish. In the Israeli kitchen, however, soup is likely to be made from vegetables, fish, cheese, or lentils, to be clear or creamed, either delicate or thick in texture.

We can see evidence of these problems in *The Arab-Israeli Cuisine*— the first Arab cookbook in Hebrew—which was written by Nawal Abu-Ghoch, edited by Nira Rousso, and published in 1996 by Keter. Abu-Ghoch accepts the popular image of Arab cuisine in Jewish Israeli society as consisting of salads and grilled meat, and she raises some of the problems involved with translating Arab culinary knowledge (such as the matter of courses) in a manner that the Jewish public might understand. In an attempt to sell the idea of Arab food to Jews and to bridge the gap between members of the two cultures, Abu-Ghoch explains the differences between occasional meals and planned ones, describing how the presence of a guest determines the menu and the role of the meal as an axis around which the social event is constructed. She also deals with the seasonality of the Palestinian kitchen, its appliances and equipment, the practice of reclining and eating with one's fingers, and the simultaneous serving of all dishes. The book does not attempt to impart a unique Palestinian culinary experience but rather to enrich the domestic Jewish menu with new dishes. Thus, Abu-Ghoch classifies dishes according to categories that are familiar to the book's potential public: the chapter on soups does not indicate that the role of soup in the Palestinian kitchen differs from that in the European kitchen, and it includes dishes, like *frike*, that are not perceived in Palestinian society as resembling soup. Likewise, the chapter on pies—a category foreign to the Palestinian kitchen—presents baked goods made from dough and filled with spiced vegetables or meat as the Palestinian version of pies. Furthermore, recipes based upon herbs are missing from the book; it contains only two types of *kubeh*; seasonings are restrained; and in the chapter on stuffed vegetables, there is no recipe for stuffed pumpkin, a Palestinian classic, but there is one for stuffed tomatoes and for cabbage leaves with a vegetarian filling, which I did not come across during my fieldwork.

In the more recent cookbook written by Miriam Hinnawi, who is introduced as "the wife of Hashem Hinnawi from Galilee," the editor says that a section of dishes made of wild herbs and plants was included despite the Jewish public's lack of familiarity with those dishes.[18] It was felt that a Palestinian cookbook without such a section would be incomplete. Husam Abbas and Nira Rousso made the same decision when compiling their joint cookbook.[19] In addition to a section on herbs, the two texts included sections on all major aspects of Palestinian cookery, including pickles, stuffed vegetables, grains, sweets, and salads. Abbas and Rousso dedicated entire sections to eggplant, various preparations of hummus and tahini, egg dishes, and *labaneh*. These cookbooks went one step further than Abu-Ghoch's book by presenting a more varied version of the Palestinian kitchen, inviting Jews to try out the recipes and assuming that at least some of their potential audience would be ready to try something new. However, both books also included a section of soups, despite the fact that Palestinians do not consider soups to be part of the meal.

The feeling among my interviewees was that, in the end, the Palestinian dishes adopted by the Jewish Israeli public were those that fit most easily into the familiar categories. Amal, an accountant from Majd al-Kurum, complains about the different manner in which Jews eat hummus and *labaneh*. Whereas Jews spread hummus over bread or use it as a sandwich filling, Palestinians see hummus as a meal in itself and scoop it with either pita bread or a spoon. As for *labaneh*, she says:

> We eat *labaneh* for breakfast—you eat it for supper together with an egg or in a restaurant with hummus. For you, falafel is food. For us, it's something you eat with food. You took from us only what suited you.

Yet another difficulty in documenting Palestinian culinary knowledge and disseminating it among the Jewish public has to do with the sociopolitical relationship between Palestinians and Jews in Israel. Palestinians, who struggle for recognition as a distinct ethnic group with rights, worry that recording existing culinary knowledge will not only change the character of their kitchen and hasten the disappearance of gastronomic learning through observation and trial and error but will also encourage and reinforce the appropriation of Palestinian culture by Jews. In other words, Palestinians fear that Palestinian cookbooks offer a source of income for Jewish entrepreneurs who value their knowledge because of its potential to generate profit. Consequently, Palestinian knowledge may be appropriated, revised, and incorporated into popular Jewish

Israeli lore—just as happened to hummus, falafel, and *labaneh*. Nonculinary entities—such as long embroidered dresses, copper trays, and the land itself—shared a similar fate: they have been appropriated as part of an Israeliness to which the Palestinian citizens of Israel have no claim.

Naggwi, a restaurant owner in Umm al-Fahm, believes it is likely that Jewish food writers or chefs will commercialize traditional Palestinian dishes—for instance, by freezing *melukhiye* and presenting it as their own discovery:

> If a Palestinian were to commercialize a food unknown to Jews, no one would buy it. Our situation is such that in order for you to eat our food, you need to appropriate it. Even we call Arab restaurants "Mizrahi restaurants." You started it, and we followed.

In a process typical of relations between ethnic groups and dominant ones, more and more private entrepreneurs are discovering the potential in commercializing and industrializing ethnic foods. International food companies choose to present frozen or fast-food versions of ethnic food, claiming that their modern incarnation will ensure their survival in public awareness. An economic entrepreneur who uses available technological means to create commercial pseudo-ethnic food enables circulation of the minority group's culinary knowledge among a wider public. In this way, advanced technology makes it possible to prepare food with a traditional aroma, as we have seen in the case of *couscouson* and *sha'ariya*. Paradoxically, without the intervention of the economic entrepreneur, the traditional food will disappear.[20] The inclusion of a traditional dish in the culinary literature enables its dissemination, though perhaps at the expense of authenticity. For that reason, even before the publication of the books by Miriam Hinnawi and Husam Abas and Nira Rousso, many of my informants expected that the publication of a book of Palestinian cooking by either a Jewish or Palestinian entrepreneur would be well received. Rana from Acre, who is married to a restaurant owner, comments:

> If there's a cookbook of ours, in Arabic, the young women will buy it—those who are studying and haven't time to learn to cook from their mothers. The recipes in Palestinian women's magazines are nothing but advertisements for food companies, not Palestinian dishes. And if there are Palestinian dishes, they're presented with modern products. It makes me laugh.

Prepackaged and industrialized ethnic food, of course, threatens the culinary knowledge and skill that is generally passed on from generation to generation. However, it also makes it possible to document and disseminate that knowledge, on the condition that the information is distributed in a form that serves the entrepreneur. At the same time, the high price, the prior existence of knowledge in the home, and the absence of a culture fostering cooking according to written recipes all ensure that the publication of a cookbook in Arabic will be a financial loss. A leading publisher agreed to tell me his opinion on the subject anonymously:

> Publishing an Arab cookbook in Arabic is very complicated. It's not by chance that there are so many books on the market without there being an Arab cookbook. To tell you the truth, and I know well, there isn't so much to write about their cuisine: hummus, tahini, *shishlik*, *seniyeh*. What will we add that's new?

In reference to my mention of dishes made of wild herbs, vegetables, stuffed dough, and meat, he smiled and "assured" me that no Jewish Israeli is going to prepare *hubeizeh* and that one does not need a Palestinian cookbook to prepare *mjadara*, which has become popular among Jews. Moreover, Arab women do not need a cookbook in order to prepare these dishes. When I ask about *melukhiye,* he says:

> Who's going to eat it? It's not appealing and not tasty either. It would be very difficult to sell the Arab kitchen as being tasty or exotic. It doesn't have what the Chinese or Japanese kitchen has, for example.

From what this publisher says, one can understand that the Israeli public, although claiming to "know them very well," still does not regard the Palestinian citizens of Israel as an ethnic group whose culture is a subject of sufficient curiosity to enrich its own culinary repertoire. Neither is there a need among members of the Palestinian community to publish a cookbook as such. The absence of written culinary information from the Palestinian kitchen may be seen as another manifestation of intercultural tension; Palestinian food is considered to be an additional medium through which the property of the Palestinian public in Israel is being appropriated. Palestinian citizens of Israel live with a feeling that the cultural conquest is gaining strength, and that with it, the only culinary knowledge they possess will be taken over, becoming the domain of a Jewish-Israeli public that will continue to ignore its original owners.

THE PERSONAL IS POLITICAL

The fear that Palestinian food will be appropriated and transformed into an integral part of the Jewish Israeli diet emerges out of a political constellation in which the boundary between personal and public-political space is hazy and fragile. It is difficult for Palestinians in Israel to experience encounters with Jews on a personal level, in part because they interpret such encounters in political terms. This situation is more complicated for Palestinian women than for Palestinian men. The blurring of the boundary between public and private is fed by a dual network of oppression that perpetuates the personal and political inferiority of Palestinian women and prevents their full inclusion within Israeli society. They are oppressed both as women and as Palestinians, and their personal experiences reflect their inferiority both in male-female relations in Palestinian society and in Jewish-Palestinian relations in the public sphere.

Arabiya, a social worker living in the Triangle area, and her husband, a banker, used to share one car. Because her husband's job entailed an hour-long daily commute, they decided that he would drive to work and she would travel by public transportation. But Arabiya had several experiences on public transit that led her to take out a loan and purchase a second car. For instance, she used to travel to her clients by taking a taxi operated by a driver she recognized as reliable. One day he wondered out loud why he was driving her from one man's house to another. Arabiya suspected he doubted her mode of conduct:

> You could tell him, "Mister, it's not your business." We can't because he would be insulted and would tell everyone that I wander around and see men. And where we live, everything is small and everyone knows me. I can't tell him that.

Arabiya felt threatened by the driver's questions, even though her legitimate occupation entails traveling from house to house and meeting with both men and women. A question that seemed innocent and informative to me had embarrassing implications for her as she imagined the driver had thought she was behaving immorally, and she knew that any reaction on her part—confirmation or denial—would strengthen his suspicions. She felt that being a woman prevented her from defining herself through her profession, as she would have done had she encountered him in the context of her working relations, thereby gaining the trust and respect she deserved.

Arabiya goes on to illustrate the ways in which private experience can be absorbed in political discourse. She mentions an extreme encounter with a security officer that sharpened her observation of what she calls "Jewish sector perceptions" and the sense that in the blink of an eye her difference could be emphasized and exploited for discriminatory purposes. One day, she tells me, she traveled to Jerusalem with a religious woman from her village. They needed to change buses at the train station in Tel Aviv and the woman wanted a soft drink. When they tried to enter the terminal, the security guard stopped them and asked for their identity cards. Arabiya, whose style of dress resembled that of her Jewish colleagues, had rarely been stopped before. The other woman, who dressed according to religious conventions, was familiar with the procedure. Arabiya confronted the guard and asked why he was checking their identification cards, but the guard refused to provide any explanation. When she reminded him that she traveled to Jerusalem often and he had never asked to see her papers before, the guard said she should have been checked. When they arrived at the Ministry of Education in Jerusalem, the same thing happened again. Arabiya refused to show her papers on the grounds that she was a regular visitor to the ministry and had never been asked to identify herself before. To the guard's response that he had not been aware of her ethnicity and therefore had neglected his duty to check her documents, she responded with anger and aggression:

> When we came back to the central bus station in Jerusalem, everyone was standing outside because there was a suspicious object inside. As we entered, they stopped us again and I began to yell at the soldier, who then threatened to arrest me. There was a circle of people around us, staring, and no one said a word. The next day, I went to the bank, took out a loan and bought a car.

Arabiya interprets the constant suspicion toward Palestinians in Israel with a sense that Palestinians are "guilty until proven innocent." She argues that it is impossible to separate the personal dimension of life from the political one when Palestinians are singled out in public as being dangerous and hostile just because of their appearance, and without any connection to their actions. The suspicion is reinforced the more the difference stands out. In the past, when she traveled alone, the security officer at the Ministry of Education perceived her as a Jew and never searched her or checked her documents. The incidental revelation of her Arab origins suddenly made her strange and dangerous, without her behavior changing in any way.

Perhaps these anecdotes provide some explanation as to why so many Palestinian women I spoke with were reluctant to share culinary knowledge outside their community. As long as Palestinians feel that they lack control over their personal lives and that their movement around Israel is limited, they are unable to disconnect their personal identities from their political ones. Not only is Palestinian food unattractive in the eyes of the Jewish majority; Palestinians also choose to keep their food, their language, and their culture to themselves or else to share them with the Jewish majority only selectively, because doing so provides a sense of preserving privacy and control over the conditions of their lives. Arabiya does not object to sharing dishes and sharing her culinary knowledge with others, but she demands to be treated as an equal in exchange:

> It's impossible to respect my food without respecting me. When people belittle me, they belittle my food as well. A portion of falafel costs less than a slice of pizza, and the falafel takes more work to prepare. But our work is cheap . . .

Arabiya is not the only one who feels that way. Salah, a fisherman and restaurant owner from Ajami (an Arab neighborhood in Jaffa), sees a direct connection between food and politics. As long as Palestinians cannot separate personal experiences from political ones, he argues, there is no point in presenting authentic Arab dishes in Arab restaurants:

> There is alienation between Israelis and Palestinians. The Israeli is afraid of me, feels uncomfortable. In 1948 we opened our homes for Jewish families to enter and have somewhere to live but when they got set up, they left and went away. That gap needs to be closed before I serve you my home food and write my cookbook.

Ali, the principal of a school in the Triangle area, adds that writing cookbooks is like recording one's historical heritage. In his opinion, (Jewish) Israeli society does not allow all its constituent social groups to narrate their heritage—only those whose unique identity does not challenge the web of power relations. He observes political developments with mixed feelings. His happiness over Israeli recognition of a Palestinian political entity is mixed with uncertainty. Will there be recognition of the Palestinian right to be different and culturally unique? Will there be recognition of their history? Who will write Palestinian history, and the history of relations between Israelis and Palestinians? Ali mentions the presence today of a third generation of Palestinians for whom the state of Israel is an accepted fact. This generation, he observes, is one that has learned how to use the state's mechanisms to put its case on the public agenda. The state has, to a certain extent, made peace with the idea of a Palestinian cultural entity as long as it does not call into question the existence of an Israeli state.

Palestinians are gaining recognition in the state of Israel and attempting to use state mechanisms to ameliorate their position. New voices are speaking and writing about the Palestinian heritage and encouraging the Palestinization of Arab citizens of Israel. As part of this process, there have been attempts to construct a museum of Palestinian heritage in the Triangle area and to celebrate the "Week of Palestinian Tradition" that has existed for several years in the West Bank. Although Ali is pleased by the growing interest in Palestinian tradition, he is critical of the ways in which Palestinian culture and history are presented:

> Only those whose heritage is not accepted have a heritage week, as if you're entitled to feel human for one week a year. In order to be proud of our heritage and begin to write it down we need to be aware of the fact that we are Palestinians who live in the state of Israel with our heritage, and you need to accept us as we are. Perhaps then you'll show an interest and books will be written about food.

Along with bringing forward Palestinian history and heritage for the Palestinian population, Palestinian entrepreneurs sought ways of attracting Jewish tourists to Palestinian culture and food. Some opened bed-and-breakfast facilities after realizing that strategy had worked for the kibbutzim. This way, Palestinians citizens of Israel were able to realize two complementary objectives: they included themselves within the borders of local tourism and claimed to be part of Israeli society. However, in summarizing his eight years of experience, a Palestinian hotel owner in Nazareth says that his clientele was mostly pilgrims and Arabs. Only a few Jews came, most of whom were "what you would call 'bleeding hearts' ":

> I wanted families and built facilities for children; I offered free meals for children in my restaurant. I contacted the Ministry of Tourism and asked them to send me leaflets on the Galilee region and programs and events in Galilee. I asked a graphic artist to prepare a map for me that would show the route from my hotel to nearby places. I wanted to integrate into the tourist industry in Israel and sell what I had to offer.

This goal was widespread, especially in Galilee. Villages like Deir Hanna, Arrabe, Sakhnin, the Druze village of Beit Jann, and others offered bed and breakfasts with views, history, pleasant aromas, and an exotic experience by means of "typical" Arab-style hospitality. Entrepreneurs planned vacation villages, restaurants, and hotels. The tourist destination was accompanied by a display of the Arab village as a traditional setting for the Jewish public who had come to experience

152 | Part Two

something different.[21] The visitor was not perceived as a customer but rather as a guest. Samir, a teacher from Kaokab who also ran a bed and breakfast, invited his guests to join him at the family table, served coffee and cold drinks, and sometimes conversed with his guests until the middle of the night.

Three social factors, then, shape the flow of culinary knowledge from the Palestinian public to the Jewish public. The first factor is the social marginality felt by the Palestinian citizens of Israel, which hinders and filters the flow of knowledge. The second factor is Palestinians' feeling that Jewish Israeli society does not encourage them to preserve and develop their cultural uniqueness. The third factor is the link between the private and public-political dimensions among Palestinian citizens of Israel, which is also expressed in their attitude toward culinary heritage.

"TRADITION, TRADITION . . ."

As noted, a return to traditional culinary heritage is typical of the third and fourth generations of immigrant groups, who seek to rediscover their roots. Even though the Palestinian citizens of Israel were not cut off from their culinary culture, that culture evolved and changed during hard times. Furthermore, after Palestinians were exposed to industrial foods that could replace traditional cooking practices, some of their culinary knowledge was abandoned. When their economic situation improved and the political arena calmed, tradition could become an exotic commodity whose purpose was to add spice to daily life while becoming a product sold outside the community.

The ability to maneuver between tradition and modernity within culinary space and the possibility of mobilizing culinary tradition for existential and political struggle offer Palestinians in Israel a sense of power and the feeling that they control their own living conditions, even if only in one particular sphere. Their close connection to the land and their farming ingenuity gave them an advantage over the Jews, especially during difficult times. During the austerity period in the early 1950s, for example, the Palestinian citizens of Israel got by more easily than their Jewish counterparts did. While the Jews had to change their eating habits and replace roast meat with lentil patties, the Palestinians continued to eat as they had been used to eating. They even sold their food ration coupons to Jews, since they had no need of the rations themselves. Ismail, the owner of an auto repair garage in Jaffa, reports:

> We would give the Jews our ration stamps, and they would pay us. One gave me clothes he had received from America that were too small for his children. We didn't need the stamps. We had oil from the olives; we would make *zibda* [butter] ourselves; we also made cheese and *laban* ourselves. Everything stayed the same.

According to Nawaf, a senior official in the Bureau of Education, there is a connection between the economic situation and the mobilization of traditional culinary knowledge. In his opinion, a return to culinary tradition takes place during both difficult times and relatively prosperous ones, though each period has its own interpretation of the role of traditional food. During difficult times, traditional food—however tasty it may be—symbolizes economic distress, whereas when people are better off, it is possible to return to tradition in search of the exotic, either out of nostalgia or a sense of the need to preserve it. Nawaf recalls that when he was a child his family used to eat lentils and *ful*, and in the spring they varied their food with wild plants. No one was really well off and families ate meat on festive occasions only. When Palestinian society entered a period of prosperity, there was a rush for meat, and now people eat meat on a daily basis. When poverty is no longer a threat, he says, the return to tradition is taken as something exotic. All of a sudden people started serving bulgur, which would have been taken as an insult fifteen years ago. But now people have become curious about the food their ancestors used to eat:

> At one time everyone went out to harvest *akub*, but it came to symbolize poverty. Only those who didn't have enough money harvested *akub*. Today, when we already have all we need, we again are going out to harvest *akub*. Now it's sport, not something to be ashamed of. It's exotic.

As Palestinians return to traditional culinary knowledge, food becomes a political medium through which to express opposition to the regime. Under such circumstances, food demonstrates the power of the minority. Amal, a political activist from Galilee, is fully aware of the role food plays in the Palestinian struggle against Israeli authorities. Being familiar with the land and its produce, Palestinians are not as dependent on food supplies as Jewish Israelis are. When the Druze protested the annexation of the Golan Heights and refused to accept

Israeli identification cards, she recalls, food played a major part in their struggle:

> Do you remember how activists of Hadash [the Israeli Arab-Jewish party] traveled with members of Forum and Campus [political organizations that originated at the University of Tel Aviv] to bring flour, rice, oil, and milk? It's impossible to starve us because we go out to the garden, to the fields, pick herbs and greens and cook them. We know our land and know how to use what there is around us, and you can't break us by cutting food supplies.

When Palestinian citizens of Israel mobilize their culinary tradition to promote political aims, they emphasize its being a cuisine of poverty, based on simple and seasonal food. However, when they use their cuisine as a resource of entrepreneurship—by opening restaurants, for example—they emphasize its richness and basic dishes are shunted aside.

Traditional dishes have come to represent the food of the poor and marginalized. Restaurant menus tend to include a limited repertoire built around the dishes Jewish Israelis associate with Palestinian food: hummus, tahini, falafel, salads, kebabs, *shishlik,* steak, chicken liver, lamb chops, *seniyeh,* grilled or fried chicken, and sometimes stuffed vegetables. The uniformity of the menu is surprising in view of the fact that Palestinian restaurateurs in different regions of Israel serve different clienteles. In Jaffa, Lod, and Ramla, for example, there is a large presence of Jewish diners, whereas in Nazareth restaurateurs usually direct their efforts toward local consumers. Only a limited number of the restaurants that are aimed at a Jewish public have begun, in recent years, to reach outside the boundaries of the usual menu and offer traditional dishes or dishes made from wild plants.

Despite the fact that Palestinian restaurant menus for both Jews and Palestinians are relatively uniform, the food takes on distinct meanings for each customer: in the Jewish sector, cheap Palestinian restaurants serve workers, often at lunch; in the Palestinian sector, every meal in a restaurant is a festive occasion. While sitting in cafés and eating hummus at a restaurant near home is common among men in Palestinian society, a family visit to a restaurant is an act of intimacy and luxury. As such, traditional and simple dishes are absent from the Arab restaurant, and they are replaced by meat dishes that are usually eaten on holidays, especially roasted or fried meat. Instead of chicken, Arab families order *shawarma* or hummus with meat. *Shishlik* and kebabs are also popular, and in Acre, there is a demand for broiled fish. Issa, the owner of a restaurant in Nazareth, says:

> If people saw *melukhiye* or *olesh*, they'd laugh—that's something they eat all the time at home. In a restaurant they want something they won't be eating at home. For example, *shawarma*, *kebab*, *shishlik*. It's difficult to prepare the meat at home in a way that will taste good.

Amin, the owner of a restaurant in Umm al-Fahm, adds:

> My clientele wants to show respect for the woman. So I won't serve things the woman makes at home. I'll serve what she doesn't eat at home, so she'll feel like a queen.

The menu of a restaurant in the village of Arrabe lists such dishes as *maklubeh*, *mjadara* made from bulgur, and, when it is in season, *akub*. But in practice, neither *maklubeh* nor *akub* is served. Hashem, the owner of a restaurant in Nazareth, explains:

> Neither Arabs nor Jews ask for it. We eat it at home and therefore don't want it in a restaurant. The Jews aren't familiar with it and are a little hesitant.

The content of the Palestinian restaurant menu emerges from the status of the woman as the keeper of culinary knowledge and the expectations connected with her role. Offering a menu of familiar home dishes in a restaurant is likely to be interpreted as challenging the woman's ability to satisfy the culinary needs of her family and as casting doubt upon her gastronomic knowledge. The absence of home dishes from the menu is an affirmation of the woman's ability to fulfill her traditional role and appreciation of her distinct skills as a home cook. Perhaps that is why Farid, the owner of a restaurant east of Acre, says jokingly that good stuffed vegetables are not to be found in restaurants; stuffed vegetables prepared by male cooks lack the feminine touch so essential in this dish. Lila, a woman in her early twenties who runs a cafeteria on a college campus in the Jewish sector, adds that women will never eat at a restaurant food that they prepare at home, as it would immediately imply that they neglect their domestic roles:

> Neither would a man do that, as people would think his wife wasn't cooking for him. The husband needs to be certain that his wife knows how to prepare food at home. My fiancé keeps asking me if I already know how to prepare this dish and that dish, and I'm learning. When I get married I intend to cook for him and to stop working.

For Palestinians in Israel, eating in a restaurant implies that a certain intimacy exists between the diners. Young couples engaged to be married will not dine in public in their home villages. Neither will women sit alone in a restaurant. Rather, they will go to a restaurant in a Jewish area. According to Miriam from Arrabe:

> We drive to Hadera or Netanya and eat pizza or steak, but we won't dine in a restaurant in our village before we're married. I heard that in Jaffa and Haifa they do sit together before they're married. They are modern; the women there also wear miniskirts.

Varda, from a village in Galilee, adds:

> My father is very modern. I'm already engaged for the second time. But when I told him that my fiancé was taking me to a restaurant, he said: "Just don't eat here in the village; it would humiliate me. Go to Nahariya."

Daily contact with Jews enables young Palestinians to take up modern patterns of eating in restaurants without challenging the Palestinian tradition. On one hand, the shared meal symbolizes intimacy or an attempt to establish intimacy. On the other hand, it defines the boundaries of intimacy, such as whether one wants a closer relationship with a particular person or at what stage of the relationship intimacy is possible. Eating in Jewish sector areas affords young Palestinian couples a way to meet without flying in the face of tradition. Similarly, it is more acceptable for two women to eat together in a Jewish area than to sit together in a restaurant in their own village. The reaction aroused by a Danish woman, who is married to an Arab physician, sitting in a café in the village indicates the powerful significance of her act. A neighbor of the couple, also a doctor, told me:

> She came to the village and began to frequent the café in the morning, together with all the men. She came in wearing shorts and sat and laughed with all of them. She didn't understand that this isn't done here, that she was harming her husband's reputation and that of his family.

For Palestinian women, eating in a restaurant is an escape from housework and the daily routine. The restaurant need not be expensive. Pizzerias, sandwich bars, inexpensive eateries, cafés, and cafeterias are all perceived for this purpose as being restaurants. Fatan, a kindergarten teacher from Galilee, explains:

> When we are done with the shopping, at the shopping center, my husband says to me, "Let's go to a restaurant." We'll grab a bite—sometimes it's pizza, sometimes lasagna, sometimes only coffee and a cream cake. On

special occasions, we drive to an Italian restaurant in Nazareth; the food there is very good.

Mahmoud, a senior official in the Ministry of Education, describes eating at a restaurant as an opportunity to spend some time alone with his wife and give her his complete attention:

> From time to time I say to my wife: "Put on something nice, and let's drive to a restaurant." She puts on perfume and lipstick, and we drive to the restaurant and eat, just the two of us without the kids. That's how I show her my respect.

The restaurant thus fulfills different roles in the Palestinian and Jewish sectors. In the Jewish sector, lunch in a restaurant is likely to be perceived as a routine and legitimate alternative to a meal at home, which also allows families in which both adults work to make do with a light evening meal. In Palestinian society, a meal in any restaurant is seen as a break in routine and a gesture of intimacy—something Jewish society associates only with meals in elite restaurants. For Palestinians, eating at a restaurant testifies to close relations among the diners and provides a way to take time out from the daily tasks. By means of the restaurant, the boundaries of intimate relations are redefined, and the traditional tasks of the woman are revalidated. The ability of the Palestinian public in Israel to make differential use of a restaurant in the Jewish sector from one in the Arab sector enables it to simultaneously adopt modern behavior and preserve traditional patterns, especially in relations between men and women.

Palestinian restaurants serving a Jewish public also avoid traditional dishes eaten in the Palestinian home, but for different reasons. The prevailing view among Palestinian restaurateurs is that the Jewish public is not interested in most Palestinian food, tending to stay with only the most familiar, and now sometimes industrialized, dishes, such as hummus or *labaneh* on bread. Walid, a restaurateur who lives in the Triangle and manages two restaurants near Tel Aviv, claims to have regular customers who have eaten at his restaurant for years, yet who do not dare to order anything beyond the two or three dishes they are used to eating:

> There's one customer who even brings his wife in the evening and his mistress around noon and trusts me not to say a word. We're like friends—but when I invite him to taste something different, he makes a face as if the idea is disgusting. He always eats hummus and *shishlik*.

Walid is not alone. Other Palestinian restaurateurs also feel that Jewish customers' relationship to Palestinian food suggests a lack of appreciation or respect for Palestinian culture as a whole. The fact that Jewish customers compose their meals from a limited selection of Palestinian dishes and that Palestinian restaurateurs do not expand the menu for fear of endangering their business is understood as a rejection of the Palestinian people and an expression of disinterest. Palestinians feel that the Jewish public opinion comes from political and cultural tension, and not from the food itself. While Jews now readily eat Japanese, Chinese, and Thai food, Palestinian food is still seen as foreign, hostile, and even dirty. These perceptions will change, according to restaurateurs, only if the political conditions in Israel change.

One of the nephews of the Younes family, one of the most famous Palestinian restaurateurs in Israel, struggled for the stomachs of Jewish customers. Under the supervision of his uncle, he opened a restaurant in Ramat Aviv, an upper-middle-class neighborhood near the campus of the University of Tel Aviv. Although the food was identical to the food served at all the other restaurants owned by Younes, and the place was previously a Mizrahi restaurant, he says that people avoided eating there. Another member of the Younes family went through a similar experience. He took over a restaurant on Ben Yehuda Street in Tel Aviv, where a Chinese restaurant had attracted many diners. According to my informant, it took him three days to clean the place. Although the previous owner had kept the place it dirty, it was always packed with customers, but hardly anyone visited the new restaurant:

> I think maybe it was because we're Palestinians, and Jews think that it's not clean and not tasty if the place is run by Palestinians. And I think they didn't want to pay us as much as they paid in restaurants owned by Jews.

Palestinian entrepreneurs who manage cafeterias in commercial settings and cater to a steady Jewish clientele rarely serve Palestinian home dishes unfamiliar to Jews. One might think that because their Jewish clientele is steady and heterogeneous, it might be possible to build relations of culinary trust. But because the cafeteria is a commercial, profit-oriented venture, it needs to present a repertoire that matches the Jewish public's perception of what constitutes the noon meal. It cannot be an arena for culinary experimentation. Paradoxically, there is a wide belief that in the limited repertoire of the cafeteria, as opposed to the restaurant, Palestinian cooks prepare better dishes that Jewish cooks do. According to Nahalan, the owner of a cafeteria in a large company, many of his regular customers wish he would hire a Palestinian cook, assuming the food would be tastier. However, whenever he offers new dishes he avoids referring to them by their Arab names for fear that his customers will reject them. Therefore, *maftoul* becomes "chickpeas with bulgur," and he rarely goes beyond serving baked fish with cabbage salad or *mjadara*. Moreover, since the place needs to be kosher he has learned to use

> vegetarian schnitzel (made of soybeans) to make *seniyeh*. Those dishes are popular. Sometimes if Palestinians are working here, we prepare something for them, but not for everyone.

Traditional Palestinian foods are not always consistent with Jewish aesthetics of eating. Even the appearance of a dish can deter diners and thereby reinforce prejudices. The owner of a flourishing restaurant near Tel Aviv says he avoids serving dishes that are not visually attractive, such as *frike* or *melukhiye*, to his Jewish customers because their look is not appealing:

> A dish that has a pleasant appearance is much easier to offer. It's not only the fact that *frike* doesn't look good. Who would choose a dish made out of green wheat or green liquid that looks like that? It's easier to offer something that doesn't look attractive when you are powerful.[22]

When I tell him that *cholent* does not look very good either, yet more and more Ashkenazi Jews deliberately go to restaurants on Saturday noontime to eat it, he attributes it to the search of groups who are in the process of losing their cultural and political hegemony for their roots[23]:

> Fifteen years ago you didn't eat *cholent* at a restaurant. It was for you, something to be ashamed of. You ate it at home. Now that everybody is eating Mizrahi food and listening to Mizrahi music you realized you, too, had a culture to nourish.

Many Palestinians believe that Palestinian food will only become popular and fully appreciated in Israel when an authoritative cultural agent, such as a celebrity chef, extols its virtues. Palestinian food will become more popular, expensive, and prestigious only if it is legitimated by Jews, who are recognized for their gastronomic expertise. In the United States, for example, ethnic kitchens became popular not only because the status of minorities improved over the years but also because an authoritative source—a cultural arbiter—recognized a particular culinary tradition as worthy of admiration.[24]

What will enable this to happen in Israel? My Palestinian interviewees claim that the acceptance of Palestinian cookery in the public sphere depends on its resemblance to cuisines that Jewish Israelis already like. Mustapha, the owner of a Jaffa restaurant, often eats in trendy restaurants in Tel Aviv that he has "read about in the newspapers." The presence of a Jewish patron, he argues, is essential to raise Palestinian food to the threshold of public recognition and enable the Palestinian restaurateur to "up his prices":

> If I weren't ashamed, I would go to Aharoni and say to him: "Let's open an elegant restaurant and dress up the staff with our traditional costumes.[25] We'll serve lots of meat and charge the kind of prices you usually charge." If Aharoni went for it, there would be money in it. If I were to open a luxurious restaurant, who would come?

Another restaurant owner from Jaffa, a descendant of a family of restaurateurs, tells me that the owner of a luxurious restaurant, which closed about five years ago, used to buy two hundred portions of hummus from him every now and then:

> I sold it to her for ten shekels per portion while at that time you would have eaten a portion of hummus in my place for seven shekels. She'd pay me. She would charge at least twenty-five shekels. Her clientele wouldn't pay me twenty-five shekels for hummus.

Recognition by a Jewish culinary authority is likely to contribute to the broad public recognition of Palestinian food and to a willingness on the part of the Jewish public to pay more for a meal at a Palestinian restaurant. This process could also expand the repertoire in Palestinian restaurants to include dishes that are rarely found there today. The fact that Palestinian restaurateurs do not receive professional recognition indicates a pervasive suspicion and lack of trust towards the entire Palestinian sector. The existence of culinary knowledge on a domestic level not only frees Palestinians from the need to document it in writing; the culinary tradition penetrates political discourse, and in the hands of the Palestinian citizens of Israel, it becomes a means for enabling them to control the conditions of their lives, to ensure their existence as a separate cultural and national entity, and to prevent their culture from becoming the appropriated territory identified with Israeliness that excludes the Palestinian public. In this way the barrier between private and public spaces is reproduced, private experience acquires political significance, and tradition is mobilized to establish national pride alongside the struggle for survival.

Conclusion

At the opening of this book I described the uncomfortable feeling I had sitting in Samira's home. I realized she was under the impression that I had come to steal her recipes, and I felt like a colonialist intruder. The uncomfortable feeling brought on by that meeting did not disappear entirely when I was writing this book. Throughout my fieldwork and writing, I kept wondering whether I was successful in grasping the subtleties and particular meanings embedded in the cultural and political worlds of the Palestinian citizens of Israel who were never actually accepted within Israeli society. I opened with the hope that you, the reader, would finish the book with the understanding that food is not only a collection of proteins, carbohydrates, calories, and minerals, but that alongside its taste and aroma it also reveals political processes, social beliefs, and the economic order. I hope that I have achieved my objective.

In the course of my work on the book, many of my acquaintances argued that there was not much point in writing a book on Palestinian cookery for an Israeli audience because Israelis were familiar with Palestinian food—which, to them, very much resembled the food of Mizrahi Jews. The common use of rice in the two cuisines, as well as shared foods such as *kubeh*, dishes made from wild herbs, and salads helped support the validity of their assertions. But behind their argument lay ignorance not only about what constituted and influenced the Palestinian kitchen in Israel but also with the political processes that influence

Mizrahi kitchens in Israel. Jewish Israelis, the reader has learned, are not only unfamiliar with basic Palestinian dishes; they are, for the most part, unwilling to familiarize themselves with them. Claims of similarities between Mizrahi and Palestinian kitchens were based on ignorance of the latter and revealed the ease with which many Jews ignore the distinctive features of Palestinian culture in general and its cuisine in particular. Therefore, it was essential that I refrain from comparing the two kitchens and give the Palestinian kitchen its space in the Israeli culinary scene. Also, because the Palestinian public in Israel has never given much emphasis to the differences between Ashkenazi and Mizrahi Jews, nor differentiated between their kitchens, comparison between the Palestinian cuisine and that of Mizrahi Jews seemed superfluous.[1]

One of the arguments of this book is that the entry of "Jewish" dishes into the Palestinian kitchen in Israel was limited to those that suited the structure of the meal and the eating habits that prevailed in Palestinian society. Moreover, in contrast to other societies in which the food of immigrants has been gradually absorbed into the culinary repertoire of the host cultures, most Jewish Israelis remain ignorant about Palestinian dishes. The sustainability of Arab dishes and culinary traditions was essential in preserving a distinctive identity and culture. In the case of immigration, the preservation of immigrants' cuisine was meant to provide a sense of familiarity and comfort in the face of a new political and economic situation. In light of political processes that accelerated feelings of exclusion from Israeli society and conditioned acceptance in affirming loyalty to the state of Israel, food practices became means for expressing resistance to political oppression and attempts by state agents to obliterate cultural heritage. The fact that a similar process occurred when it came to Jewish acceptance of Arab dishes was another example of the role food had come to play in the interactions and relationships between Jews and Palestinians in Israel.[2]

However, while Palestinian dishes in Israel were preserved over the years in the domestic sphere only, the food of Mizrahi Jews became a symbol of the culture of the Mizrahi community and an inexpensive, popular cuisine offered to people outside the community. Mizrahi dishes that required much preparation disappeared from everyday life and became nostalgic, while exotic dishes were prepared for special occasions or eaten outside the home. Some wild plants also returned to the diet, as a result of increased awareness about health foods and not as part of the process of establishing a distinct Mizrahi ethnic identity. The perception that ethnic kitchens as a rule were healthier brought back an appreciation of wild herbs, which are now cultivated and sold to markets and food chains and have come to serve the needs of both immigrants of Mizrahi origin and those who determine taste in cooking and in restaurants. Palestinian cookery, although healthy and full of ingredients praised by fans of the Mediterranean diet, lags behind. Major culinary authorities in the local food scene often disregard its accordance with current health trends. The disrespect toward Palestinian cookery in Israel is, therefore, a good example of how identity politics and social inferiority determine both the inclusion and exclusion of ethnic cuisines in the culinary scene.

Unlike the role of food among the Palestinian public in Israel, the role of food among Mizrahi Jews in the struggle for social equality or cultural recognition has been limited or even nonexistent. Only recently have young Mizrahi chefs started mobilizing their food with the aim of establishing what they refer to as an emerging Israeli cuisine based on upgrading their mothers' cooking. This happened in large part because young Mizrahi Jews felt secure enough to return to their native dishes at the same time that ethnic cooking in general became an exotic pursuit and young restaurant critics sought out a new subject to discuss. Only recently has the desire to develop a distinct political and ethnic identity become part of the process.[3]

The case of Palestinians in Israel was different. Palestinian cookery in Israel, in addition to being a means of survival, has always been mobilized to negotiate position and terms of inclusion in Israeli society. On the one hand, it has played a role in developing a distinct national-cultural identity among Palestinians in Israel, who keep up with domestic cookery and refuse to share certain culinary assets with the Jews among whom they live. On the other hand, and without contradicting the aim of preserving cultural uniqueness and distinction, Palestinian entrepreneurs aimed, by means of food, to build bridges between the two groups that were so close geographically but perceived in their own eyes as far apart politically and culturally.

Selective acceptance of the ethnic kitchen along with its often inferior social standing is not limited to the attitude of Jewish Israeli society toward the Arab kitchen. Many ethnic kitchens are perceived negatively by the absorbing society and thus are preserved primarily in the private domain.[4] In Palestinian homes, women are the agents of culinary knowledge who create, develop, and disseminate that knowledge from generation to generation. Unlike restaurant culinary knowledge, domestic culinary knowledge rests on a reservoir of products and dishes that reflect the economic and technological conditions of the home, as well as the slow changes that occur in the cultural sphere and in ways of thinking about food. This knowledge, which emerges from and feeds into women's collective memory and personal experience, leads to the establishment of a cuisine that links the generations. The kitchen becomes the place where women gain social appreciation and honor at the level of the home and the community.

However, it is important to emphasize that the Palestinian citizens of Israel do not perceive modernization as a break with tradition but rather as a means to improve living conditions and access a higher standard of living. Adopting a modern approach to cooking is not seen as antithetical to preserving the old; it is not an affront to a religious revival, nor a threat to male dominance in the household and the community or to the nationalism stirring among parts of the Palestinian public in Israel. Change in the Palestinian kitchen is expressed in the gradual disappearance of simple domestic technology in favor of new technologies, such as microwaves and processed foods that have lessened the work of women and enabled them to prepare traditional foods in a more efficient manner.

While women transmit culinary traditions from generation to generation, men are in charge of positioning Palestinian cookery in the public sphere alongside other cuisines with the aim of building intercultural culinary bridges, on the one hand, and showing Palestinian cuisine's distinctive features, on the other hand. Male restaurateurs are the agents who disseminate Palestinian culinary knowledge as they define its character, boundaries, and the techniques that will enable it to preserve its distinctiveness and at the same time to be accepted by other groups.

Palestinian restaurants in Israel have managed to serve both Palestinian and Jewish Israeli diners. And while the menu at both types of restaurants is quite similar, they represent different cultural functions for each party. A Palestinian entrepreneur who opens a restaurant directed at his own people will serve food that differs from food served inside the Palestinian home, thus liberating the woman for a day from the burden of cooking for the family. Because eating in a restaurant is perceived in the Palestinian sector in Israel as a festive occasion, diners prefer to eat meat dishes or dishes that are not often prepared at home. A Palestinian restaurateur aiming for a Jewish clientele serves similar dishes because he adapts the menu to the tastes of this public and chooses a menu filled with foods already consumed by Jewish Israelis. Many restaurateurs also recognize that Jews most commonly consume Palestinian food on lunch breaks and not for festive occasions. The commercial success of the Palestinian restaurateur in this case depends upon his ability to make use of his culture in a way that will interest the Jewish public, as well as on the openness that the latter reveals toward the Palestinian Arabs and their status in the wider society.

I believe this book contributes to the understanding that food is one of many cultural elements to consider when studying the relationship between a dominant national group and an ethnic minority. Like language and traditional customs, the national kitchen and ethnic cuisine are means for constructing historical consciousness and identity—whether local or diasporic—that create a sense of identity, transmitted from one generation to the next. Globalization is sometimes perceived as standing above national traditions in general and culinary traditions in particular, but it can also emphasize old traditions, rejuvenate national and ethnic cuisines, and provide a means of disseminating culinary knowledge to a broader audience. It is therefore interesting to examine what has happened to Palestinian food and how it has been mobilized to construct a distinctive national identity and to enable Palestinians to better their positions in Israel.

The study of the Palestinian cuisine, I believe, is part of a broad body of studies that show that cuisines are not monolithic creations containing the unique historic dimension of a society, limited by geographical, historical, and cultural-national boundaries. On the contrary, these studies strongly call to look at cuisines as texts containing diverse and sometimes even contradictory elements in their geographic, political, cultural, social, cognitive, and associative levels. The cuisine contains contradictions whose unique combination in frying pan or dish is what imparts to them their distinctive identity, be it "French," "Italian," "American," or "Palestinian." The cuisine is created through mobilization, adaptation, and an exchange of elements and their uses that historically may be foreign to one another. The consumer interprets and creates the cuisine, leaning on the cultural context from which he derives significance. In this way, falafel becomes, for Jewish Israelis, a distinct dish served with tahini and salads, and, for Americans, a vegetarian substitute for hamburger—both modes of serving estranged from the Palestinian serving of falafel.

This book constructs the culinary narrative of the Palestinian citizens of Israel and recognizes it as representing Palestinian collective culture. It is of particular interest because of its extraculinary constituents. First, the culinary narrative, as presented in this book, is the product of three or four generations that brought the trauma of dispossession from their land into the heart of collective national memory and used it as a means of constructing culture and a sense of exile. Second, exposure to and accessibility of democratic mechanisms, as stated previously, enabled Palestinian citizens of the state of Israel to demand cultural recognition. The fact that Palestinians remained outside the Israeli collective is thus what transformed the culinary sphere into an arena in which it was possible to attempt to connect to Israeli culture and be part of the cultural processes taking shape within it; at the same time, Palestinian citizens of Israel were able to dominate in this sphere in which Jewish society had limited entry and control.

Moreover, this study helps us understand that Palestinian food in Israel plays two roles. From a Jewish standpoint, it serves as a means to define Palestinian citizens as different and to appropriate those dishes from their kitchen that do not contradict the eating habits of the developing Israeli kitchen. In the view of Palestinian citizens of Israel, their kitchen serves as a means of articulating their independent definition and preserving their identity as distinct from the Jewish-Israeli entity. The political discourse around the Palestinian kitchen becomes a tool enabling dominant Jewish cultural agents to define the ethnic group and for members of the group itself to establish their renewed self-definition in view of the constant political, social, and economic changes occurring in Israel.

A study of Palestinian food in the state of Israel is also a good case study of social groups whose sense of exile has become central to their identity. It is a case that combines within it longings for a state that has not yet arisen and for an unclear future that needs to be created. The struggle to define the future is carried on through the use of symbols, culture, and religious practices that have not been established within the boundaries of a Palestinian nation-state. The preservation of Palestinian food in the domestic sphere and its controlled exposure outside the Palestinian community indicate the limited ability of Palestinian citizens of Israel to be absorbed within Jewish society. They live in a nation-state, but their identity crosses political and cultural boundaries and is based upon symbols unique to their community.

I began this book on a personal note and I shall end it in the same register, with a short personal story. Precisely because it deals with everyday reality, this story emphasizes the role of food as a symbol of the relation of estrangement between Palestinians and Jews in Israel. In the summer of 2000, shortly before the al-Aqsa Intifada broke out, I was sitting with several friends at a restaurant of which I am especially fond in an Arab town in Galilee. The menu was standard, but a brief paragraph at the bottom caught my attention. Under the category of "special dishes," the restaurant owner recommended trying two dishes that went beyond the boundaries of the familiar: *fattoush* and *maklubeh*. I ordered both of them. The waiter asked me if I was certain I wanted these foods. I said I was, and he went to the kitchen to enter my order. Several minutes later, the restaurant owner arrived at our table and asked who had ordered *fattoush* and *maklubeh*. I identified myself. To the surprise of my friends, he tried challenging my knowledge of Palestinian food. I passed the test with flying colors. Once he realized I was familiar with the dishes I had ordered, he suggested, as a gesture of friendship, that I allow him to choose our food. After several minutes, our table was filled with dishes that did not appear on the menu and that none of the Jewish clientele of the restaurant had ever before had the chance to eat. Until then, the owner said, no one had ever ordered either of the two dishes that I ordered: "They had not even asked me what they were. You were the first and only one, and you even knew what they were." Because of that, the restaurant had actually stopped preparing them. The dish of *maklubeh* I was served was made possible only because, entirely by chance, the owner's wife had prepared *maklubeh* at home that day, and the owner asked her to bring it to the restaurant for my friends and me. The food was excellent, and my friends felt that a new gastronomic world had opened up before them. The owner refused payment from us, and he came around reluctantly only after I told him explicitly that his refusal to accept payment would be understood as saying that he did not want me to return to his restaurant.

I have chosen to end with this story mostly because of the happiness my familiarity with his food caused the restaurateur. Because of this familiarity, my friends were exposed to a new gastronomic world, of whose existence they had not been aware until that day and which ipso facto they had never tried. This world had been opened gradually in small controlled steps since the Oslo Accords, but it has been blocked again with the appearance of the al-Aqsa Intifada, which turned every order of hummus in Umm al-Fahm into an anti-Zionist act in the eyes of significant parts of the Jewish public and, for others, an act signifying desire for rapprochement and communication.

As complex and multilayered as the relationships between Palestinians and Jews in Israel are and as marginal as the Palestinian citizens of Israel feel, I would still like to end this book in an optimistic spirit. The future awaiting both Jews and Palestinians in Israel is not easy and a lot of issues that stand between us are hard to resolve. Some never will be resolved. However, I find hope in the preservation of Palestinian cuisine and food practices and the resistance to their appropriation by Israeli culinary agents. In upholding their food and making moderate and recent attempts to expose dishes that are traditionally eaten in the domestic sphere, Palestinian culinary agents ensure that the fate of the long embroidered dress, the copper trays, and the land itself—which have been appropriated to an Israeliness of a kind in which Palestinian citizens of Israel have no part—will not be the fate of Palestinian food.

Notes

PREFACE TO THE ORIGINAL EDITION

1. All those interviewed will be referred to in this book by first name only. In order to protect their privacy, I have changed their names and places of residence.

2. See the glossary at the end of the book for descriptions of these and other Palestinian dishes.

INTRODUCTION

1. Gvion (2006, 2009a).
2. Douglas (1975, 1984).
3. Hobsbawm and Ranger (1989).
4. Fitzgerald (1979).
5. Said (1978).
6. Young (1990).
7. Stam and Shohat (1994).
8. Fanon (1967).
9. B. Anderson (1997); Guibernau and Rex (1997: 1–12).
10. Cusack (2003); Mennell (1985).
11. Goody (1982; 1986: 74–128); Mennell (1985).
12. Braudel (1979).
13. Hooker (1981).
14. Barthes (1983).
15. Bennett and Bhabha (1998: 43–44); Braziel and Mannur (2003); Cornell and Hartmann (1998: 250); Giroux (1998: 178); Taylor (1994).
16. Safran (1991).

17. Levi and Weingrod (2005).

18. Clifford (1994); Levi and Weingrod (2005).

19. Goldberg (1994); Radhakrishnan (2003).

20. Dyson (1994); Giroux (1998: 179–181); Manalansan (2003).

21. Boyarin and Boyarin (2003); Smith (1997).

22. Gibau (2005); Rex (1997: 274–275); Tölölyan (1991: 4–5).

23. Macias (2004); May (2000); Vincent (1974).

24. Nelson and Tienda (1988); Pierre (2004); Pyke and Dang (2003).

25. Bonacich (1972); Jabareen (2006); Lewin-Epstein and Semyonov (1992).

26. Eldering (1998); Kim (2004).

27. al-Haj (1997); Bishara (1993); Gvion (2009a); Haidar (2005); Rabinowitz and Abu Baker (2002).

28. Smooha (2004); Yiftachel (1999).

29. Ghanem (2001); Jabareen (2006); Pappé (1994).

30. Abu-Saad (2006); Lustick (1980); Rouhana (1998); Yiftachel (1999).

31. Kemp (1999: 328–331, 336–338); Sa'di (2003).

32. Bishara (1993).

33. Al-Haj (1997b).

34. Blumen and Halevi (2005); Ghanem (2001); Jabareen (2006); Sa'ar (2005).

35. Bishara (1993).

36. Stein (1998).

37. Jabareen (2006); Levy (2005); Rabinowitz and Abu Baker (2002).

38. Al-Haj (1997b); Gvion (2006, 2009a); Rabinowitz and Abu Baker (2002); Sa'di (2003).

39. Gvion (2006, 2009a); Lewin-Epstein and Semyonov (1992).

40. Kimmerling (1993).

41. Jabareen (2006); Levy (2005).

42. Al-Haj (1997b); Lewin-Epstein, al-Haj, and Semyonov (1994: 140); Shavit (1992); Swirski (1990).

43. Wikipedia contributors, "First Intifada," *Wikipedia, The Free Encyclopedia*, http://en.wikipedia.org/wiki/First_Intifada (accessed May 18, 2012).

44. Al-Haj (1997b); Bishara (1993); Smooha (1989, 1992).

45. Rabinowitz and Abu Baker (2002).

46. Wikipedia contributors, "Second Intifada," *Wikipedia, The Free Encyclopedia*, http://en.wikipedia.org/wiki/Second_Intifada (accessed May 18, 2012).

47. Al-Haj (1997b); Jabareen (2006). The United Nations as well as many governments and international organizations refer to the territories occupied by the Israeli army after the Six-Day War of 1967 as the Occupied Territories. The Occupied Territories consist of the West Bank, the Gaza Strip, much of the Golan Heights, and, until 1982, the Sinai Peninsula. The West Bank and Gaza Strip are also referred to as the Palestinian Territories or Occupied Palestinian Territory and form the basis of the Palestinian state. They are ruled by the Palestinian Authority, the European Union, and the U.N. Security Council. Wikipedia contributors, "Occupied Territories," *Wikipedia, The Free Encyclopedia*, http://en.wikipedia.org/wiki/Israeli-occupied_territories (accessed May 18, 2012).

48. Al-Haj (1997b).
49. Gavison (1999); Lustick (1980).
50. Al-Haj (1997b); Rabinowitz and Abu Baker (2002); Sa'di (2003).
51. Bishara (1993, 1996); Hammack (2006); Levy (2005).
52. Barbas (2003); Belasco (1987); Levenstein (1987).
53. Appadurai (1988); Belasco (2002).
54. Barbas (2003); Gvion and Trostler (2008); Levenstein (1987); Lu and Fine (1995); Raspa (1984).
55. Gvion (2006).
56. Van den Berghe (1984).
57. Sutton (2001).
58. Fragner (1994); Sutton (2001).
59. Levenstein (1987).
60. Dallalfar (1994); Mankekar (2002).
61. Goode, Theophano, and Curtis (1984); Moore (1984); Raspa (1984).
62. Wheeler and Swee Poh (1983).
63. Gillette (2005).
64. Prosterman (1984).
65. Caldwell (2004); Lozada (2005); Yan (2005).
66. Gaytán (2008); Lem (2007); Liu and Lin (2009); Yano (2007).
67. Conlin (1986).
68. Lem (2007); Liu and Lin (2009); Lou (2007).
69. Conlin (1986: 181–189).
70. Belasco (1987).
71. Ferreri (2002); Gaytán (2008); Lind and Barham (2004); Pilcher (2002).
72. Harbottle (1997).
73. Bardenstein (2002); Gvion (2002, 2009c); Inness (2001).
74. Barthes (1982).
75. Goody (1986); Gvion (2002); Inness (2001); Mennell (1985).
76. Theophano (2001).
77. Goode, Theophano, and Curtis (1984); Ray (2004).
78. Bardenstein (2002); Gans (1979); Prosterman (1984); Sutton (2001); Wheeler and Swee Poh (1983).
79. Gans (1979).
80. Kitcharoen (2007); Lem (2007); Mohanty (1988); Spivak (1988); Suleri (1992).
81. Habermas (1986).
82. Foucault (1979).
83. Banner (1973); Leschziner (2007); Mennell (1985).
84. Lyotard (1988).
85. Gvion (2009c); Gvion and Trostler (2008).
86. Karaosmanoglu (2009); Zubaida (1994a, 1994b).
87. Lu and Fine (1995).
88. Gaytán (2008).
89. The term *mixed city* refers to a town in which both Jews and Arabs live, such as Jaffa, Lod, Ramla, Acre, Haifa, or Jerusalem.

PART I. WHAT PALESTINIAN WOMEN MUST KNOW

1. Gvion (2006).

2. E. Anderson (1980, 1984); Murcott (1983d); Bromberger (1994); Maclagan (1994); Yamani (1994).

3. Counihan (1999); Lindenbaum (1977).

CHAPTER I. WOMEN'S WAYS OF KNOWING

1. For example, once Mexican women overcame their initial reluctance toward commercially produced tortillas, they gradually stopped preparing tortillas at home, even though the commercial tortillas were nutritionally deficient and their use impacted negatively on the nourishment of Mexican farmers. See Pilcher (2002).

2. Aubaile-Sallenave (1994); Perry (1994).

3. Bryld (2003); Negash and Niehof (2004).

4. Aubaile-Sallenave (1994).

5. Burnett (1979).

6. The "wonder pot" was invented in Israel during the 1950s, the period of national austerity. It is an appliance that makes it possible to bake on a gas or kerosene burner. The central part is an aluminum pot shaped like a Bundt pan. An electric wonder pot, developed later, dispensed with the burner. Wikipedia contributors, "Wonder Pot," *Wikipedia, The Free Encyclopedia*, http://en.wikipedia.org/wiki/Wonder_Pot (accessed May 18, 2012).

7. Gvion (2006).

8. Dishes made of mostly vegetables with a little meat enriched with the protein provided by legumes are not unique to the Palestinian kitchen. These dishes are typical especially of the kitchens of displaced immigrants or of low-income minority groups. Immigrants who arrived in America during the nineteenth century and the beginning of the twentieth century were compelled, for economic reasons, to forgo meat in favor of vegetable dishes mixed with meat or plant protein. Immigrants from Eastern Europe cooked stews of vegetables, grits, and pork, and Italians enjoyed pastas with cheese—an eating habit that initially aroused criticism among American dieticians. Vegetarian diets, as they found expression in the United States, also evolved during periods of economic crisis, and not only for ideological reasons. See Gvion (2002).

9. The Palestinian citizens of Israel were not the only ones who exchanged bulgur for rice. Sami Zubaida (1994b) notes that in the past, bulgur had been a basic ingredient of the daily menu in Greater Syria, Anatolia, and northern Iraq. Bulgur was the basis for vegetable stew and a cheap substitute for rice. During the 1940s, these regions experienced changes in production patterns, land management, and the marketing of agricultural produce that led to rice becoming a staple in the Middle Eastern menu. Rice was not necessarily served as a substitute for wheat, but rather as an addition. In Middle Eastern cuisine, wheat is part of every meal, either as bread or in one cooked form or another. Rice, on the other hand, may be a side dish or an integral part of one or another of the dishes served, but it does not always appear on the table.

10. Fiddes (1997); Twigg (1983); Willetts (1997).

11. Murcott (1983a).

12. Gvion (2002, 2009a); Gvion-Rosenberg (1991).

13. At the level of female culinary knowledge, the meal is evidence of the ability to translate into practical knowledge not only the theoretical knowledge of cooking but also the semiotic system and cultural beliefs in which food is enmeshed. See Burgoyne and Clarke (1983); Delamont (1983); Douglas and Nicod (1974); Martens and Warde (1997); Murcott (1983b, 1983d, 1997); Wood (1995).

14. Inness (2001); Pitt-Rivers (1977); Wood (1995); Yamani (1997).

15. Burgoyne and Clarke (1983).

16. For example, the accepted norm in Western meals is that the side dishes accompanying the meat consist of carbohydrates and vegetables. The simultaneous serving of two carbohydrates, such as rice and potatoes or noodles, is rare and is thought of as being in poor taste or as lacking understanding in matters of food and nutrition. This norm stems from the cultural assumption that these three foods have the same function in the meal and contain similar nutrients. In Palestinian cuisine, on the other hand, rice, potatoes, and noodles are not perceived as resembling one another. As in Chinese, Japanese, Cuban, Indonesian, Brazilian, or Indian cuisine, rice is a staple that is compatible with every other food and is considered not a side dish but rather a vital component. Potatoes are treated as vegetables, just like squash, carrots, or onions.

17. In his analysis of the development of table manners from the seventeenth century onward, Norbert Elias (1978) claims that they reflect the rise of the individual and of personal territory for activity. In the Middle Ages it was customary for diners sitting alongside one another to share dishes and glasses. Diners cut off portions of meat with their own knives and using their own hands. In the eighteenth century, people began to use forks as utensils to help cut meat, allowing the hand to disappear from the collective plate. Still, diners saw the central platter and the space between personal plates as communal. At the end of the eighteenth century, the use of a personal fork was introduced, along with a personal plate and a personal portion. This individuation was accompanied by an increased blurring of the form of the animal being served as food, until the connection between the animal and the meat on the plate was something located only in the mind of the diner.

18. Charsley (1997); Delamont (1983); Prosterman (1984).

CHAPTER 2. THE SOCIAL SPHERE

1. The social demand that women cook and provide food for their families receives special emphasis in times of family crisis or when women fail to fulfill this demand due to economic distress. In a study of battered English women, Rhian Ellis (1983) found that women who do not have a hot meal ready when their husbands come home, or whose meals do not meet the standards set by their husbands, are more likely to be hit by them. Jacqueline Burgoyne and David Clark (1983), who studied divorce in English society, show that most of the arguments between couples before divorce took place at mealtimes, which

thereby develop into a verbal battlefield. In second marriages, on the other hand, mealtimes become occasions for pleasant family meetings for the couple. Temma Kaplan (1982) connected the economic crisis in Spain with female protest. She showed how women took to the streets to protest the rising prices of housing and food, which prevented them from fulfilling their traditional role.

2. Willard Moore (1984) studied a community of Russian immigrants in the United States and discovered a similar social pattern: Older women who were excellent cooks were invited to prepare the traditional noodles for the main religious ceremonies of the community. The women met in the church kitchen a few days before the event and prepared the noodles together. Requesting their assistance was in itself a form of community valuation.

CHAPTER 3. *LABNEH* WITH LIGHT BREAD AND *KNAFEH* FROM WHITE CHEESE

1. Modernization is a historical process in which developing societies, whose members engage in intertwined spheres of activity and whose worldview is primarily religious, gradually become knowledge societies, organized around professions and expert knowledge. See Habermas (1986). By glorifying the new over the old, modernity transforms newness into a fundamental value that redefines other values. Modernity, in contrast to tradition, sanctifies progress rather than faith in a transcendental power. See Vattimo (1988: 95–107). Increased professionalism and secularism, as well as the elevation of the new to a sacred level, have led modernity to be identified with the capitalist economy, as expressed through the wide distribution of goods and ideas (Simmel [1971: 3–15]), an increase in social mobility, and a change in the organization of relations between ethnic groups.

2. Among these were the Ibn al-Balad ("Sons of the Village") movement, the National Committee of Chairmen of Arab Local Authorities, and the follow-up committees that sprang up around the latter. On the question of the Arab minority in Israel, see al-Haj (1997); Bishara (1993); Soen (2005a).

3. This particular kind of cheese is very popular as a spread.

4. *Samneh* imparts a strong taste and aroma to the dish. It is still possible to find *samneh* in grocery stores in Jaffa and in the villages, even though in recent years its use has diminished. *Samneh* is expensive in comparison with oil, butter, and margarine.

5. An example of this is the changing attitude toward Italian food in the United States. When Italian immigrants first arrived in the United States at the end of the nineteenth century, and for a long time afterward, their menu was perceived as unbalanced and even dangerous to health, and American nutritionists regarded Italian culinary habits with amazement and suspicion. Social workers and home economists were specially trained to help Italian immigrants change their eating habits. Members of the first generation refused to do so. However, members of the second and third generations, who had institutionalized their ethnic identity as Italian Americans, adopted elements of American cuisine while continuing to preserve Italian characteristics in their foods, such as high consumption of pasta in white or red sauce. During World War I, Ameri-

cans discovered that eating pasta had certain advantages, such as providing a nutritious meal without meat, and they adapted it and other Italian dishes until their Italian origins were blurred. See Goode, Theophano, and Curtis (1984); Gvion (2002, 2009c); Levenstein (1987).

6. Bardenstein (2002); Gvion (2009a); Gvion and Trostler (2008). The arrival of McDonald's in Turkey is an example of how modernization contributed to the revival of traditional Turkish foods that had been disappearing from the popular culinary repertoire. Fast food was a source of inspiration for local entrepreneurs, who began to apply the fast-food principle to traditional dishes such as kebabs, soups, stews, local cheeses, eggplant fried with yogurt, and baklava. Fast-food versions of these dishes became even more popular than McDonald's. Like hamburgers, these foods were inexpensive, portable, and able to be eaten quickly and while standing. Similarly, in China, the entry of international fast-food enterprises brought the growth of fast-food chains purveying Chinese food, claiming that it was healthier than Western fast food. These claims did not gain many adherents because they contradicted the modern Western culture according to which the Chinese wanted to educate their children. In Russia, however, McDonald's won a place in the private sphere. Russians were influenced by McDonald's but believed that the same food prepared at home was healthier; thus they began to prepare hamburgers and milkshakes in private homes. See Caldwell (2004); Chase (1994); Lozada (2005); Watson and Caldwell (2005); Yan (2005).

7. The disappearance of complicated traditional dishes is typical of kitchens encountering modern cooking technologies. See Lind and Barham (2004); Pilcher (2002).

8. These organs hint at some direct connection between the animal and the meat we eat. See Elias (1978).

9. This return is possible only after the minority group has accepted the dominant culture. Once that happens, a return to tradition is no longer perceived as a challenge to the dominant group. I discuss this at length in the next chapter. See Gvion and Trostler (2008); Lu and Fine (1995).

10. Gvion (2009b, 2013).

CHAPTER 4. ENCOUNTERING ISRAELI JEWS

1. The Tadmor Culinary Institute is a major school of culinary arts in Israel that trains cooks to work in cafeterias and small restaurants. Many of its students are Palestinian citizens of Israel.

2. Gvion (2009c); Gvion and Trostler (2008).

3. Restaurants and cookbooks provide examples of how the culinary knowledge of minority and ethnic groups is selected, sorted, analyzed, adapted, and transmitted to the consuming and reading public. Processing the culinary knowledge of ethnic and minority groups into written form not only introduces it to people outside the ethnic community but also enables the detachment of the ethnic group's culinary knowledge from its owners and subjects it to the principles of the dominant culture. The process culminates with the return of the original knowledge, devoid of authenticity, to its original owners. Cookbooks

and restaurants are thus a part of the process of institutionalizing the exchange relations between ethnic culinary knowledge and the knowledge of the dominant group in accordance with the nature of the relations between these groups.

4. Gans (1979); Macias (2004); Merino (2004); Pierre (2004).

5. In the postmodern era, ethnic identity becomes a store of popular knowledge that ethnic groups convert into a resource to be shared with other groups. Food is a convenient reservoir of ethnic knowledge that may be a public good, since it does not challenge the foundations of the dominant society but rather adds an exotic dimension through which ethnic groups tell their story and share the information in their possession with the surrounding society. Still, when ethnic knowledge is appropriated by the general public, the minority group's control of the texts of its culture and its past becomes limited. Usually, it is not the minority group that gathers, adapts, or disseminates its culinary knowledge; instead, members of the dominant group sort this knowledge, adapt it to their own culture, spice it with an exotic flavor, and sell it to the general public as "ethnic food." Minority groups tend to accept the situation because their livelihood sometimes depends on the consumption of their food by the dominant group.

6. Generally, it is men who earn their living from cooking in the public sphere and thus transmit ethnic culinary knowledge, defining its character, boundaries, and techniques and establishing both its uniqueness and its appeal to other groups. Such ethnic economics imparts a sense of security by virtue of its foundation on an accessible reservoir of knowledge and encourages the creation of social circles within the group that serve as a resource for earning a livelihood. As the economic situation improves, the circles expand to include members of the wider society. See Fine (1996); Gvion and Trostler (2008); Harbottle (1997); Mankekar (2002); Van den Berghe (1984).

7. May (2000).

8. In general, Chinese restaurateurs in the United States are willing to forgo authenticity in favor of a more popular culinary repertoire that appeals to the average palate while imparting an exotic dimension to the restaurant's décor. The design of the restaurant is modeled on the image the dominant group has bestowed upon the ethnic group while emphasizing the lines of difference between them, and it often has an appearance that is similar to other restaurants of the same ethnicity. See Lu and Fine (1995).

9. The decline of domestic farming, along with limited mobility in the public sector, compelled Palestinians in Israel to find alternative sources of income. The turn to culinary sources was limited for several reasons. First, economic hardship and an instrumental perception of food prevented eating in a restaurant from developing as a familial experience until after their economic situation had improved. In addition, the Jewish public perceived Palestinians to be a hostile minority, and therefore also treated their food with suspicion. For a more detailed discussion of this subject, see the introductory chapter of this book.

10. In using the term *ethnic economy*, I refer to immigrants' use of their culture or special expertise to develop means of making a living, freeing them from dependence on the lower ends of the job market. Arlene Dallalfar (1994), in her study of Iranian immigrants in the United States, shows how Iranian

immigrants made a living and sustained their culture by opening stores, travel agencies, and Persian language schools. Also see Kitcharoen (2007); Lem (2007); Lovell-Troy (1990); Yano (2007).

11. Cookbooks are presented as reservoirs of a minority historical and cultural knowledge that exists alongside the formal history of the national group within which they live. Peter Heine (1994) ponders the question of whether an Arab cookbook is one that is written in Arabic or one containing recipes of Arab dishes. In France, Arabic cookbooks written in French offer Lebanese and Algerian recipes. See Gvion (2009c).

The few cookbooks that were published in the Middle East from the sixteenth through the eighteenth centuries were written by court chefs, as were cookbooks from Europe during that time. The canonic Arab culinary literature during the sixteenth century evolved from a combination of two written sources from the Abbasid period (750 CE to 1258 CE). Because only the most complex recipes are included in these cookbooks, it is impossible to learn from them about the eating habits of the lower classes. See Fragner (1994); Zubaida and Tapper (1994: 4). Cookbooks in Iran between the sixteenth and eighteenth centuries reported on technological developments that enabled changes in the dishes and were written by chefs famous for their ability to prepare gourmet dishes.

Cookbooks intended for women began to appear in Iran during the 1920s, following exposure to European influences. These cookbooks interwove Iranian recipes and French ones. Iranian cookbooks in European languages were also published. Most were written by Iranians living abroad who wanted to encourage preservation of their traditional kitchen and to invoke nostalgia for their origins. See Fragner (1994: 56–68). A similar trend was found in Egypt during the nineteenth century, when female authors combined local recipes with European ones in their books. See Zubaida (1994a: 37). One example is the book by Josephine Richard, the granddaughter of a Frenchman who converted to Islam.

12. Rabinowitz and Abu Baker (2002); Reiter and Aharoni (1991); Soen (2005b).

13. Douglas (1975).

14. Ben-Ze'ev (2004).

15. Gvion (2009a).

16. Gvion (2013).

17. Kitchens that have organized knowledge for the purpose of recording and preserving it have, in the course of modernization, altered their cooking and measuring practices. This process is especially evident in the United States, where the growing interest in the kitchens of various ethnic groups has been accompanied by culinary authority: along with measuring quantities and documenting recipes, this process has organized intuitive knowledge in written form in a way that every American reader can understand and use. The written recipe is a text that indicates a form of social organization. Until the end of the nineteenth century, each recipe in a Western cookbook appeared as a chapter of a book; it occupied a number of pages and included such instructions as "While the meat is cooking in water, go down to the cellar and take a handful of flour and butter the size of an egg . . ." or "Go out to the yard and pluck

three stems of parsley and two stems of rosemary and add them to the dish." At the beginning of the twentieth century, the recipe as we know it appeared: text distinguishing graphically between the list of ingredients and the instructions for preparation. The graphic separation reflects a cognitive division in the organization of the modern household, such as the fact that this household does not rely on daily cooking, and cooking according to written recipes is not an integral part of daily life. Many ingredients, including basic ones, are not to be found at all times in the domestic pantry, let alone in the home garden. See Gvion (2009c); Gvion-Rosenberg (1991).

18. Hinnawi (2006).

19. Abbas and Rousso (2006).

20. Lind and Barham (2004); Pilcher (2002).

21. Stein (1998).

22. Over the past few years, I have come across several restaurants that have started serving *frike* and *maklubeh*. These restaurants cater either to professional middle-class Palestinians who no longer prepare those dishes at home or to Jews who are familiar with the dishes because they have eaten them in the homes of Palestinian friends.

23. *Cholent* is the Eastern European version of cassoulet. It consists of meat, beans, chickpeas, wheat or oats, onions, potatoes, eggs, and goose fat, all cooked overnight on a low flame. It looks horrible. Surprisingly, it tastes great, and one cannot move for a week after eating it.

24. Thus, during the 1920s and 1930s, Americans began writing and taking chefs of ethnic origin under their wing. The ethnic chefs cooked, and the American writers measured quantities and cooking times, substituted familiar ingredients for those that were foreign to the American palate, and wrote introductions to books in which they praised the quality of the food and especially its suitability to the needs of the middle class. It was only during the 1940s that ethnic chefs began to write texts independently, and even then, they adhered to the formula already set in place for them: pseudo-authentic food that had been adapted to the American public. During the 1960s, immigrants stopped being a part of the American discourse on ethnic food, as American food writers argued that immigrants were no longer familiar with current culinary trends in their home countries. This being the case, American writers began to travel around the world gathering recipes, collecting them into books as representative of ethnic food in its authentic form, without the intervention of American change agents. See Gvion-Rosenberg (1991).

25. Aharoni is an Israeli chef famous for introducing Chinese cookery to the Israeli public. Aharoni hosts a popular cooking show, writes a food column in a major newspaper, and has published many cookbooks.

CONCLUSION

1. In regions such as the Negev, and in cities such as Jaffa, Ramla, and Lod, Palestinian food is influenced by the Egyptian kitchen; in northern parts of the country, it is influenced by Syrian and Lebanese kitchens. On the other hand, the majority of Mizrahi Jews came to Israel from countries of the Maghreb

and from Iraq, Kurdistan, Yemen, and Iran, rather than from Egypt, Lebanon, and Syria. For this reason, perhaps, *melukhiye* is familiar not to Jewish citizens of Israel in general but only to those from Egypt. Kurdish and Iraqi Jews introduced *kubeh* soup, as well as round and flat *kubeh;* North African Jews contributed to the popularity of couscous, made from semolina and served over a soup rich in vegetables. These are different in essence from the Palestinian *kubeh* in Israel and from *mugrabiya*—the Palestinian-Israeli version of couscous. Yet many Jewish Israelis disregard these differences and see Palestinian cookery as similar to Mizrahi cuisines.

2. The changes that occurred in the food of Mizrahi Jews in Israel and the way in which that food was absorbed by the Ashkenazi public are typical of immigrant kitchens. Among the first generation of Jews from Mizrahi communities, women continued to cook, as much as they could, the food they had eaten in their land of origin, and the eating habits of the family underwent only a few changes, in response to a lack of certain ingredients. The second generation was already exposed to other foods and began to request them at home, so that new dishes entered their kitchens. When the daughters of this generation grew up, they often chose to cook dishes other than those their mothers had been accustomed to cooking in the homes where they grew up, or they prepared the same dishes but used advanced technology that shortened the cooking time. The third generation associated the traditional dishes with foods they used to eat at grandma's house on special occasions, and their love of these dishes became part of the nostalgia they developed for their cultural roots.

3. Gvion (2013).

4. Barbas (2003); Gvion (2006); Harbottle (1997).

Glossary of Culinary Terms

AFSHI A dish made from the head, feet, and intestines of a cow. The cow parts are cleaned until they are white; filled with rice; seasoned with black pepper, cumin, and cinnamon; and cooked in water. When the dish is almost ready, *fati* (dry crumbled bread) is added to thicken it.

AKUB A thorny plant with edible stems and florets. After the thorns are removed and the edible parts are cleaned, they are fried with onion, garlic, and lemon. *Akub* is eaten with bread and *laban*, used as a filling for dough, added to a salad, or fried with lamb or veal and served with rice.

ARUM A spicy wild plant that is used as a condiment for meat.

BAHARAT A mixture of spices used to season meat and rice dishes.

BAKLAVA A pastry made of phyllo dough filled with nuts and seasoned with honey and cinnamon.

BLILI A dish consisting of chickpeas cooked with bulgur and either lamb or beef, *blili* is eaten hot or cold with *laban* and raw onions. Those wishing to avoid the expense of meat can prepare *blili ful*—a dish of green fava beans and bulgur.

BSARA A dish made from dried fava beans that have been soaked in water with baking soda and cooked until soft. Dried *melukhiye* is added to the *ful* along with a mixture of crushed garlic, lemon, and hot pepper. The result is a soup-like dish that is eaten with bread and vegetables.

BULGUR Cracked wheat, used to make *kubeh*, tabbouleh, and *mjadara*. In preparing bulgur, the first step is to remove the stones, husks, straw, and any other foreign granules. The wheat is then cooked and scattered on the roof to dry. Once it is dry, it is cleaned a second time and stored in sacks. In the past, it was customary to prepare a supply of bulgur to last an entire year.

COUSCOUSON See *mugrabiya*.

DUKKAH A mixture of *zaatar,* olive oil, and sesame seeds in which bread is dipped.

FALAFEL Fried patties made of either garbanzo beans or fava beans and eaten with hummus. Israelis stuff pita bread with falafel to which tahini sauce and a chopped vegetable salad is added.

FATTOUSH A vegetable salad made of cucumbers, tomatoes, onion, parsley, and mint seasoned with olive oil and lemon juice. Pieces of grilled pita are added to the salad, and in Galilee, cheese is put on top.

FRIKE Cooked green wheat flour used as an alternative to rice. Sometimes *frike* is added to meat soup or chicken soup to make a complete meal.

FUAREH In this dish, tripe is washed thoroughly with water and cleaned with spices until it turns white. The tripe is then stuffed with rice and pine nuts, almonds, or pieces of meat. The stuffed tripe pieces are sewn shut and cooked in water seasoned with black pepper, *baharat,* and cinnamon.

FUL A dish made of cooked fava beans, warm tahini, olive oil, lemon, and parsley, to which some add a hard-boiled egg. *Ful* was originally eaten as a late breakfast after returning from the field, as it is very filling.

HINDBAH A wild herb that grows in the fields after it rains, *hindbah* is stir-fried with olive oil and lemon and generally served as part of a complete meal with rice, *laban,* bread, and a salad.

HUBEIZEH A sharp-tasting wild plant that grows during the winter in most parts of Israel. Its leaves are dark green and rich in iron, and it improves the function of the intestines. *Hubeizeh* is often fried with onions, dill, salt, and pepper, or in lemon juice with a little salt, and served with cold *laban.* The Bedouin used the leaves to prepare a thick soup that was eaten with sheep's-milk *laban* and eggs fried in *samneh.*

HUMMUS A paste made of cooked garbanzo beans, tahini, lemon, cumin, and garlic. Traditionally, Palestinians ate hummus for a late breakfast after working in the field. Now it is eaten as part of a meal.

HURFESH One among many wild herbs that are picked in the field, lightly fried in olive oil, and seasoned with lemon. As with many other herbs, it is served with rice, *laban,* and a vegetable salad.

JARISHA Also called *lubatiyeh* or *shulbato, jarisha* is a popular version of *mjadara* made from bulgur and without lentils. Onions are fried either in corn oil or olive oil, to which bulgur and tomato juice are added.

JIBJIB A firm and sour mixture of bulgur and *laban* made from dried sheep's milk that is used to prepare various dishes. To reconstitute *jibjib* as *laban,* a piece is cut off, crushed, and boiled in water until it is the thickness of powdered milk. The mixture is added to lamb soup to thicken and sour it.

JIBNE *Jibne,* or Arab cheese, is a salty, hard white cheese with a consistency and flavor that can be varied according to the needs of a particular dish. *Jibne* provides a supply of cheese for eating and cooking even during periods when goat's milk is scarce. For sweet dishes, the cheese is soaked in water that is changed every few minutes to remove its saltiness and then kneaded until it reaches the desired consistency.

KA'EK Cookies made of semolina dough filled with nuts or dates and formed into the shape of a bagel.

KARAIN A dish made from lamb's feet that have been cleaned and boiled in water. While the feet are boiling, stuffed grape leaves and squash are prepared. The softened lamb's feet are layered in a pot with the stuffed vegetables until the pot is full.

KAWA'IR See *kubeh*.

KHOSI A side dish of lamb meat and onion that is fried in olive oil and eaten alongside *kubeniyeh*.

KIRSHE A dish made of sheep's stomach filled with rice. The tripe is washed and cleaned with spices until it turns white. Then it is filled with rice and pine nuts, almonds, or pieces of meat; sewn shut; and cooked in water with black pepper, *baharat*, and cinnamon.

KISHIK Boiled sheep's milk to which is added all the bulgur the liquid can absorb, and then dried. When dry, a large, heavy stone is placed on the cheese for several days to remove any remaining liquid. When the mass is completely dry, it is wrapped in salt, strung on a cord, and hung in the sun to finish drying. To reconstitute *kishik* so it can be used as a substitute for *laban*, a piece is chopped very fine and mixed with water until it becomes a liquid with the consistency of *laban*.

KNAFEH A sweet dish made of *kada'if* (dry thin noodles) and Arab cheese. It is baked in the oven and served hot.

KOBAB Roasted *kubeh* prepared from semolina dough filled with fried sheep meat and pine nuts and seasoned with cumin and *baharat*.

KOFTA Grilled meat seasoned with salt, pepper, cinnamon, and *baharat*. Originally *kofta* was prepared from sheep meat, but now many use turkey meat.

KORA See *kubeh*.

KUBEH This is the most widely known dish that combines bulgur flour and a stuffing. The mixture may be left as dough or shaped into croquettes *(kawa'ir)*, patties *(kora)*, or a pie. Lamb is the only meat deemed suitable for proper *kubeh*. In the absence of lamb, veal may be used as a substitute.

KUBEH BATATA A dish consisting of layers of mashed potatoes alternated with layers of meat fried with onion and spices. Bread crumbs and margarine are sprinkled over the top layer of mashed potatoes.

KUBEH KAZABI See *kubeh tehili*.

KUBEH SENIYEH A dish consisting of layers of bulgur, or bulgur mixed with ground lamb, and layers of *khosi* baked in a pan in the oven.

KUBEH TEHILI "Mock *kubeh*," also known as *sarasira, kubeh kazabi,* or *false kubeh,* is defined as poor man's *kubeh* because it contains no meat. Its preparation follows that of classic *kubeh*: dough made from bulgur with a meat-like filling. Sometimes the patties contain just bulgur filled with potato, onion, and spices, or chickpeas cooked with onions and spices. The patties or croquettes are cooked in *laban* with garlic and mint. *Kubeh tehili bandora* is made from uncooked bulgur mixed with onion and tomato and seasoned with *baharat, marda'ush,* and mint.

KUBENIYEH A mixture of bulgur, very fresh raw lamb meat, hot red pepper, nutmeg, and cinnamon. The lamb is cut into small pieces, minced by hand, and mixed with finely ground bulgur. Croquettes are formed from this mixture and served uncooked alongside *khosi*. When eating, the diner takes some of the *kubeniyeh* and mixes it with the *khosi*.

LABAN A cultured dairy product, like yogurt, that is made of goat's milk and has the consistency of kefir. It is used especially as a sauce for meat and vegetable dishes.

LABANEH A cheese made from goat's milk. The milk is put into bags that are hung up in order to drain the liquid. After the liquid has been removed, salt is added and balls are formed. The finished *labaneh* balls are stored in bottles and covered with olive oil.

LENTIL SOUP A thick soup made from red lentils that constitutes a meal in itself. Lentils are cooked in water with fried onions, *baharat*, salt, and bouillon powder or cumin, until the lentils fall apart and form a very thick soup. See also *rishta*.

LUBATIYEH See *jarisha*.

MA'AMUL Cookies made from semolina flour filled with nuts or dates.

MAFUNE See *maklubeh*.

M'KHAMAR In this dish, cooked chicken is cut and placed on large flat bread. Onion, pine nuts, sumac, or red pepper are put on top, and the dish is grilled in the oven until it turns red.

MAKHSHI Stuffed vegetables. Squash, small green pumpkins, eggplant, grape leaves, carrots, cabbage, tomatoes, or potatoes are stuffed with a mixture of rice and seasoned lamb or veal, and cooked in liquid, sometimes with the addition of a tomato.

MAKLUBEH A rice dish in which cubed or thickly sliced vegetables are placed on the bottom of the pot, with rice on top, and covered with water. When ready, the pot is inverted over a large plate, and the resulting dish resembles a cake. Ingredients suitable for *maklubeh* include chickpeas, eggplant, cauliflower, tomatoes, and potatoes. When fish is used instead of vegetables, the dish is called *mafune* or *saidiye*. A variation with meat is called *matfune*.

MANSAF Rice covered with lamb meat that has been fried with onions and pine nuts.

MATFUNE See *maklubeh*.

MELUKHIYE A popular cultivated plant. The small leaves are cleaned with a cloth as soon as possible after purchase and dried in the sun to prevent them from absorbing liquid. After drying, the leaves are finely chopped and fried or cooked as soup. During the frying or cooking, the leaves exude a liquid that thickens the dish. *Melukhiye* may be served as soup alongside a meat dish, or it may be mixed with meat or chicken and served with rice and *laban*.

MENAZALI Slices of eggplant fried with tomatoes, onions, and sometimes chickpeas. *Menazali halabiah* consists of sliced fried eggplant layered with fried onions and lamb seasoned with *baharat* and black pepper. Slices of tomato and meat form the top layer, water is added, and the dish is cooked.

MENAZALI HALABIAH See *menazali*.

MJADARA A dish made from lentils and grains (rice or, more commonly in northern Israel, bulgur) and served either dry or as a soup. In Jaffa and the Triangle area, a dry version of *mjadara* is made with rice and small green lentils. In this version, fried (or even burnt) onions are added to lentils and rice that have been cooked in water with salt and cumin. See also *yalanji*.

MUGRABIYA The Palestinian version of *couscous, mugrabiya* consists of a soup made of chickpeas and chicken, each of which is cooked in a separate pot and served over *couscouson*. The *couscouson* are prepared by rolling grains of bulgur and semolina in flour until they separate from one another. The separated grains are steamed over the chicken soup. The soup is seasoned with *baharat*, cumin, turmeric, and cinnamon. For serving, the plate is filled with *couscouson*, and soup is ladled over it. Fried onions, chickpeas, and a piece of meat are added.

MUSAKA In this Palestinian variation on the Greek moussaka, slices of eggplant are attached to each other at the base to form a kind of sandwich, which is filled with seasoned ground meat that has been fried or cooked in goat's-milk *laban*.

OLESH Also known as chicory, *olesh* is a wild plant used for salads.

PTITIM Tiny squares or circles of pasta that many Israelis eat as a side dish with meat. *Ptitim* are especially popular among children.

RISHTA A version of lentil soup in which green lentils are cooked with onions and seasoned with salt, pepper, and chicken bouillon powder. Thin strips of dough are added to the soup to create noodles.

SAIDIYE See *maklubeh*.

SAMBUSAK Triangles of flaky pastry stuffed with meat and baked in the oven.

SARASIRA See *kubeh tehili*.

SELIKA A wild plant whose stem is boiled in water and then seasoned with garlic and lemon.

SENIYEH *Seniyeh*, which literally means "tray," is a dish made of ground sheep meat seasoned with pepper and *baharat* and either baked or cooked on the stove with either tomatoes or tahini sauce on top.

SFIKHAH *Sfikhah* consists of pieces of phyllo pastry in the form of circles or squares on which ground meat seasoned with salt, cinnamon, and pepper is placed. It may be left open or made from two layers of dough stuffed with meat and is baked in the oven.

SHAWARMA *Shawarma* is a popular dish eaten in restaurants. It consists of a combination of meats and meat fat all grilled on a spit for many hours. The meat is served either on a plate or as a sandwich.

SHISHBARAK Dumplings filled with seasoned ground meat and then cooked in *laban* seasoned with mint.

SHISHLIK Pieces of lamb meat or beef roasted on skewers.

SHULBATO See *jarisha*.

STUFFED VEGETABLES See *makhshi*.

SUNARA A thorny plant that grows near the home and is found mostly in Galilee. It can be eaten as is, as a salad seasoned with olive oil and lemon, or fried with onion, salt, pepper, and mushrooms. This dish serves as a main course and is eaten with rice and *laban*.

TABBOULEH A salad made of fine bulgur, a lot of parsley, and a little bit of mint and seasoned with olive oil, lemon, salt, and pepper. Some also add onions, tomatoes, and cucumbers.

TAHINI A sesame paste that is usually mixed with water, lemon, garlic, and a little bit of salt. It is either eaten as a dish in itself or added to hummus, *seniyeh*, cauliflower, or other vegetables.

TRIDI A dish made from vegetables left over from stuffing. Small pieces of the leftover flesh of vegetables, such as squash or eggplants, are fried, sometimes with chickpeas, seasoned with lemon juice and spices, and served with pita.

YALANJI A version of *mjadara* made from bulgur to which finally diced tomato, onion, parsley, and mint have been added. *Yalanji* may also be used as a filling for grape leaves.

ZAATAR A mixture of dried herbs (mostly sage) and sesame seeds, *zaatar* is used as a spice mostly for *labaneh*.

Works Cited

Abbas, Husam, and Nira Rousso. 2006. *Lamb, Mint and Pine-Nuts: The Flavors of the Israeli-Arab Cuisine* (in Hebrew). Tel Aviv, Israel: Yedioth Aharonot.

Abu-Ghoch, Nawal. 1996. *The Arab-Israeli Cuisine* (in Hebrew). Jerusalem: Keter.

Abu-Saad, Ismael. 2006. "State-Controlled Education and Identity Formation among the Palestinian Arab Minority in Israel." *American Behavioral Scientist* 49 (8): 1085–1100.

Al-Haj, Majid. 1997a. "Family Styles in the Arab Society in Israel" (in Hebrew). In *Jews and Arabs in Israel*, edited by R. Hochman, 203–204. Jerusalem: Academon.

———. 1997b. "Identity and Orientation among the Arabs in Israel: The Case of Double Periphery." *State, Government and International Relations* 41–42:103–122.

Allan, Tony. 1994. "Food Production in the Middle East." In Zubaida and Tapper 1994, 19–31.

Anderson, Benedict. 1997. "The Nation and the Origins of National Consciousness." In *The Ethnicity Reader: Nationalism, Multiculturalism and Migration*, edited by Montserrat Guibernau and John Rex, 43–51. Cambridge, UK: Polity Press.

Anderson, Eugene N. 1980. "Heating and Cooling Foods in Hong Kong and Taiwan." *Social Science Information* 19 (2): 237–268.

———. 1984. "Heating and Cooling Foods Re-Examined." *Social Science Information* 23 (4–5): 755–773.

Appadurai, Arjun. 1988. "How to Make a National Cuisine: Cookbooks in Contemporary India." *Comparative Studies in Society and History* 30:3–24.

Aubaile-Sallenave, Françoise. 1994. "Al-Kishk: The Past and the Present of a Complex Culinary Practice." In Zubaida and Tapper 1994, 105–139.

Banner, Lois W. 1973. "Why Women Have Not Been Great Chefs." *South Atlantic Quarterly* 72 (2): 198–212.

Barbas, Samantha. 2003. " 'I'll Take Chop Suey': Restaurants as Agents of Culinary and Cultural Change." *Journal of Popular Culture* 36 (4): 669–686.

Bardenstein, Carol. 2002. "The Gender of Nostalgia." *Signs* 28 (11): 353–386.

Barthes, Roland. 1982. *Image Music Text*. London: Flamingo.

———. 1983. *Mythologies*. England: Paladin.

Belasco, Warren J. 1987. "Ethnic Fast Foods: The Corporate Melting Pot." *Food and Food Ways* 2 (1): 1–30.

———. 2002. *Food Nations: Selling Taste in Consumer Societies*. New York: Routledge.

Bennett, David, and Homi K. Bhabha. 1998. "Liberalism and Minority Culture: Reflection on 'Culture's In Between.' " In *Multicultural States: Rethinking Difference and Identity*, edited by David Bennett, 37–47. London: Routledge.

Ben-Ze'ev, Efrat. 2004. "The Politics of Taste and Smell: Palestinian Rites of Return." In *The Politics of Food*, edited by Marianne E. Lien and Brigitte Nerlich, 141–160. Oxford: Berg.

Bishara, Azmi. 1993. "On the Question of the Arab Minority in Israel" (in Hebrew). *Teoria Ubikoret* 3:7–20.

———. 1996. "The Israeli Arab: Scrutinizing a Divided Political Dialogue" (in Hebrew). In *Zionism: A Modern Polemic, Research and Ideological Approaches*, edited by P. Ginosar and A. Bareli. Beer-Sheva: The Ben Gurion Legacy Institute.

Blumen, Orna, and Sharon Halevi. 2005. "Negotiating National Boundaries: Palestinian and Jewish Women's Studies Students in Israel." *Identities* 12:505–538.

Bonacich, Edna. 1972. "A Theory of Ethnic Antagonism: The Split Labor Market." *American Sociological Review* 37: 547–559.

Boyarin, Daniel, and Jonathan Boyarin. 2003. "Diaspora: Generation and the Ground of Jewish Diaspora." In *Theorizing Diaspora: A Reader*, edited by Jana Evans Braziel and Anita Mannur, 85–118. Malden, MA: Blackwell.

Braudel, Fernand. 1979. *The Structures of Everyday Life*. New York: Harper and Row.

Braziel, Jana Evans, and Anita Mannur, eds. 2003. *Theorizing Diaspora: A Reader*. Malden, MA: Blackwell.

Bromberger, Christian. 1994. "Eating Habits and Cultural Boundaries in Northern Iran." In Zubaida and Tapper 1994, 185–201.

Brown, Linda Keller, and Kay Mussell, eds. 1984. *Ethnic and Regional Foodways in the United States: The Performance of Group Identity*. Knoxville: University of Tennessee Press.

Bryld, Erik. 2003. "Potentials, Problems, and Policy Implications for Urban Agriculture in Developing Countries." *Agriculture and Human Values* 20:79–86.

Burgoyne, Jacqueline, and David Clarke. 1983. "You Are What You Eat: Food and Family Reconstruction." In Murcott 1983c, 152–163.

Burnett, John. 1979. *Plenty and Want: A Social History of Diet in England from 1815 to the Present Day.* London: Scolar Press.

Caldwell, Melissa L. 2004. "Domesticating the French Fry: McDonald's and Consumerism in Moscow." *Journal of Consumer Culture* 4 (1): 5–26.

Caplan, Patricia, ed. 1997. *Food, Health and Identity.* London: Routledge.

Charsley, Simon. 1997. "Marriages, Weddings and Their Cakes." In Caplan 1997, 50–70.

Chase, Holly. 1994. "The *Meyhane* or McDonald's? Changes in Eating Habits and the Evolution of Fast Food in Istanbul." In Zubaida and Tapper 1994, 73–86.

Clifford, James. 1994. "Diasporas." *Cultural Anthropology* 9 (3): 302–338.

Conlin, Joseph R. 1986. *Bacon, Beans, and Galantines: Food and Foodways on the Western Mining Frontier.* Reno: University of Nevada Press.

Cooper, Ann. 1998. *"A Woman's Place is in the Kitchen": The Evolution of Women Chefs.* New York: Van Nostrand Reinhold.

Cornell, Stephen, and Douglas Hartmann. 1998. *Ethnicity and Race: Making Identities in a Changing World.* London: Pine Forge Press.

Counihan, Carole. 1999. *The Anthropology of Food and Body: Gender, Meaning, and Power.* New York: Routledge.

Cusack, Igor. 2003. "Pots, Pens and 'Eating Out the Body': Cuisine and the Gendering of African Nations." *Nations and Nationalism* 9 (2): 277–296.

Dallalfar, Arlene. 1994. "Iranian Women as Immigrant Entrepreneurs." *Gender and Society* 8 (4): 541–561.

Delamont, Sara 1983. "Lobster, Chicken, Cake and Tears: Deciphering Wedding Meals." In Murcott 1983c, 141–151.

Douglas, Mary. 1974. "Food as an Art Form." *The Studio:* 83–88.

———. 1975. "Deciphering a Meal." In *Implicit Meanings: Essays in Anthropology,* 249–279. London: Routledge.

———. 1977. "Beans Means Thinks." *The Listener:* 292–293.

———. 1984. *Food in the Social Order: Studies of Food and Festivities in Three American Communities.* New York: Russell Sage Foundation.

Douglas, Mary, and Michael Nicod. 1974. "Taking the Biscuit: The Structure of British Meals." *New Society* 30: 744–747.

Dyson, Michael Eric. 1994. "Essentialism and the Complexities of Racial Identity." In *Multiculturalism: A Critical Reader,* edited by David Theo Goldberg, 218–229. Oxford: Blackwell.

Eldering, Lotty. 1998. "Mixed Messages: Moroccan Children in the Netherlands Living in Two Worlds." In *Ethnic Identity and Power: Cultural Contexts of Political Action in School and Society,* edited by Yali Zou and Enrique T. Trueba, 259–282. Albany: State University of New York Press.

Elias, Norbert. 1978. *The History of Manners.* New York: Pantheon.

Ellis, Rhian. 1983. "The Way to a Man's Heart: Food in the Violent Home." In Murcott 1983c, 164–171.

Fanon, Frantz. 1967. *The Wretched of the Earth.* Harmondsworth: Penguin.

Farb, Peter, and George Armelagos. 1980. *Consuming Passions: The Anthropology of Eating.* New York: Washington Square Press.

Ferrero, Sylvia. 2002. "*Comida sin par.* Consumption of Mexican Food in Los Angeles: 'Foodscapes' in a Transnational Consumer Society." In *Food Nations: Selling Taste in Consumer Societies,* edited by Warren Belasco and Philip Scranton, 194–219. New York: Routledge.

Fiddes, Nick. 1997. "Declining Meat: Past, Present . . . and Future Imperfect?" In Caplan 1997, 252–266.

Fine, Gary Alan. 1985. "Occupational Aesthetics: How Trade School Students Learn to Cook." *Urban Life* 14 (1): 3–31.

———. 1996. *Kitchens: The Culture of Restaurant Work.* Berkeley: University of California Press.

Fitzgerald, Frances. 1979. *America Revised.* New York: Vintage Books.

Foucault, Michel. 1979. *Discipline and Punish: The Birth of the Prison.* New York.

Fragner, Bert. 1994. "From the Caucasus to the Roof of the World: A Culinary Adventure." In Zubaida and Tapper 1994, 49–62.

Gamarnikow, Eva, David Morgan, June Purvis, and Daphne Taylorson, eds. 1983. *The Public and the Private.* London: Heinemann.

Gans, Herbert. 1979. "Symbolic Ethnicity: The Future of Ethnic Groups and Cultures in America." *Ethnic and Racial Studies* 2 (1): 1–20.

Gavison, Ruth. 1999. "Jewish and Democratic? A Rejoinder to the 'Ethnic Democracy' Debate." *Israel Studies* 4 (1): 44–72.

Gaytán, Marie Sarita. 2008. "From Sombreros to Sincronizadas: Authenticity, Ethnicity, and the Mexican Restaurant Industry." *Journal of Contemporary Ethnography* 37 (3): 314–341.

Ghanem, As'ad. 2001. *The Palestinian-Arab Minority in Israel, 1948–2000.* Albany: State University of New York Press.

Gibau, Gina Sánchez. 2005. "Contested Identities: Narratives of Race and Ethnicity in the Cape Verdean Diaspora." *Identities: Global Studies in Culture and Power* 12:405–438.

Gillette, Maris Boyd. 2005. "Children's Food and Islamic Dietary Restrictions in Xi'an." In *The Cultural Politics of Food and Eating: A Reader,* edited by James L. Watson and Melissa L. Caldwell, 106–121. Malden, MA: Blackwell.

Giroux, Henry A. 1998. "The Politics of National Identity and the Pedagogy of Multiculturalism in the USA." In *Multicultural States: Rethinking Difference and Identity,* edited by David Bennett, 178–194. London: Routledge.

Goldberg, David Theo. 1994. *Multiculturalism: A Critical Reader.* Oxford: Blackwell.

Goody, Jack. 1982. *Cooking, Cuisine, and Class: A Study in Comparative Sociology.* Cambridge, UK: Cambridge University Press.

———. 1986. *The Domestication of the Savage Mind.* Cambridge, UK: Cambridge University Press.

Goode, Judith, Janet Theophano, and Karen Curtis. 1984. "A Framework for the Analysis of Continuity and Change in Shared Sociocultural Rules for Food Use: The Italian-American Pattern." In Brown and Mussell 1984, 66–88.

Guibernau, Montserrat, and John Rex. 1997. *The Ethnicity Reader: Nationalism, Multiculturalism and Migration.* Cambridge, UK: Polity Press.

Gvion, Liora. 2002. "Who's Afraid of Cooking Vegetables? Changing Conceptions of American Vegetarianism—1850–1990." *European Journal of American Culture* 21 (3): 146–159.

———. 2006. "Cuisines of Poverty as Means of Empowerment: Arab Food in Israel." *Agriculture and Human Values* 23 (3): 299–312.

———. 2009a. "Narrating Modernity and Tradition: The Case of Palestinian Food in Israel." *Identities.* 16 (4): 391–413.

———. 2009b. "Organised Leisure as Promoting Nostalgia: Israeli Senior Citizens Singing in Yiddish." *Leisure Studies* 28 (1): 51–65.

———. 2009c. "What's Cooking in America? Cookbooks Narrate Ethnicity: 1850–1990." *Food, Culture and Society.* 12 (1): 53–76.

———. 2013. "Is there Jewish Food in Israel?" *Studies in Contemporary Jewry* 28 (forthcoming).

Gvion, Liora, and Naomi Trostler. 2008. "From Spaghetti and Meatballs through Hawaiian Pizza to Sushi: The Changing Nature of Ethnicity in American Restaurants." *Journal of Popular Culture* 41 (6): 950–974.

Gvion-Rosenberg, L. 1991. "Telling the Story of Ethnicity: American Cookbooks, 1850–1990." PhD diss., SUNY Stony Brook.

Habermas, Jürgen. 1986. "Modernity—An Incomplete Project." In *The Anti-Aesthetic: Essays on Postmodern Culture,* edited by Hal Foster, 3–15. Port Townsend, WA: Bay Press.

Haidar, Aziz, ed. 2005. *Arab Society in Israel: Population, Society, Economy* (in Hebrew). Jerusalem: Van Leer.

Hammack, Phillip L. 2006. "Identity, Conflict, and Coexistence: Life Stories of Israeli and Palestinian Adolescents." *Journal of Adolescent Research* 21 (4): 323–369.

Harbottle, Lynn. 1997. "Fast Food/Spoiled Identity: Iranian Migrants in the British Catering Trade." In Caplan 1997, 87–110.

Heine, Peter. 1994. "The Revival of Traditional Cooking in Modern Arabic Cookbooks." In Zubaida and Tapper 1994, 143–152.

Hinnawi, Miriam. 2006. *Arab Cuisine from the Heart of Galilee* (in Hebrew). Israel: Modan Publishing.

Hobsbawm, Eric J., and Terence O. Ranger. 1989. *The Invention of Tradition.* Cambridge, MA: Cambridge University Press.

Hochman, Rami. 1988. *Jews and Arabs in Israel* (in Hebrew). Jerusalem: Academon.

Hooker, Richard James. 1981. *Food and Drink in America: A History.* Indianapolis, IN: Bobbs-Merrill.

Inness, Sherrie A. 2001. *Kitchen Culture in America: Popular Representations of Food, Gender, and Race.* Philadelphia: University of Pennsylvania Press.

Jabareen, Yousef T. 2006. "Law and Education: Critical Perspectives on Arab Palestinian Education in Israel." *American Behavioral Scientist* 49 (8): 1052–1074.

Kaplan, Temma. 1982. "Female Consciousness and Collective Action: The Case of Barcelona, 1910–1918." *Signs* 7 (3): 545–566.

Karaosmanoglu, Defne. 2009. "Eating the Past: Multiple Spaces, Multiple Times—Performing 'Ottomanness' in Istanbul." *International Journal of Cultural Studies* 12 (4): 339–358.

Kemp, Adriana. 1999. "The Mirror Language of the Border: State Territoriality and National Minorities" (in Hebrew). *Israeli Sociology* 2 (1): 319–349.

Kim, Claire Jean. 2004. "Imagining Race and Nation in Multiculturalist America." *Ethnic and Racial Studies* 27(6): 987–1005.

Kimmerling, Baruch. 1993. "Militarism in Israeli Society" (in Hebrew). *Theory and Criticism* 4:123–140.

Kitcharoen, Patreeya. 2007. "An Ethnography of Restaurant Workers: Thai Women in England." *Asian and Pacific Migration Journal* 16 (4): 555–557.

Kressel, Gideon. 1981. "The Ecological and Cultural Adaptation of Bedouin in the Process of Urbanization in Central Israel" (in Hebrew). In *The Arabs in Israel: Continuity and Change*, edited by Aharon Layish, 140–167. Jerusalem: Magness Press.

Layish, Aharon. 1988. "The Woman and the Family" (in Hebrew). In *Jews and Arabs in Israel*, edited by R. Hochman, 146–153. Jerusalem: Academon.

Lem, Winnie. 2007. "Daughters, Duty and Deference in the Franco-Chinese Restaurant." In *The Restaurants Book: Ethnographies of Where We Eat*, edited by David Beriss and David Sutton, 133–150. Oxford: Berg.

Leschziner, Vanina. 2007. "Kitchen Stories: Patterns of Recognition in Contemporary High Cuisine." *Sociological Forum* 22 (1): 78–102.

Levenstein, Harvey A. 1987. "The American Response to Italian Food, 1880–1930." *Food and Foodways* 1 (1): 1–23.

———. 1988. *Revolution at the Table: The Transformation of the American Diet*. New York: Oxford University Press.

———. 1993. *Paradox of Plenty: A Social History of Eating in Modern America*. New York: Oxford University Press.

Levi, André, and Alex Weingrod, eds. 2005. *Homelands and Diasporas: Holy Lands and Other Places*. Stanford, CA: Stanford University Press.

Lévi-Strauss, Claude. 1966. "The Culinary Triangle." *New Society* 8:937–940.

Levy, Gal. 2005. "From Subjects to Citizens: On Educational Reforms and the Demarcation of the 'Israeli-Arabs.' " *Citizenship Studies* 9 (3): 271–291.

Lewin-Epstein, Noah, Maged Al-Haj, and Moshe Semyonov. 1994. *Arabs in the Labor Market* (in Hebrew). Jerusalem: Haidar.

Lewin-Epstein, Noah, and Moshe Semyonov. 1992. "Local Labor Markets, Ethnic Segregation, and Income Inequality." *Social Forces* 70 (4): 1101–1119.

Lind, David, and Elizabeth Barham. 2004. "The Social Life of the Tortilla: Food Cultural Politics, and Contested Commodification." *Agriculture and Human Values* 21 (1): 47–60.

Lindenbaum, Shirley. 1977. "The Last Course: Nutrition and Anthropology in Asia." In *Nutrition and Anthropology in Action*, edited by Thomas K. Fitzgerald, 141–155. Assen, Amsterdam: Van Gorcum.

Liu, Haiming, and Lin Lianlian. 2009. "Food, Culinary Identity, and Transnational Culture: Chinese Restaurant Business in Southern California." *Journal of Asian American Studies* 12 (2): 135–162.

Lou, Jia. 2007. "Revitalizing Chinatown into a Heterotopia: A Geosemiotic Analysis of Shop Signs in Washington D.C.'s Chinatown." *Space and Culture* 10 (2): 170–194.

Lovell-Troy, Lawrence A. 1990. *The Social Basis of Ethnic Enterprise: Greeks in the Pizza Business*. New York: Taylor and Francis.

Lozada, Eriberto. 2005. "Globalized Childhood? Kentucky Fried Chicken in Beijing." In *The Cultural Politics of Food and Eating: A Reader*, edited by James L. Watson and Melissa L. Caldwell, 163–179. Malden, MA: Blackwell.

Lu, Shun, and Gary Alan Fine. 1995. "The Presentation of Ethnic Authenticity: Chinese Food as a Social Accomplishment." *The Sociological Quarterly* 36 (3): 535–553.

Lustick, Ian. 1980. *Arabs in the Jewish State: Israel's Control of a National Minority*. Austin: University of Texas Press.

Lyotard, Jean-François. 1988. *The Postmodern Condition: A Report on Knowledge*. Minneapolis: University of Minnesota Press.

Macias, Thomas. 2004. "*Imaginandose Mexicano:* The Symbolic Context of Mexican American Ethnicity Beyond the Second Generation." *Qualitative Sociology* 27 (3): 299–315.

Maclagan, Ianthe. 1994. "Food and Gender in a Yemeni Community." In Zubaida and Tapper 1994, 159–172.

Manalansan, Martin F. 2003. "In the Shadows of Stonewall: Examining Gay Transnational Politics and the Diasporic Dilemma." In *Theorizing Diaspora: A Reader*, edited by Jana Evans Braziel and Anita Mannur, 207–227. Malden, MA Blackwell.

Mankekar, Purnima. 2002. " 'India Shopping': Indian Grocery Stores and Transnational Configurations of Belonging." *Ethnos* 67 (1): 75–98.

Martens, Lydia, and Alan Warde. 1997. "Urban Pleasure? On the Meaning of Eating Out in a Northern City." In Caplan 1997, 131–150.

May, Reuben A. Buford. 2000. "Race Talk and Local Collective Memory among African American Men in a Neighborhood Tavern." *Qualitative Sociology* 23 (2): 201–214.

Mennell, Stephen. 1985. *All Manners of Food: Eating and Taste in England and France from the Middle Ages to the Present*. Oxford: Basil Blackwell.

Merino, Asunción. 2004. "Politics of Identity and Identity Policies in Europe: The Case of Peruvian Immigrants in Spain." *Identities: Global Studies in Culture and Power* 11 (2): 241–264.

Mohanty, Chandra Talpade. 1988. "Under Western Eyes: Feminist Scholarship and Colonial Discourses." *Feminist Review* 30:61–88.

Moore, Willard B. 1984. "Metaphor and Changing Reality: The Foodways and Beliefs of the Russian Molokans in the United States." In Brown and Mussell 1984, 91–112.

Murcott, Anne. 1983a. "Cooking and the Cooked: A Note on the Domestic Preparation of Meals." In Murcott 1983c, 178–185.

———. 1983b. " 'It's a Pleasure to Cook For Him. . . ': Food, Mealtimes and Gender in Some South Wales Households." In *The Public and the Private*, edited by Eva Gamarnikow et al, 78–90. London: Heinemann.

————, ed. 1983c. *The Sociology of Food and Eating: Essays on the Sociogical Significance of Food*. Aldershot, England: Gower.

————. 1983d. "Women's Place: Cookbooks' Images of Technique and Technology in the British Kitchen." *Women's Studies International Forum* 6 (1): 33–39.

————. 1997. "Family Meals—A Thing of the Past?" In Caplan 1997, 32–49.

Negash, Almaz, and Anke Niehof. 2004. "The Significance of Enset Culture and Biodiversity for Rural Household Food and Livelihood Security in Southwestern Ethiopia." *Agriculture and Human Values* 21 (1): 61–71.

Nelson, Candace, and Marta Tienda. 1988. "The Structuring of Hispanic Ethnicity: Historical and Contemporary Perspectives." In *Ethnicity and Race in the U.S.A.*, edited by Richard D. Alba, 49–74. New York: Routledge.

Pappé, Ilan. 1994. *The Making of the Arab-Israeli Conflict, 1947–1951*. London: I. B. Tauris.

Perry, Charles. 1994. "The Taste for Layered Bread among the Nomadic Turks and the Central Asian Origins of Baklava." In Zubaida and Tapper 1994, 87–92.

Pierre, Jemima. 2004. "Black Immigrants in the United States and the 'Cultural Narratives' of Ethnicity." *Identities: Global Studies in Culture and Power* 11: 141–170.

Pilcher, Jeffrey M. 2002. "Industrial *Tortillas* and Folkloric Pepsi: The Nutritional Consequences of Hybrid Cuisines in Mexico." In *Food Nations: Selling Taste in Consumer Societies*, edited by Warren Belasco and Philip Scranton, 222–239. New York: Routledge.

Pitt-Rivers, Julian. 1977. "The Law of Hospitality." In *The Fate of Shechem, or the Politics of Sex: Essays on the Anthropology of the Mediterannean*. Cambridge, UK: Cambridge University Press.

Prosterman, Leslie. 1984. "Food and Celebration: A Kosher Caterer as Mediator of Communal Traditions." In Brown and Mussell 1984, 128–142.

Pyke, Karen, and Tran Dang. 2003. " 'FOB' and 'Whitewashed': Identity and Internalized Racism among Second Generation Asian Americans." *Qualitative Sociology* 26 (2): 147–172.

Rabinowitz, Dan, and H. Abu Baker. 2002. *The Stand Tall Generation: The Palestinian Citizens of Israel Today* (in Hebrew). Jerusalem: Keter.

Radhakrishnan, R. 2003. "Ethnicity in an Age of Diaspora." In *Theorizing Diaspora: A Reader*, edited by Jana Evans Braziel and Anita Mannur, 119–131. Malden, MA: Blackwell.

Raspa, Richard. 1984. "Exotic Foods among Italian-Americans in Mormon Utah: Food as Nostalgic Enactment of Identity." In Brown and Mussell 1984, 185–194.

Ray, Krishnendu. 2004. *The Migrant's Table: Meals and Memories in Bengali-American Households*. Philadelphia: Temple University Press.

Reiter, Yitzhak, and Reuven Aharoni. 1991. *The Political Life of Arabs in Israel* (in Hebrew). Beit Berl: Institute for Israeli Arab Studies.

Rex, John. 1997. "The Nature of Ethnicity in the Project of Migration." In *The Ethnicity Reader: Nationalism, Multiculturalism and Migration*, edited by Montserrat Guibernau and John Rex, 269–283. Cambridge, UK: Polity Press.

Root, Waverly, and Richard de Rochemont. 1976. *Eating In America: A History*. New York: Morrow.

Rosenfeld, Henry. 1981. "Change, Barriers to Change, and Contradictions in the Arab Village Family" (in Hebrew). In *The Arabs in Israel: Continuity and Change*, edited by Aharon Layish, 76–103. Jerusalem: Magness Press.

Rouhana, Nadin. 1998. "Israel and Its Arab Citizens: Predicaments in the Relationship between Ethnic States and Ethnonational Minorities." *Third World Quarterly* 19 (2): 277–296.

Sa'ar, Amalia. 2005. "Postcolonial Feminism, the Politics of Identification, and the Liberal Bargain." *Gender and Society* 19 (5): 680–700.

Sa'di, Ahmad. 2003. "The Incorporation of the Palestinian Minority by the State of Israel, 1948–1970." *Social Text* 21(2): 75–94.

Safran, William. 1991. "Diasporas in Modern Societies: Myths of Homeland and Return." *Diaspora* 1 (1): 83–99.

Said, Edward. 1978. *Orientalism*. London: Routledge and Kegan Paul.

Schwartz-Cowan, Ruth. 1983. *More Work for Mother: The Ironies of Household Technology from the Open Hearth to the Microwave*. New York: Basic Books.

Senghor, Léopold Sédar. 1994. "Negritude: A Humanism of the Twentieth Century." In *Colonial Discourse and Post-Colonial Theory*, edited by Patrick Williams and Laura Chrisman, 27–35. New York: Columbia University Press.

Shavit, Yossi. 1992. "Arabs in the Israeli Economy: A Study of the Enclave Hypothesis." Israel Social Science Research 7 (1–2): 45–66.

Shohat, Ella. 2001. *Forbidden Reminiscences: A Collection of Essays* (in Hebrew). Israel: Bimat Kedem Lesifrut.

Simmel, Georg. 1971. "The Conflict in Modern Culture." In *Georg Simmel: On Individuality and Social Forms*, edited by Donald N. Levine, 375–394. Chicago: University of Chicago Press.

Smith, Anthony D. 1997. "Structure and Persistence of *Ethnie*." In *The Ethnicity Reader: Nationalism, Multiculturalism and Migration*, edited by Montserrat Guibernau and John Rex, 27–33. Cambridge, UK: Polity Press.

Smooha, Sammy. 1978. *Israel: Pluralism and Conflict*. Berkeley: University of California Press.

———. 1989. *Arabs and Jews in Israel*. Vol. 1, *Conflicting and Shared Attitudes in a Divided Society*. Boulder: Westview Press.

———. 1992. *Arabs and Jews in Israel*. Vol. 2, *Change and Continuity in Mutual Intolerance*. Boulder: Westview Press.

———. 2004. *Arab-Jewish Relations in Israel* (in Hebrew). Haifa: The Jewish Arab Center.

Soen, Dan. 2005a. *The Book of Arab Society in Israel* (in Hebrew). Jerusalem: Van Leer.

———. 2005b. *Israel: From Welfare State to Social Darwinism* (in Hebrew). Tel Aviv: Cherikover.

Song, Miri. 2004. "Introduction: Who's at the Bottom? Examining Claims about Racial Hierarchy." *Ethnic and Racial Studies* 27 (6): 859–877.

Spivak, Gayatri Chakravorty. 1988. "Can the Subaltern Speak?" In *Marxism and the Interpretation of Culture,* edited by Cary Nelson and Lawrence Grossberg, 271–313. Urbana: University of Illinois Press

Stam, Robert, and Ella Shohat. 1994. "Contested Histories: Eurocentrism, Multiculturalism, and the Media." In *Multiculturalism: A Critical Reader,* edited by David Theo Goldberg, 296–324. Oxford: Blackwell.

Stein, Rebecca. 1998. "National Itineraries, Itinerant Nations: Israeli Tourism and Palestinian Cultural Production." *Social Text* 16 (3): 91–124.

Suleri, Sara. 1992. "Woman Skin Deep: Feminism and the Postcolonial Condition." *Critical Inquiry* 18 (4): 756–769.

Sutton, David E. 2001. *Remembrance of Repasts: An Anthropology of Food and Memory.* Oxford: Berg.

Swirski, Shlomo. 1990. *Education in Israel: Schooling for Inequality* (in Hebrew). Tel-Aviv: Breirot.

Taylor, Charles, et al. 1994. *Multiculturalism: Examining the Politics of Recognition.* Edited and introduced by Amy Gutmann. Princeton: Princeton University Press.

Theophano, Janet. 2001. "Home Cooking: Boston Baked Beans and Sizzling Rice Soup as Recipes for Pride and Prejudice." In *Kitchen Culture in America: Popular Representations of Food, Gender, and Race,* edited by Sherrie A. Inness, 139–156. Philadelphia: University of Pennsylvania Press.

Tölölyan, Khachig. 1991. "The Nation-State and Its Others: In Lieu of a Preface." *Diaspora* 1 (1): 3–7.

Twigg, Julia. 1983. "Vegetarianism and the Meanings of Meat." In Murcott 1983c, 18–30.

Van den Berghe, Pierre L. 1984. "Ethnic Cuisine: Culture in Nature." *Ethnic and Racial Studies* 7 (3): 387–397.

Vattimo, Gianni. 1988. *The End of Modernity: Nihilism and Hermeneutics in Postmodern Culture.* Oxford: Polity Press.

Vincent, Joan. 1974. "The Structuring of Ethnicity." *Human Organization* 33 (4): 375–379.

Watson, James L., and Melissa L. Caldwell. 2005. *The Cultural Politics of Food and Eating: A Reader.* Malden, MA: Blackwell.

Wheeler, Erica, and Tan Swee Poh. 1983. "Food for Equilibrium: The Dietary Principles and Practice of Chinese Families in London." In Murcott 1983c, 84–94.

Willetts, Anna. 1997. " 'Bacon Sandwiches Got the Better of Me': Meat-Eating and Vegetarianism in South-East London." In Caplan 1997, 111–130.

Williams, Brett. 1984. "Why Migrant Women Feed Their Husbands Tamales: Foodways as a Basis for a Revisionist View of Tejano Family Life." In Brown and Mussell 1984, 113–126.

Wood, Roy C. 1995. *The Sociology of the Meal.* Edinburgh: Edinburgh University Press.

Yamani, Mai. 1994. "You Are What You Cook: Cuisine and Class in Mecca." In Zubaida and Tapper 1994, 173–184.

Yan, Yunxiang. 2005. "Of Hamburger and Social Space: Consuming McDonald's in Beijing." In *The Cultural Politics of Food and Eating: A Reader,* edited by James L. Watson and Melissa L. Caldwell, 80–103. Malden, MA: Blackwell.

Yano, Christine R. 2007. "Side-Dish Kitchen: Japanese American Delicatessens and the Culture of Nostalgia." In *The Restaurants Book: Ethnographies of Where We Eat,* edited by David Beriss and David Sutton, 47–64. Oxford: Berg.

Yiftachel, Oren. 1999. " 'Ethnocracy': The Politics of Judaizing Israel/Palestine." *Constellations: An International Journal of Critical and Democratic Theory* 6 (3): 364–390.

Young, Robert. 1990. *White Mythologies: Writing History and the West.* London: Routledge.

Zubaida, Sami. 1994a. "National, Communal and Global Dimensions in Middle Eastern Food Cultures." In Zubaida and Tapper 1994, 33–45.

———. 1994b. "Rice in the Culinary Cultures of the Middle East." In Zubaida and Tapper 1994, 93–104.

Zubaida, Sami, and Richard Tapper, eds. 1994. *Culinary Cultures of the Middle East.* London: I. B. Tauris.

Index

"mock *kubeh*," 57
modernity, 19, 63, 101–4, 174n1; cake preparation symbolizing, 123; and consumption of industrial food products, 106; infusing food with historical dimension, 123–24; modes, 98–101; and status symbols, 108; and tradition in culinary space, 152
modernization, 174n1; fostering nostalgia, 123; and organized kitchen knowledge, 177–78n17; and the Palestinian citizenry in Israel, 6–7, 23, 164; women's perception of time in, 126
monetary economy, 9, 30, 31, 36, 62
Moore, Willard, 174n2
mothers, 12, 31–32, 35, 103, 115; and baking bread, 38; help in cooking, 27, 79, 86; help in domestic duties, 78; teacher daughter to cook, 40, 87, 88, 139; and weddings, 68–69
mothers-in-law, supervising brides, 73–74, 86, 88
mugrabiya, 48, 91, 103–4, 109, 146, 179n1
Murcott, Anne, 51
musaka, 42
Muslims, 76; Chinese, 12; eating *burbara*, 16
myth of returning home, 4, 5

Nasser, Abdel, 99
National Committee of Chairmen of Arab Local Authorities, 174n2
national consciousness, 3, 102
national cuisines, 3, 20–21
national identity, 3, 4; and culinary knowledge 1, 10; Palestinians in Israel, 6, 7, 10, 99, 100, 130
national liberation: and distinct female identity, 18; and local culture, 4
nation-states, 3–4
Nazareth, 151, 154
Negev, 178n1
nostalgia, 13, 47, 123, 127, 128, 177n11; and dishes symbolizing ethnic culture, 57, 103, 125, 127, 128, 153, 179n2
nutrition, 63, 112, 118, 119, 122, 173n16

Occupied Territories, 9, 23, 170n47; and Muslim Palestinians in Israel, 9
olesh, 59, 155
Orientalism (Said), 2

Palestinian cuisine, 1, 162, 164, 165, 168, 173n16; cultural perceptions shaping,

49; development in Israel, 16–17, 20, 22; disrespect of, 163 and globalization, 15; "Jewish" dishes in, variations, 10, 141. *See also* cultural knowledge; dishes
Palestinians in Israel: adopting modern behavior and preserving traditional patterns, 157; and boundary between personal and public-political space, 148, 150, 152; Christians, 16, 76, 77; close connection to the land, 152–54; culinary culture of, 15, 20, 21–22;culinary narrative, 165–66; cultural identity, 30; cultural uniqueness, 152, 163; defined as hostile to Israel, 17, 100, 132, 149, 158, 176n9; defining ethnic identity, 130; a diasporic minority, 18, 130; distinct ethnic group, 131; eating in Jewish sector restaurants, 155–56; feelings of exile and uprooting, 130–31, 166; identity, 6–10, 18, 23, 30, 94, 99, 100, 103, 128, 130, 133, 162–63, 165, 166; lack of respect for, 134, 158; leadership, 7; limited absorption into Israeli Jewish society, 99–100, 166; mobilization of culinary tradition, 154, 163, 165; modernity, 103; outsiderness and the culinary sphere, 126; perception of restaurant eating, 155–56, 164; personal dimension meeting with the political, 100; presentation of their culture and history, 151; relationship to their culinary heritage, 133–34; sharing culture selectively, 150; social marginality felt, 152; social practices, 29; social stratification of, 101; sociopolitical relationship with Jews, 145; status in society, 133; suspicion toward, 149
pasta, 4, 11, 15, 20–21, 115, 172n8, 174–75n5
pasteurization, 35
pita, 37
pizza, adaptation of, 116
political regimes in Israel, dual, 6
politics of identity, and daily culinary practices, 1
pork, 16
postmodernism: and the cultural sphere, 19–20
potatoes, 112, 173n16
power relations, 2, 58, 94, 134; in the home, 26, 27, 30; local, 71; and narration of heritage in Israel, 150; preserving, 26, 39; public role of

CALIFORNIA STUDIES IN FOOD AND CULTURE

Darra Goldstein, Editor